CW00802137

Britten's
*A Midsummer
Night's Dream:*
Making an Opera from
Shakespeare's Comedy

Benjamin Britten

Cartoon of Britten composing by Sir David Low, ca. 1950. Photo University of Hull Art Collection. © Solo Syndication & Literary Agency Ltd.

Britten's
A Midsummer Night's Dream:
Making an Opera from
Shakespeare's Comedy

William H. L. Godsalve

Madison • Teaneck
Fairleigh Dickinson University Press
London and Toronto: Associated University Presses

Associated University Presses
440 Forsgate Drive
Cranbury, NJ 08512

Associated University Presses
25 Sicilian Avenue
London WC1A 2QH, England

Associated University Presses
P.O. Box 338, Port Credit
Mississauga, Ontario
Canada L5G 4L8

The paper used in this publication meets the requirements
of the American National Standard for Permanence of Paper
for Printed Library Materials Z39.48-1984.

Library of Congress Cataloging-in-Publication Data

Godsalve, William H. L., 1913–
    Britten's A midsummer night's dream : making an opera from
Shakespeare's comedy / William H. L. Godsalve.
        p.   cm.
    Includes bibliographical references (p.   ) and index.
    ISBN 0-8386-3551-2 (alk. paper)
    1. Britten, Benjamin, 1913–1976. Midsummer night's dream.
2. Shakespeare, William, 1564–1616.—Adaptations. 3. Shakespeare,
William, 1564–1616. Midsummer night's dream.
ML410.B853G63   1995
782.1—dc20
                                                        94-7296
                                                        CIP
                                                        MN

PRINTED IN THE UNITED STATES OF AMERICA

With love to
Joan,
my dear wife for fifty-four years,
"something of great constancy,"
who understands and supports;

and to
Valerie, Edward, Käthe, and Karen,
our children,
fortunately spared "the blots of Nature's hand."
May they relish the 1913 vintage!

Contents

Illustrations

Tables

Examples

Preface

In this book I attempt to portray the making of an opera. I visualize Benjamin Britten and Peter Pears in 1959–1960 as they adapt Shakespeare's comedy, *A Midsummer Night's Dream,* for the operatic stage.

Britten left a few general comments on their writing of the libretto, but "airy nothing" on his compositional modus operandi. Further, before I began my study in earnest, the famous composer and the renowned tenor had been laid side by side with matching, simple black marble headstones in the extended parish churchyard in Aldeburgh, Suffolk, in their native England. Hence, when, like Oberon, I would "overhear their conference" and next would witness Britten as he, like Titania, would "music call," it had to be by the patient research of scattered facts and the exercise of restraint as the "imagination bodies forth / The forms of things unknown." Alternative conclusions, tenable yet questionable, were all too many and too frequent: I necessarily took risks, but I hope that not too often "is a bush suppos'd a bear."

This book is a re-presentation of an interdisciplinary doctoral dissertation. I hope the new form will attract and be useful to opera lovers, amateurs of English literature and of music, and students, as well as academic scholars. This is not a "how-to" book about writing opera. Such a volume would need to explain the successful procedures of many more composers working with their librettists, although it may be hoped that some dos and don'ts may surface to help an aspiring opera maker.

The great majority of writings on this genre are descriptions and evaluations of operas in their true guise, fully staged performances. A score, however meritorious, is not an opera; a performance, however unworthy, is. But a performance is the responsibility and product of many persons other than the librettist and the composer, and it is beyond the scope of this book to venture into such an unstable labyrinth. I stop short at the score, treating it as a necessary blueprint for a performance.

The book concentrates on one work, a mid-twentieth-century romantic chamber opera in English. The work has been interna-

tionally successful and critically acclaimed since its premiere in
1960. Britten was a colibrettist as well as the composer, and he
largely preserved the source text. He named the distinct steps in
the making of the opera, but not his reasons for choosing among
the wide literary and musical options open.

In the introductory chapter, several necessary preliminary topics are discussed, including some problems with the texts that require study and that involve a misleading claim by Britten. The
conventions of opera are deliberated: artificial, extravagant, high-
styled staged performances using diverse visual and aural media.
Britten considered operatic conventions critically; the study in-
quires whether and why he followed or flouted them.

The examination of the making of the opera proceeds by Britten's stages and by topics rather than by the order of events in the
plot. In chapters 2 and 3, the librettists' restructuring of Shakespeare's actions to form a new shape the composer found manageable, responsive to changed cultural forces, and receptive to
musical influences is analyzed. In chapters 4 and 5, reasons are
sought for the specific excisions and other textual adjustments
made to allow for the slower pace and other characteristics of the
sung word.

Britten always refused to say how his music works, affording
broad scope to indicate here how he achieved his goal of writing
"dramatically effective music for the theatre." In chapters 6 to 9,
the implications of the use of music are introduced, and ideas of
formal and psychological meaning in music are discovered and
examined against constructs and processes in Britten's score. Both
individual and joint functions for voices and instruments are discussed and Britten's roles as both an eclectic assimilator and an
innovator are recognized. Interdisciplinary in nature, this study
explores aspects of English literature and music and touches on
cultural influences other than the aesthetic, particularly philosophical, moral, and economic ones.

As argued in Chapter 10, Britten—with Pears, his colibrettist—
mindful of changed relevancies in mid-twentieth-century England,
succeeded in writing an aesthetically attractive opera by constructing a new, strong dramatic design (albeit with lacunae) and
by applying masterly techniques to the details of putting the drama
into music. Appendices contain ancilliary material.

A few specialized terms are employed, particularly in the chapters on music. Circumlocutions in "nontechnical" language would
be worse and probably confusing. The context of, for instance,
"horizontal dodecaphony" will make the meaning plain, and, if

"isorhythm" is too arcane a concept, any musical dictionary should clarify it. After all, Britten himself said that music demands some effort from several kinds of person; why not expect the same effort from the reader of a book about his compositional procedures?

I offer thanks to the ever-helpful and encouraging supervisor of my doctoral studies, Dr. William W. E. Slights, professor of English in the University of Saskatchewan, who bravely plunged into the unfamiliar depths of Benjamin Britten's music and continues to guide me. I thank, too, the other supportive members of my advisory committee: Dr. Herbert A. Berry, Dr. Judith R. Henderson, Dr. Peter T. Millard, and Dr. Claud A. Thompson of the Department of English, and Dr. David L. Kaplan of the Department of Music. Excepting Dr. Berry, unavoidably absent, and including Dr. Philip Brett, professor of Music in the University of California at Berkeley, these persons became the perspicacious probers whose company I enjoyed so much while defending my thesis.

I take this opportunity of thanking the persons in England who generously gave their time in interviews (reported in appendix C) to assist my research into a work by the composer they admired: Mr. Jeremy Cullum, Dr. Donald Mitchell, and Miss Rosamund Strode. Paul S. Wilson, librarian of the Britten-Pears Library (since regrettably deceased), must be thanked for making visits to Aldeburgh so rewarding and pleasant. I gratefully acknowledge constructive comments from two of my publishers' readers, Dr. C. J. Gianakaris and Dr. Gary Schmidgall, and their copyeditor Richard E. Jones. There have been, naturally, many other helpers, too numerous to name individually: I thank them and hope they do not feel that I have misapplied their contribution.

The extensive quotations from Britten's article "A New Britten Opera" (*Observer* Weekend Review, 5 June 1960) and all other extracts from the writings of Benjamin Britten are copyright © the Britten-Pears Foundation. They are quoted by kind permission of the Britten-Pears Foundation and may not be reproduced further without the written authorization of the Foundation.

Specific thanks are offered to Boosey & Hawkes Music Publishers Limited for permission to quote from the published opera score, to the Penguin Group for clarifying the out-of-copyright status of The Shakespeare text and the Droeshout engraving, to Miss Rosamund Strode for approving the report of interviews with her and to the Solo Syndication & Literary Agency and the University of Hull Art Collection for the use of the cartoon of Britten composing.

General thanks are offered to others, not named here—including the authors, editors, and compilers mentioned in the Works Cited—for the use of their words or ideas in small packages that nevertheless help to clarify the initial enigma of Britten's genius.

Reference Symbols

GENERAL
In general, a parenthetical reference is to a page number in the work indicated or implied in the sentence and described in the list of works cited.

SOURCE TEXT
The text of the play in Harrison's Shakespeare edition, the "source text," has no printed lineation. References consist of a number indicating the page in Harrison, a semicolon, and numbers indicating the act, scene, and line in *The Riverside Shakespeare.* (A lineation added to Harrison would match *Riverside's* closely, except in extended prose passages.) For example, Oberon's "I know a bank" is referenced "(40; 2.1.249)."

WORKING LIBRETTO
References to the Britten-Pears Library's unpublished working libretto are to the archivist's microfilm frame reference numbers (added in pencil).

LIBRETTO
References to Boosey & Hawkes's published booklet, the "libretto," consist of the printed page number, a period, and the line, not numbered by the publisher but counted from the top including settings, stage directions, and speech headings. For example, the first of the three references to "sixpence a day" is "(41.9)."

SCORE
References to the Boosey & Hawkes published full score, the "score," are to page numbers rather than to the rehearsal numbers, which repeat for each act. Named notes, instruments, performers, or text make the references precise. In examples 7.3, 7.4, and 7.5 and tables 9.2 and E.6, measure numbers [in brackets] are added.

CROSS-REFERENCES

Where two possibly indefinite references occur together, the respective works are indicated by a prefixed "H" for Harrison, "L" for libretto, and "S" for score.

NOTES

Superscript figures indicate end-of-chapter notes.

Britten's
*A Midsummer
Night's Dream:*
Making an Opera from
Shakespeare's Comedy

1

Introduction

Music . . . demands . . . from a listener . . . some preparation, some effort, a journey to a special place, saving up for a
ticket, some homework on the programme perhaps, some clarification of the ears and sharpening of the instincts. It demands
as much effort on the listener's part as on the other two corners
of the triangle, this holy triangle of composer, performer and listener.

—Benjamin Britten,
*On Receiving the First
Aspen Award*

In 1964 in Aspen, Colorado, Benjamin Britten received the first
Aspen Award, established the previous year to honor "the individual anywhere in the world judged to have made the greatest contribution to the advancement of the humanities." The citation
describes Britten as "a brilliant composer, performer, and interpreter through music of human feelings, moods, and thoughts,
[who] has truly inspired man to understand, clarify and appreciate
more fully his own nature, purpose and destiny" (*Aspen,* 8). These
glowing generalities invite inquiries into Britten's specific abilities.
In particular, they prompt one to identify his opera-making procedures.

In 1959 and 1960, with Peter Pears as colibrettist, Britten
adapted Shakespeare's comedy, *A Midsummer Night's Dream,* to
the operatic stage. The making of this particular opera is an especially appropriate field of study because of how closely the Shakespearean text is followed (Peter Evans saw "almost formidable
authenticity" [236]), the supportive power of its music, and its remarkable success. The success of Britten's creative process is
proved by the resulting opera's attractiveness and its artistic merit.
Chapters to follow discover criteria for these qualities and argue
that the work possesses them; for the present, it suffices to show

evidence of its attractiveness from performance statistics and to suggest its artistic merit from critical comment.

Britten's *A Midsummer Night's Dream* has enjoyed continued popularity. Late in 1987, Boosey & Hawkes Music Publishers Limited in London, England, and eight of their branches and agents in other countries, were asked for details of rentals of scores and parts for performance. Appendix A summarizes the replies. The 142 leasings disclosed represent a yearly average of five leasings and nearly twenty-eight performances for some twenty-eight years, a remarkable performance record for a contemporary full-length, full-blown opera. In a letter dated 14 June, 1988, the manager of the Boosey & Hawkes hire library in London wrote, "the popularity of this work is undoubted." A partial updating of statistics of performances of the opera since the period discussed above appears in appendix A.

Many critics have made favorable, detailed comments on Britten's *Dream* in reviews of specific productions or in analyses of performances visualized from the score. For instance, Gary Schmidgall considers that "a composer may approach a work with just the right key to its implicit operatic potency." He continues:

> A masterpiece may result. Such was the case when Britten chose to make a version of *A Midsummer Night's Dream*, . . . one of the very few truly successful musical transformations of both Shakespearean poetry and drama. (*Literature*, 5)

Others, notably Patricia Howard, Eric Walter White, and Peter Evans, have published lengthy, complimentary accounts of the opera. The critics' readings and evaluations of the fait accompli can be enriched by an explication of the opera-making process itself. As Britten stresses in the epigraph to this chapter, the listener must make an effort, and "homework on the programme" would certainly extend to a study of the process of making an opera from a well-known comedy.

To understand in retrospect Britten's remaking of Shakespeare's *Dream* involves overcoming several difficulties, largely related to complexity. First, problems faced by librettists and composers are intricate and must be identified before measures for solving them can be explained. Second, the varied criteria for opera scattered throughout an enormous literature about the genre must be weighed. Third, the meaning of music is largely subjective, and a reader's full reward necessarily depends upon tackling some special terminology designed to describe nonverbal phenomena. Fourth, the relation of sung words to accompanying music is complex, and the success of their functioning together on a stage is dependent not only upon their joint sound but also upon the simultaneous sight of singing actors in costume, gesturing and moving amid artificially lit sets.

The complexity of opera makes its composition and its analysis all the more interesting. The mixing of media that are much alike can easily—may even necessarily—produce unintelligible confusion, but opera, using unlike components, seems to avoid this chaos. Indeed, it is easy to share Britten's own enduring opinion, stated in his introduction to Anthony Gishford's compilation on leading opera houses and personalities:

> Ever since those fruitless struggles with *Paul Bunyan* [1941] up to the immediate struggles with the problems of *Death in Venice* [1973] I have been fascinated by the most powerful medium of musical communication I know. (11)

By 1959, when Britten came to tackle Shakespeare's *A Midsummer Night's Dream,* he had mastered the complex problem of integrating disparate media.

The plan of this explication of the steps in Britten's successful creative process is, to consider operatic conventions as possible guidelines and constraints, to identify decisions affecting form and content that Britten and Peter Pears took as they worked from source to score, and to discuss their literary and musical inclusions and exclusions (by type, rather than by their order of appearance in performance) and to offer reasons for them.

What Britten does as librettist or composer in a single passage of the work often addresses several distinct textual or musical problems. These are discussed separately, hence an event or process is often referred to again in the context of a different topic. The examination demonstrates Britten's meticulous attention to detail and confirms the breadth and depth—even the deliberate ambiguity—of his artistic vision.

The conclusion is that Benjamin Britten, with Peter Pears, in the opera *A Midsummer Night's Dream,* by adapting Shakespeare's late-sixteenth-century play, restructuring the plots, excising half the words, and adding modern music to an old text, intensified the drama and made it more relevant to mid-twentieth-century English culture.

Peter Evans, in his *The Music of Benjamin Britten*, finds in Britten "fairly near a norm of indebtedness to past practice" (2), thus circuitously labeling him as mainstream. Evans points out that his very choice of Britten for analysis involves an initial intuitive prejudgment, but he hopes that his commentary "proceeds consistently from demonstrable musical facts" (5). Similar hopes are held for this analysis, which is consistent with Evans's summary appraisal of Britten's procedures:

> Britten's mastery of the art of composition remains, in his operas as elsewhere, a mastery of tonal and harmonic structures, of thematic cast, cross-reference and transformation, of resourceful textural variety and of imaginative deployment of voices and instruments—though it would be futile indeed not to show the uniquely fitting relationship of each of these to verbal and dramatic contingencies. (5)

When Evans turns to an analysis of Britten's *Dream*, he begins with a statement that the operas composed before it "can be interpreted as the composer's commentary on recurrent patterns of human behaviour, most commonly relations between individuals and the society to which they belong." He continues that the *Dream* is not essentially a musical adornment of the play and that it creates an atmosphere that cannot be mistaken for Shakespeare's (236–37). He adds that Britten employs means of intramusical unity that subsume the specific incidents that occur on the three separate planes on which the fairies, the mechanicals, and the lovers exist, whereas Shakespeare attempted no unifying cosmography (237). There is no quarrel with Evans over this.

Michael Kennedy's account of *A Midsummer Night's Dream* in *Britten* (220–22), his book on the composer's life and music, raises two matters, the first by a misleading statement. "In their masterly adaptation of Shakespeare's play as an opera libretto, Britten and Pears needed only to invent one line and to omit about half the text! . . . they have concentrated the essentials of the action into a superb framework for music." The first statement is untrue. They completely restructured the action, making the enchanted wood near Athens rather than the no-nonsense court of Theseus the opening scene and point of departure. Kennedy's oversight is confirmed by his later statement (222) that the scene change (in act 3) "takes us back into the 'ordinary' world": we were never there in the first part of the opera, not even at Quince's house, as we were in Shakespeare's opening scenes. Peter Evans repeats Kennedy's mistake by stating that everyday values are reinstated at the end; they were never there in the beginning of the opera (238).

Donald Jay Grout, in the second, one-volume edition of his *A Short History of Opera,* has some adverse comments on Britten's *Dream:* "Some mannerisms, such as glissandi in the double-basses and ostinato techniques generally, are overworked, and a certain monotony of effect results from the prevailing color of high voices; in particular the countertenor of Oberon is dramatically unconvincing" (544). These strictures are not accepted, nor are they endorsed by later critics; indeed these very features are praised—operatic beauty is truly in the ear of the listener.

Charles Hamm's *Opera* (1966), "a book about opera, not operas" (vii), virtually a textbook, is useful here in providing a vocabulary for all aspects of the genre. Hamm agrees with others in regarding opera as integrated words and music—which, over the years, have alternated in dominating a whole work. In one respect, the central task is to discover how Britten makes each component medium, turn and turn about, play a prominent but cooperative role for effective communication.

Some incidental comments of critics have wide connotations. Kennedy and several others specify the opera as the high point of Britten's preoccupation with the twin themes of night and sleep (220), and this engrossment may have been a factor in Britten's commitment to the compositional task. But his interest in the play was general and long-standing. He said; "I have always loved *A Midsummer Night's Dream, ...* I always feel [it] to be by a very young man, whatever Shakespeare's actual age when he wrote it" (Palmer, 177). The forty-six-year-old Britten was looking back at the work of the thirty-one-year-old Shakespeare![1]

Britten's experience in composing major vocal works about night, sleep, and dreams—e.g., *Serenade* (1943) and *Nocturne* (1958)—may have been a factor in his rapid composition of the opera—"seven months for everything." He could not, however, work at night: "By midnight I want to do nothing but sleep" (Palmer, 178 and 179).

Peter Evans's apt though cumbersome term "listener-spectator," reflecting the etymological limitation of the commoner term "audience," recognizes that the full apprehension of drama, including opera, requires the witness to see many things as well as to hear the text uttered. The implications of staged performance and apprehension are central to an evaluation of the composition of opera.

Other general statements by Britten himself concerning his creative process warrant citing here, to be borne in mind in later contexts. First, in an article published in the *Observer* on 5 June 1960, a few days before the premiere of the opera, he refers to the play as a masterpiece that already has a strong verbal music of its own, but "its music and the music I have written for it are at two quite different levels" (Palmer, 178), an enigmatic but suggestive statement, touching the relation between poetry and music in a setting.

Second, Britten refers to the way "local conditions can determine what you do," and his conclusion, "It is to me the local things that matter most" (Palmer, 180), can be taken to mean that he regards himself as an artist appropriately within society—that art and culture should be integrated. Moreover, in his 1964 acceptance speech, *On Receiving the First Aspen Award,* Britten asks: "How far can a composer go in . . . considering the demands of people, of humanity?" (11). He concludes: "It is the composer's duty, as a member of society, to speak to or for his fellow human beings" (12) and "Music does not exist in a vacuum, it does not exist until it is performed . . . . I prefer to study the conditions of performance and shape my music to them" (13). He elaborates, saying that any artist "demands that his art shall be accepted as an essential part of human activity, and human expression" (16), that artists should aim at pleasing people today (17), and that he does not write for posterity: "I write music, now, in Aldeburgh, for people living there, and further afield, indeed for anyone who cares to play it or listen to it" (22). These statements surely mean that the opera-making procedures for his *Dream* should be appraised as changes to Shakespeare to make the opera not only attractive but relevant to mid-twentieth-century audiences. Britten was explicit about contemporaneity in his introduction to Gishford's compilation on leading opera houses and personalities: "[Opera] has to express itself in the framework of an ever changing society" (11). The conclusion stated earlier includes the concept that Britten's opera is a modernization of Shakespeare's comedy.

In a study of the process of turning an extant literary work into an opera, three texts out of many are of primary importance, in that they must be compared with each other to determine what the librettists and the composer did. The first such text, the source text, is the written record or records of the incidents and situations that are to be incorporated into the plot and setting of the opera. The second text, the working libretto, materializes when the composer accepts a text as appropriate for setting to music. It is to be distinguished from the libretto, the "little book," which is compiled for the convenience of operagoers, representing the words in the score, or, better, the performance of the completed opera. Britten's comments in his *Observer* article suggest the importance of the working libretto text: "In writing opera, I have always found it very dangerous to start writing the music until the words are more or less fixed" (Palmer, 177). The third text appears when the composer becomes satisfied, perhaps only temporarily, with a written text in which the words, the musical notation, and other data, such as stage directions, form an integrated unit—there is now a score. Of these key texts, the source text, the working libretto, and the score, the first and third are the indispensable points of departure and arrival; the second is of major interest in the light of Britten's compositional procedures. The first two present problems, but, before discussing them, it is appropriate to note certain other texts of passing interest involved in the making of the *Dream*.

Ancillary to the main line of inquiry are numerous documents generated in the making of this opera: they will be referred to only when they throw light on those activities of the librettists and the composer that are under direct study. They are: (1) a plot summary of Shakespeare's play, antedating the working libretto, made by Pears; (2) a proposed but abandoned prologue to act 1 of the opera, by Myfanwy Piper; (3) a list of the cast contemplated for the first performance, drawn up by Britten; (4) Britten's composition sketches; (5) notes by Imogen Holst to Britten on textual discrepancies discovered when she and Martin Penny were making the vocal score and Britten's replies; (6) the manuscript vocal score; (7) the manuscript full score; and (8) proofs of the printed full score. These documents are located in the Britten-Pears Library at Aldeburgh, Suffolk, England, built after Britten's death on the grounds of his residence, The Red House. The library is briefly described in appendix D.

The problem with identifying the source text arises from a vague statement by the composer, which is misleading in view of evidence available. Britten, in his *Observer* article, describing how Pears and he wrote the working libretto, said: "We worked from many texts, but principally from facsimiles of the First Folio and the First Quarto" (Palmer, 178). As to the "many texts" and "facsimiles," the Britten-Pears Library, according to the librarian, contains only four Shakespearean editions acquired prior to 1960, which can be conveniently called the Booth, the Griggs, the Blackwell, and the Harrison. A "First Folio" volume, *Shakespeare: A Reprint of His Collected Works as Put Forth in 1623: Part I containing the Comedies* (London: Lionel Booth, 1862), purports to be a facsimile, but is really a typeset representation in old spelling, which does not state which of the many variant originals it reproduces. A

"First Quarto" volume is truly a facsimile, *Shakespeare's Midsummer Night's Dream, The First Quarto, 1600: A Facsimile in Photo-Lithography, by William Griggs* (1800), again not identifying the original. The third edition of Shakespearean texts in the library is *The Works of William Shakespeare Gathered into One Volume. Oxford, Newly Printed for the Shakespeare Head Press and Sold for the Press by Basil Blackwell* (1934). In sharp contrast to the extensive marking of the Harrison edition, discussed below, and to the frequent presence of glosses by Britten in other books he studied, in none of these three editions (Booth, Griggs, or Blackwell) is the text of the *Dream* annotated, suggesting strongly that they were not "worked from" in making the working libretto. Moreover, it is significant that the librettists produced a text in a modernized spelling matching Harrison's, and it is most unlikely that they themselves made the change from the late Elizabethan and Jacobean orthography of the first publications.

There exist in the Library two copies of *A Midsummer Night's Dream,* edited by G. B. Harrison (revised edition 1953), in the paperback Penguin Shakespeare series, one copy with the manuscript initials "BB" in the top right-hand corner of the cover, the other with "PP." (It is ironic that the voiceless consonant initials belong to the superbly voiced one!) The librarian stated that the initial are apparently holograph. In these small books the play texts are heavily edited throughout, in pencil, mainly by deletions and instructions for the relocation of sections of text. This is convincing evidence that the Harrison edition is the real source text, a conclusion supported by Palmer when he cites a facsimile of some editing by Pears of the Penguin edition (illustration 34, between pages 224–25). If further proof be required of the status of the Harrison text, Jeremy Cullum, Britten's secretary in 1959 and 1960, recollects that it was from one of these paperbacks that he, pursuant to the day-to-day instructions of the librettists, made successive drafts of the working libretto (appendix C).

Editions of the play other than those in the Britten-Pears Library have been examined. Some contain textual items that match the working libretto where it differed from Harrison, but there is no evidence to suggest that the librettists used those other editions or that the matches are due to anything more than chance. In any event, the First Quarto (*Q*1) and the First Folio (*F*1) of Shakespeare's *Dream* are "good" texts (i.e., probably, at least, closely authoritative), so later editions of this play do not differ greatly, and the recognition of any particular edition as source text is not likely to cause major errors.

The shortage of editions and genuine facsimiles in an otherwise full and carefully kept archive, the existence of the librettists' heavily annotated copies of a specific edition of Shakespeare's play, and the recollection of the person who typed the working libretto are strong reasons to regard what Britten wrote in the *Observer* article as a distortion and to recognize that the real source text of the working libretto is one specific edition of the play, the Harrison Penguin edition.

Turning from the source text to the libretto, there are difficulties of different kinds. The document that the Britten-Pears Library designates as the *Dream*'s working libretto can be seen only at the library, which will not supply a facsimile copy of archival material. The document, in typescript, is considerably amended in manuscript, the changes often, but not always, identifiable as being in Britten's hand. There is a microfilm copy, and, of its sixty frames, only nine do not show manuscript changes.[2] Of the fifty-one amended frames, sixteen contain changes more significant than spelling corrections, added or deleted stage directions, or isolated word changes. For most of the revisions, it is difficult, if not impossible, to say whether they were made in fixing the working libretto or later during composition, an important obscurity when examining the composer's modus operandi.

A reprint copy (showing, on the last page, "Westerham [Kent] Press 2M/4/62") of the Boosey & Hawkes 1960 libretto, published for use at the first performance, has been annotated with departures from the library's working libretto. Many of the departures, such as spelling and punctuation, are of no consequence, particularly in a text destined to be disciplined by music and to be sung. Stage directions are more numerous and more explicit in the printed booklet. Errors common to both documents suggest that the printed booklet was prepared directly from the amended working libretto rather than from the score. Both fail to show the words "Amen, amen to that fair prayer say I," sung by Hermia in her sleep, an echo of Lysander's declaration a dozen lines earlier in the play (43; 2.2.61), most probably inserted by Britten during composition, on which occasion he omitted to make his usual addition to the working libretto. Both documents fail to include Theseus's line, "To while away this long age of three hours," justifying his call for masques, but it is in the score (410). Its omission from the working libretto is probably a typist's error, caught during composition, when, again, Britten did not correct the working libretto. In the source text (89; 5.1.372), Puck says, "the wolf beholds the moon." The working libretto has "beholds," but the printed libretto

(50.33) and the score (473) have "behowls." Britten could not have based the change on $Q1$ or $F1$ both of which have "beholds," and it may safely be assumed that he failed to record on the working libretto an inspiration suggesting a sound image he received during composition.

All in all the differences between the libretti are such as to suggest that the published booklet may be accepted as a sufficiently close representation of the library's document: indeed different circumstances combine to justify, even to compel, this practical course. Britten had some precompositional musical ideas; he required that the words of the working libretto be only "more or less" fixed. Cullum suggested that Britten began composition before the libretto was finished, and the precise timing of the manuscript changes to Cullum's typescript cannot be established. In the author's perspective, one is dealing with a modern language adaptation of a modern edition of the play that had been published only seven years earlier. All in all, textual minutiae can and should be ignored in favor of a concentration on changes of far greater significance, namely: restructuring Shakespeare's complex of plots, excisions and retentions of his text, and setting the remaining words to music. The intermediate key text, regarded as the "more or less fixed" words that Britten demanded before beginning detailed composition, will therefore be the Boosey & Hawkes published libretto, which, unless the context requires otherwise, is termed simply "the libretto."

Identification of the best score to be used presents few difficulties. The easily read vocal score by Imogen Holst and Martin Penny was published by Boosey & Hawkes in 1960. It is available, and Britten's acknowledgment (Aldeburgh, 15 April 1960) authenticates it, but it fails to reveal the details of orchestration. There is a personal conducting score of Britten's in the library that reveals his specific thoughts on certain aspects of performance, but it is not readily accessible. In the circumstances, it is most appropriate to accept as the third key text the Boosey & Hawkes printed full score (London, 1960), also subscribed "Aldeburgh, April 15th 1960." This study is based on a 1961 reprint that incorporates some corrections of minor printer's errors (documented in the library's collection of printer's proofs) that Britten himself approved. A few minor errors persist.[3] This score is regarded as the final text towards which the librettists' and the composer's efforts were directed.

The texts of both the play and the opera are only blueprints for performance, since the reality of drama is the unfolding totality of personal and impersonal things heard and seen on stage. For well-known reasons beyond the scope of this book to describe, the experience of a listener-spectator (Peter Evan's term is apt here) in the opera house must be different from that of a score reader in the closet. Partial performances in the shape of sound recordings of plays and operas provide only partial experiences, and even audiovisual media fail to generate the sense of being part of a group seeing and hearing a drama in a theater or an opera house. Moreover, only a live performance can permit the playgoers or operagoers and the players, individually and as groups, to react with each other. This interaction is recognized in the very acknowledgment of any meaning in the texts, and, when the connection is not merely implicit but open, as in Puck's epilogue (91; 5.1.423), it must be recognized. Particular performances however—and every performance is in some way particular—are irreducibly varied, and discretion advises safety through concentration on the score. Britten himself said to Elizabeth Forbes in a 1967 interview that he had "seen some productions of his operas . . . which contained a great many ideas never dreamt of by him or his librettist" (16).

This book is not concerned with a systematic study of Britten's life or with biographical details of others involved in the making of his *Dream*. Many books contain chronologies of his life and works: one of the most useful is that in the recently published *A Britten Source Book* compiled by John Evans, Philip Reed, and Paul Wilson (1987). More recent still, but naturally silent on the composition of this opera, is *Letters from a Life: The Selected Letters and Diaries of Benjamin Britten 1913–1976* (1991) in two volumes covering the years 1923–39 and 1939–45. In the introduction, the editor-in-chief, Donald Mitchell, believes that "Britten's impulse to . . . accurate self-documentation" resulted in "our having access to an autobiography embodied in the letters and diaries" (56–57).

Some relevant personal matters, however, must be put in context. Adapting Theseus's words, to make the opera-makers more true than strange (78; 5.1.2) and to give to persons who might otherwise seem "airy nothings" a local habitation and a name (79; 5.1.16), biographical notes of Benjamin Britten, Jeremy Cullum, Imogen Holst, Donald Mitchell, Peter Pears, Rosamund Strode, and Paul Wilson are provided in appendix B. It is beyond the scope of this study to trace Britten's musical development, though mention is made of his previous interest in night, sleep, and dreams, exemplified in his *Serenade* and *Nocturne*.

Three persons who knew Britten and Pears well were interviewed. Jeremy Cullum typed the working libretto for the *Dream;* Donald Mitchell, a longtime friend of Britten's, is an authority on his music; Rosamund Strode was Britten's music assistant and continued as keeper of manuscripts and archivist at the Britten-Pears Library. Notes of the interviews with Cullum and Strode which contain matters of both general and specific interest, are in appendix C. Some merely peripheral material has been retained because it is not otherwise available.

A critical look at operatic conventions is appropriate. In order to enrich an examination of the things Britten and Pears did to make their operatic *Dream* from Shakespeare's, it is relevant to understand their major options for changes, to discover any probable major expectations for the new work as an adaptation, and to note how far the expectations are realized. The change options can be particularized in one manner by recognizing the elements of a drama, while the expectations for the composition can be rationalized to some degree in the light of operatic conventions.

The very relevance of comparing Britten's *Dream* with operatic standards depends, however, upon its being indeed an opera within received definitions. Grout defined opera as "a *drama in music:* a dramatic action, exhibited on a stage with scenery by actors in costume, the words conveyed entirely or for the most part by singing, and the whole sustained and amplified by orchestral music" (4). Other definitions of the genre are similar. In 1981 Robert Donington, in *The Rise of Opera,* described it as "staged drama unfolding integrally in words and music" (20). Joseph Kerman, in both editions of his *Opera as Drama,* stated that "opera is properly a musical form of drama" (1956, 3; 1988, 1). (Unless otherwise indicated, subsequent references to Kerman are to the 1988 edition.) Finally, Herbert Lindenberger, in *Opera: The Extravagant Art,* by opening with a reference to the power opera has exercised on its audiences (9) and by ending with a reference to it as "among the performative genres" (284), clearly concurs in the essential concept of opera as staged drama.

The acceptance of Britten's *Dream* as generically an opera is based on its outward features, its reception as an opera by critics generally, and Britten's own *Observer* article, written between the completion of composition and the first performance. His precompositional intentions are clear: "Last August it was decided that for this year's [the 1960] Aldeburgh Festival I should write a full-length opera for the opening of the reconstructed Jubilee Hall" (Palmer, 177). Later in the article, he refers to the work as an opera, albeit a small-scale one, that he and Pears had made (Palmer, 178–79).

Evan Senior, however, a critic who reviewed the world premiere, rejected the label "an opera" in favor of "a masque." He praised "the beautiful and well-produced entertainment" and the "magical evocative qualities" of the music. "But," he wrote, "not one moment of this music pushes the action forward to the slightest degree. It is purely comment on what is happening . . ." This characteristic violates his criterion for operatic music, which "must carry the development of the material forward in purely musical thrust and purely musical develpment." He concludes, "If it can be called anything, it should be called a Masque—not an opera" (10). Senior's views on the proper role of music in opera as music drama, which coincide with those of other critics, can be accepted and it can be recognized that he may see the court's and the lovers' verbal commentary on the tradesmen's tragedy as masquelike audience participation—even as a vicarious joining-in by the theatre audience that is characteristic of court masques in Renaissance England. The main thrust of the work, however, remains the comedy of the lovers' triumph over patriarchal tyranny and self-ignorance: the audiences do not leave their seats. Moreover, Britten's music does carry the development forward, as Senior failed to see, and it does "articulate the drama," according to a requirement of Kerman's.

The foregoing definitions of opera name or suggest its key elements, which, in turn, provide a vocabulary for analysis—categories for the makers' options for changes and labels for the fields within which operatic conventions can be organized, albeit roughly. (The more important of the elements shown below are italicised.)

DRAMA, a staged performance, encompassing:
CHARACTERS, represented by
PLAYERS in
COSTUME and MAKE-UP,
ACTING, by means of
SUNG WORDS, MOVEMENT, and GESTURE, an
ACTION (situations, events, and processes) forming a
PLOT (a structured story or fable) within a
SETTING (comprising one or more places and times) represented by

SCENERY and PROPERTIES, constituting, on occasion,
SPECTACLE; all accompanied by
MUSIC of an
ORCHESTRA.

With the possible exceptions of "drama" and "plot," these elements are immediate perceptions by the senses of sight and hearing that generate emotions, prompt comprehension by reason, and lead to the consideration of further elements. These, often criteria-forming, may include;

FORM (on large and small scales) and
CONTENT, which together may appear chaotic, varied, unified, or homogeneous;
THEMES and *MOTIVES;*
INTERELEMENTAL RELATIONS, especially between the music and the words, or, better, the drama;
REPRESENTATION, true or false, general or specialized, of the real world;
IMAGINATION;
LANGUAGE, VERSE OR *PROSE,* especially its rhythm, sound, and metaphor;
THEATER, as the medium for presenting opera directly to its
AUDIENCE, and indirectly to its
PATRONS;
DIDACTICISM and ENTERTAINMENT; and
VALUES, aesthetic and moral.

Many of the elements are closely interrelated, forming functional systems and are properly considered together. These elements, with the exception of sung words and accompanying music, are also parts of plays, and, thus, the changes in their characteristics and importance when being newly deployed in opera are features for study.

Another value of this identification of operatic elements lies in recognizing that each element or each combination of elements has distinctive attributes, ranging widely in kind and force. Further, the distinctive nature of an attribute may give it or its parent element special status as an operatic convention or a criterion.

The useful, commonly used term "convention" for a certain quality in an opera needs to be taken in context. Its basic connotation implies something received although unnatural or even ridiculous, such as sung words that would be spoken in real life or continuous accompanying orchestral music. As a convention, such a distinctive characteristic emits no pejorative overtones, and it often constitutes part of a class definition.

The reception of an operatic feature, conventional or not, is usually limited, confined to a subgenre of opera during a restricted period of time in a particular country or region. The approval is subjectively based and is rarely, if ever, unanimous. If an attribute, conventional or not, is necessarily present to an optimal extent in order for the work to achieve popular or critical acclaim or both, it may be considered a value-charged criterion.

Britten, in his Aspen Award acceptance speech, said "I . . . take note of the human circumstances of music, of its environment and conventions" (11). Thus, while discovering his modus operandi it is surely relevant to examine how far he and Pears respected or defied those operatic conventions that might be expected to limit, validate, or enfranchise their vision. The mature Shakespearean comedies, like all artistic genres, had their contemporary conventions, and one may sometimes regard Britten's compliance with or rejection of an operatic convention as the perpetuation or abandonment of a convention of the earlier special dramatic genre. One should certainly bear in mind the precompositional decision that the source was to be a well-known Renaissance drama and that familiar but somewhat archaic language was to carry over into the opera.

For the present, in view of the lack of certainty regarding many operatic attributes, including conventions, the discussion is confined to identifying—usually simply naming—the major conventions of mid-twentieth-century romantic chamber opera in English, the subgenre of Britten's *Dream*. The "chamber" restraint was no doubt deliberate—to facilitate performance. Indeed, a larger-scale Covent Garden staging, shortly following the premiere, received some adverse criticism based on the lost intimacy. At the same time, it should be recognized that some attributes had and continue to have wider currency. Later, when discussing specific events in the makers' literary and musical procedures, some of the ensuing attributes of their product, remarkable or mundane, will be compared with the conventional operatic expectations—both those identified here and others.

The operatic attributes, including conventions, of concern here are indicated below in a list of descriptive synonyms, characteristics, or functions applicable to the respective operatic elements. The listed attributes are stated briefly—some, as a result, perhaps too dogmatically. Indeed, Kerman concludes the later edition of

his book in the light of a lifetime of experience: "Objective operatic
criticism is not a concept anyone will buy today, if they ever would.
The best we can do is cultivate observation, pray for insight, and
keep subjectivity as honest as we can" (228). These cautionary
words must be noted while persisting in an evaluative analysis.
Some attributes are followed by a reference to the authority for a
statement—often selected from several available—from which the
attribute is recognized. Other attributes are based on the same or
other authorities, but all ultimately rest on the subjective opinions
of operagoers. Ideally, many attributes are present in a given work
simply to an adequate degree, neither lacking nor excessive to an
extent that substantially reduces the opera's reception. Similarly,
optimally, many attributes fluctuate within the work, present to
different extents at different times, generating directed development.

DRAMA
  dramma per musica, drama by means of music (Grout, 1)
CHARACTERS
  merely sketched in verbally (Grout, 4)
  eloquently passionate (Schmidgall, *Literature,* (20)
  assume more formal, often heroic, stances (Lindenberger, 19)
SUNG WORDS
  a sine qua non
  singing is received, although unnatural, even ridiculous in re-
    ality
  "wholly a third . . . nearly always get lost" (Richard Strauss
    in Lindenberger, 29)
  rhythm of the music overrides the rhythm of the words
  recitative differs basically from aria, respectively emphasizing
    intelligibility for narration and musicality for comment
ACTION, FORMING A PLOT
  must be dramatic (Kerman, 1956 and 1988, passim)
  "dramatic" implies exciting, unified, continuous, and com-
    pleted
  multiple action is good; must be unified (Doran, re drama gen-
    erally, 294; Weiner, passim)
  simplicity (Schmidgall, *Literature,* 19)
  elements should be interdependent and balanced
  affective, containing passion (Harries and Harries, 275); with
    crises; emotional moments (Smith, 99), epiphanic moments
    (Schmidgall, *Literature,* 11–12), and magical transformations
    (Lindenberger, 46–47)

dramatic tempo is slower to make room for the music to function (Grout, 5)
SETTING
exotic (Lindenberger, 51)
SPECTACLE
rhetorical set pieces are favored: prayer, plea, lament, raging,
cursing, conspiratorial oath-taking, soliloquy, and mad
scenes (Lindenberger, 31–32)
MUSIC of an ORCHESTRA
continuous
functional (Langer, Copland, Meyer, Wallace Berry)
interesting in itself
articulates the action
integrated with other elements
"dramatically effective music for the theatre" (Britten,
Aspen, 11)
leitmotivs are useful
may reinstate rhetoric cut from the source
FORM
plot is simplified
opera centres on episodes: dances, choruses, ensembles, and
spectacles (Grout, 4)
paratactic rather than hypotactic, links excised from source
text
disjunctiveness: number opera, scenic form is popular in mid-
twentieth-century (Smith, 401), a reaction against *durch-
komponierte* (through-composed) opera
ceremonious acts are favored—form before
content (Lindenberger, 27)
CONTENT
range of topics is virtually unlimited
love is the most popular subject
exotic material is favored (Lindenberger, 51)
lyric, explosive, and hyperbolic moments are good (Schmidgall, *Literature,* 11)
prosaic or rhetorical niceties are not good (Schmidgall, *Literature,* 11)
supernatural material must be limited (Lindenberger, 47–48)
philosophical, aesthetic, and conceptual materials are unsuit-
able (Schmidgall, *Literature,* 17)
classical references and allusions are problematic: "[we] had
endless trouble with the references" (Britten in Palmer, 178)

INTERELEMENTAL RELATIONS
  deeper meaning is possible from the mixed medium (Cone in
    Grout, 6)
  "the music of a song destroys the verbal music of the poem
    utterly" (Tippett in Smith, xiii)
REPRESENTATION of the REAL WORLD
  opera is embedded in society
  opera is "conditioned . . . by the ideals and desires of those
    upon whom it depends" (Grout, 2)
  the composer is in society (Britten, *Aspen,* 16)
  distancing from the real world is prevalent
  representation tends towards overt artifice and exaggeration
    (Lindenberger, 15),
  illusion, imagery, loftiness; stylization (Grout, 2)
  representation tends to be false rather than true, even pessi-
    mistic, satirical,
  cynical, and nihilistic (Smith, 384–85)
  uses other arts: dance, scenic design, and theatrical arts
  materially expensive, luxurious
  contemporary relevance is essential: modernization, topical-
    ity, originality, and novelty may be good (Peter Evans, 2–3)
  source is expendable, rewriting rather than reduction often
    best (Harries and Harries, 288)
LANGUAGE
  understandable, intelligible (Britten, "On Writing," 7)
  the use of English is desirable (Britten, "On Writing," 7)
  modernized spelling
  too conspicuously "poetic" is a disadvantage (Harries and
    Harries, 286)
  sound of words is important (Grout, 5)
  vowels at certain pitches may cause difficulties
  pace is generally slower to allow music to function (Lindenber-
    ger, 40)
THEATER
  theatrical arts are important
  coups de théâtre are desirable
AUDIENCE
  an integral part of a performance
  members use several senses to apprehend and several intellec-
    tual skills to comprehend
PATRONS
  required, opera is dependent upon them

DIDACTICISM
   music should be useful (Britten, *Aspen,* 21–22)
   opera can be didactic
   challenge to the audience to understand is didactic
   "I have . . . strong points of view to which I find opera can
     give expression" (Britten, "On Writing," 7)
ENTERTAINMENT
   opera should be attractive, pleasing
VALUES
   aesthetic value of internal beauty is required (Peter Evans, 3)
   can reveal moral values, mainly through exempla and caution-
     ary situations
   provides enrichment and embellishment of civilized life
     (Grout, 1)

At some risk of inviting accusations, on the one hand, of failure to recognize irreconcilability, and, on the other, of oversimplification, inflexibility, and dogmatism—but encouraged by Hamm's conclusion that "many of the basic concepts and structures of opera have carried through various periods of music history" (217)—this chapter concludes with the perception of central conventions, criteria even, to be observed in making an aesthetically good mid-twentieth-century opera according to the weight of opinion in the literature:

1. The libretto portrays action that is dramatic, and it provides throughout opportunities for the music to perform its functions.
2. The music is interesting, and it functions in its own distinctive manner in a cooperative, equal partnership with the words.
3. The opera is an organic compound of all its balanced elements working in multiple unity and displaying variety in unity.
4. As a cultural artifact, a close-to-the-score performance seriously affects its audience—which must be regarded as an integral part of the performance—by its contemporary relevance and by displaying at least some novel features.

These criteria are things not indispensable, but may be ignored at the composer's peril: "each a frequent hallmark rather than a sine qua non" (Schmidgall, *Literature,* 10). A final distillation is offered by repeating the words of the maturer Kerman. Still proclaiming opera as drama he concludes: "Drama requires not only the presentation of action, but an insight into its quality by means of response to action. Only the presentation of such quality justifies the dramatic endeavor; and in the best dramas, the response seems imaginative, true, illuminating, and fully matched to the action" (212). It must be added that the insight into the quality should suggest a cultural response that is evaluative.

Notes

1. There is no reason to doubt that Britten's love of Shakespeare's *Dream* was based on a long acquaintance. Britten obviously meant to name the *Dream* rather than the *Merchant* in his diary entry of 21 May, 1930, when in the school orchestra at Gresham's School: "We are doing Selecs [Selections] Purcell's *Fairy Queen* music for the play, Merchant of Venice" (Mitchell and Reed, 2: 1225).

2. The ratios of amended to total frames, by act, are: $1 = 11/19$, $2 = 20/21$, and $3 = 20/20$, the lower incidence in the first act no doubt reflecting its extra typing.

3. Errata in the Boosey & Hawks full score, 1961 edition:

Page 9, measure 4, the first group of fairies' final note when they "serve the Fairy Queen" should be a C♯ rather than a C♮;

page 51, measure 9, the cellos need a bass clef sign;

page 287, the oboist should be instructed: "Take English Horn", to prepare for the entry of that instrument at page 311;

page 389, measure 1, clarinet numbers are required; and

page 391, measure 3 (end), a cautionary tenor clef sign is required.

2
Restructuring the Play: Aims and Options

Britten . . . innegabilmente silenzioso; certo una personalità
schiva, con una netta avversione a lasciarsi coinvolgere in dispute ideologiche o a propagandare la propria musica. . . . pre-
ferendo lasciare che le sue composizioni parlassero da sole.
— Donald Mitchell, "Benjamin Britten:
l'innovatore silenzioso"

Britten . . . undeniably silent; truly a shy person, with a clear
aversion to allowing himself to become involved in ideological
arguments or to promoting his own music . . . . preferring to
allow his compositions to speak for themselves.
— Donald Mitchell, "Benjamin Britten:
The Silent Innovator"
(author's translation)

Britten's often noted reluctance to discuss his music, particularly
its interpretation, is underlined in the epigraph to this chapter from
Mitchell's article in the program book of the fifty-first Maggio Musicale Florentia 1988 (31). Britten, however, did leave some piece-
meal clues to his working procedures, particularly in the *Observer*
article, written between the composition and the first performance
of his *Dream* (Palmer, 177–80). The article deals extensively with
making the libretto, Britten's first and only venture into the field
of libretto writing. This and the next chapter draw from it to examine one step in that exercise, the reshaping of Shakespeare's play—
the reordering of substantial units of text affecting the characters'
staging, as distinct from the excising and modifying of lesser passages discussed in later chapters.

First, in his approach to writing opera Britten had always found
that it was "very dangerous to start writing the music until the
words [had been] more or less fixed." He elaborated, saying that

when he had worked with independent librettists they had "blocked the opera out in the way that an artist might block out a picture" (Palmer, 177). A synopsis of the opera in Pears's hand, to be discussed later, indicates that some initial blocking out was done here.

These statements suggest that the making of the libretto could and should be examined as a distinct process. Such a course is contrary to other analyses in depth of the *Dream,* but Howard examined Britten's approach to his libretti separately in her 1969 book on his operas (230–34). Also, the neglected recognition of libretti motivated Smith to defend them as art works in his book *The Tenth Muse.* With this opera it is not possible to argue for a separation on the grounds that distinct persons were concerned with the libretto and the score, for it is assumed that one person— and that Britten rather than Pears—had the last word concerning the libretto. This assumption follows Philip Brett's conclusion after he had studied closely original documents related to the making of the libretto for *Peter Grimes:*

> Montagu Slater [the librettist] cannot have been prepared for the consequences of writing for such a strong-willed composer . . . . Despite the comments . . . of his team of supporters—Pears, Slater, Crozier, Duncan and perhaps others— . . . it was Britten himself who made all the decisions. (87)

Peter Porter concludes likewise:

> All the operas on which [Britten's] world reputation are based are entirely his in idea, inspiration, lay-out and dramatic emphasis. His librettists whether poets, novelists, producers or scholars, tailored their books to his minutely worked-out requirements. (9)

According to Cullum, Britten did begin detailed composing before the libretto was finished (appendix C), but this does not seriously weaken Britten's warning of the dangers or the argument for analysis by stages. Relying, therefore, on Britten's "words-first" opinion, it is apt to deal first and separately with the making of the libretto. But the isolation of the libretto cannot be complete in view of Britten's musical preconceptions and the fact that a librettist is expected to foresee opportunities for musical occasions and to make structural and other adaptations of the source to facilitate the composer's realizing them.

A second topic in Britten's statements about the opera makers' approach bears directly on the "words-first" question: he said that to get the play into manageable shape was the first task, and "the shape comes first" (Palmer, 177–78). These are suggestive terms. The wide connotations and implications of the term "shape" suggest that the librettists considered several different structural elements in the play as candidates for reshaping, including the character groups, the plots, and the settings (more about these later). By its nontechnical nature, the word "shape" perhaps also recognizes the ultimate interdependence of the two procedures of restructuring and excising and of the two concepts of form and content, which are sometimes initially distinguished for analytical purposes.

Britten's term "manageable" confirms that, despite facing "the tremendous challenge of those Shakespearean words" (Palmer, 178), the composer nevertheless intended to be in charge. He does not say what makes a libretto's shape manageable—though he apparently means it should be amenable to manipulation when setting it to music—but there is a clue in his goal of writing "dramatically effective music for the theatre." Surely he would concur in the general criterion that the libretto must be a text that will permit significant music to function jointly with the words in a partnership that produces opera rather than, say, a play with incidental music.

Three features of manageability of shape stand out. First, as Grout indicated, since music requires time for the deployment of its ideas, there must be room in the text for this to happen, probably as a result of a slowed down dramatic tempo. Second, since the composer may at times wish to counterpoise textual and musical forms, on both large and small scales, the libretto must include literary forms that will be recognizable and significant in collaboration with or in opposition to those of the music. Third, the dramatic action, axiomatically a constitutent of the libretto, should be unified, or at least be unifiable by being set to music.

Britten indicated, partly at least, the route to manageable shape: "basically . . . simplifying and cutting an extremely complex story" (Palmer, 177–78). Cutting makes a text shorter in unspecified ways—and not necessarily better—but simplifying is a procedure capable of definition. Britten's very view of Shakespear's *Dream* as an extremely complex story implies that the libretto should be less elaborate and involved, but there is nothing to suggest that the result should be artless, which might well make it unoperatic. Simplicity, like complexity, could be excessive in a story that Britten would adopt for setting to make a full-length opera, indeed he was prepared and apparently glad to take as a libretto "one that was ready to hand" (Palmer, 177), the *Dream* as Shakespeare left it, complex though it appeared. It is, therefore, assumed that the story in the desired libretto for the hastily required opera was to be simpler than the source, but not something noticeably simple in an absolute sense by conventional standards for the plot of an opera of its kind. A complete opera, on the other hand, if preserving the intelligibility of the words and integrating them with meaningful music, will certainly be more complex than the libretto and may well be more complex than the source—and better for it. This probability of a resurgence of complexity in the final product, either score or performance, marks simplicity as a quality that should be considered separately for libretto and opera. It provides another reason for first analyzing the libretto when examining the opera-making process in depth.

The shape that Britten desired, in addition to being manageable after simplification, was "a whole dramatic shape" (Palmer, 178). This desire recognizes the need for balance between the constituent parts and a final unity due to a natural outcome of varied, relevant, and functional elements. A dramatist's whole dramatic shape found in a source play can be improved, maintained, or marred by a a librettist's goal of simplification, and thus, when Britten stressed that he wanted the shape fixed early, he was taking precautions against a late, unpleasant surprise.

A third matter in Britten's statements concerning the approach towards making the *Dream* is his initial musical ideas. He conceded that, with the *Dream,* as with other operas, he "first had a general musical conception of the whole work" in his mind and that he "could have described the music, but not played a note" (Palmer, 178). It is postulated that, because of several specific musical possibilities already in his mind, Britten decided that the opera should open in the wood near Athens, to reveal, first, the fairies, before the court, the lovers, and the tradesmen, with these groups of dramatis personae and the setting largely portrayed by that music. This assumed librettists' approach is not the device of inventing and fitting words to an established tune, but rather, as Britten put it, more or less fixing given words in the light of describable music that could work with them as a frame and a simultaneous medium. Britten's remark about preconceived music acknowledges a background that profoundly affects the "words-first" statement; therefore, certain musical influences on the restructuring of the play text also need to be considered in this chapter.

The view is that Britten and Pears were primarily making an opera rather than converting a play; thus, at the fundamental, strategic level, they were guided by the form and content of a visualized, acceptable libretto for a visualized, acceptable opera rather than by the shape and matter of a known, loved play. The ground for this opinion is Britten's acknowledgment of the preconceived, describable music in his mind. He did know the play well, but he also appreciated its operatic possibilities—just as he did, probably a decade later, when studying and glossing another text, Mann's *Death in Venice*. From this point of view, a conceived libretto—even a visualized performance—underlay the selection and reordering of Shakespeare's character groups, plots, and settings, all of which the librettists moved around to make a whole dramatic shape that could be put into music. (This conclusion is discussed further later, in reference to an opera plot synopsis made by Pears in his Penguin play text.) In other words, based on Britten's preconception of describable music, it is a central assumption that, in making the libretto, the exercise was, primarily, one of conceiving the opera as a different communication in a different genre and, secondarily, of selecting and ordering units of action found in the play. The play provided the opera with an attractive, respectable parentage, but, more than ever in Britten's day, the offspring was free to construct its own world. An "opera from comedy" is being studied, rather than a "comedy into opera." Jonathan Miller, in seminars following the 1989 Whelen Lectures given at the University of Saskatchewan, speaking of a dramatic end product, a particular staging, endorsed this concept. He asserted that the text of a play is an artifact found by the producer, who cannot reproduce a former performance in what is necessarily a new, different context: even a living author has forfeited authority.

One may still recognize the influence of the play on the details of the libretto, but this should be regarded as a secondary, reverse process. Almost all of the comedy's content finds its way into the opera, but Shakespeare's form is drastically modified. The evidence of the annotated Penguin texts of Shakespeare's *Dream* is consistent with the conclusion that a conceived libretto with initially describable music dominated the librettists' work, for the editing of the texts came after the planning revealed by Pears's synopsis of the opera-to-be.

As a direct consequence of the librettists' reshaping, as distinct from their cuts to shorten the text, a good many of the play's speeches, particularly from the beginning of the first scene, were dropped. Thus, although a detailed discussion of the librettists' textual excisions is deferred until the later chapters, it is appropriate to outline here the main considerations in retaining and discarding text in a source, against which the cuts incidental to restructuring can be judged.

First, since opera must have a dramatic content, as stressed by

Kerman (214), the nature of the material, whether it unfolds action or pictures nonaction, governs its dramatic essentiality or expendability respectively. Another consideration in choosing text from a source to make a libretto is the fitness of the material for setting to music. A composer has a wide range of contrasting material from which to select according to his particular preference: contrast the "prolonged orgy of lust and crime" in Puccini's *Tosca* (1900) and "the mysterious, spiritual character of the drama" in Debussy's *Pelléas et Melisande* (1902) (Grout, 441 and 500). Third, the nature of the language, its capability of setting to music, can be decisive. Britten was specific on this, although he treated it as a challenge rather than a warning: "Nor did I find it daunting to be tackling a masterpiece which already has a strong verbal music of its own" (Palmer, 178).

Reordering text, as distinct from keeping or cutting it, to make a libretto from an extant literary work is based on considerations that may conflict: the meaning desired and dependent upon a particular series of events versus the effect of musical ideas inherent in a prospective musical form. The relative importance of these two forces will vary from work to work and from time to time in the same work. On this point Britten, *"l'innovatore silenzioso,"* was typically reticent, inviting speculations: "I haven't tried to put across any particular idea of the play that I could equally well express in words, but although one doesn't intend to make any special interpretation, one cannot avoid it" (Palmer, 178). Nor did he describe his preconceived music, which, he stated, he could have described.

The restructuring was subject to constraints based on audiences' conservatism. As already noted, Britten's attention to conventions invites consideration of how far he observed them and how far he was an innovator, free of these constraints. Moreover, Shakespeare's *Dream* would be widely known to members of Britten's audience from their studies in secondary school of this frequently taught "safe" play by the supreme English dramatist, chosen for its relative freedom from bawdy and, in those pre-Jan Kott days, from the more embarrassing sexual problems. It would be remembered for the inanities of the tradesmen, especially the one with the funny, anatomical name. Britten was a product of English boys' preparatory and public schools and, according to Mitchell, was from a social class corresponding to that of the lovers in the play. Britten knew the work, possibly better than most, and realized that its popular familiarity would have box office advantages—even, as Dean points out, that "a modern audience would doubtless reject an extreme upheaval of the story" (Hartnoll, 92). But opinions vary. Howard claims that a play should be radically changed to make a good opera and praises Britten's *Dream* because it "presents a single interpretation of the comprehensive material of the play, . . . its narrow reading reveals some aspects in compensatingly greater depth" (163). This opinion is worth remembering, for Howard will, finally, be found to be correct.

In their blocking out, Britten and Pears must have recognized various elements of the play that might be marshaled into alternative rearrangements to make different libretti, some more acceptable than others. A natural, manipulable unit is an action or part of an action, a plot or subplot executed by members of a character group. The interdependence of plots is important, too, especially if one of them is a candidate for amendment or exclusion, because unity may be jeopardized. Settings of place and time can also be altered.

The character groups were no doubt seen by Britten and Pears as prime targets for possible reshaping. Indeed, Britten found the play "operatically . . . especially exciting because there are three quite separate groups." He named them as the lovers, the rustics, and the fairies, stating that, in the opera, each was given "a different kind of texture and orchestral 'colour'" (Palmer, 177). It is to be hoped, however, that he might have conceded recognition to a fourth group, the court—as, for example, do Dean (Hartnoll, 118) and Schmidgall (Shakespeare, 288)—for the music for Theseus and Hippolyta is quite distinctive. The groups are worth looking at separately, for some are more interesting than others as operatic attractions, possibly requiring changed emphases.

The plots of the play are complementary to the character groups as objects of concern to the librettists bent on reshaping. A preliminary look at each of these as a separate series of events, ignoring for the moment the connections with other plots, will highlight the innate drama of each plot and focus on what would be lost if it were to be sacrificed or curtailed. This form of simplification is commonly used by librettists; however, it can leave a gap that must be filled.

Settings, both of place and time, are commonly seen as incidental to the action and are the elements of an old play most often changed in a modern production. Britten had strong views with his *Dream,* probably derived from his interest in night, sleep, and dreams. His preconceived, describable music meant that to open in an enchanted, nocturnal sylvan setting was more important than all else in determining his required reshaping. Yet he wanted to preserve as much of Shakespeare as possible—"one can only hope that one hasn't lost too much" (Palmer, 178).

Northrop Frye's references in his *Anatomy of Criticism* to sojourns in the "Green World" in Shakespeare's mature comedies were published three years before Britten composed his *Dream,* and C. L. Barber's analyses in his *Shakespeare's Festive Comedy* of indulgences in transient station-reversing festivities were published three years after the opera. Whether Britten had read or thought of these concepts is not known. If he had, his ideas for restructuring nevertheless overrode the Shakespearean pattern.

The play opens in the Athenian court. The characters in the court group with speaking parts, according to the designations in Harrison's list of "The Actors' Names," are Theseus, Duke of Athens; Hippolyta, Queen of the Amazons, betrothed to Theseus; and Philostrate, Master of the Revels to Theseus (20; 1.1.1). The Duke and the Queen represent a court as the pinnacle of society, and the Duke functions as a court of law and equity. Others are mentioned in the play's stage directions: "their train" in the Duke's and Queen's hunting scene (72; 4.1.103), and "Lords" in that scene (74; 4.1.186) and in the final court revels (77; 5.1.1). It is obviously court servants who "wind horns" before and during the hunt (72; 4.1.102 and 73; 4.1.139), and who provide a "flourish of trumpets" before the court entertainment (81; 5.1.107).

Because—for good musical reasons—the librettists decided to open the opera in the wood near Athens, they deferred the appearance of Theseus and Hippolyta until the day of their wedding, in their court, where they were eventually needed to provide and host the final coordinating entertainment. Thus Theseus and Hipployta are retained in the opera, but Theseus's role becomes little more than a cameo appearance in the opera's final scene. He becomes "a rather tin god" (Howard, 164), a fate perhaps reflecting his reduced contemporary relevance. Before his appearance, he is represented by approaching and receding offstage horn passages (identifiable as an offstage hunt by those who remember the play) to awaken the lovers and by orchestral horn fanfares in the transition scene from the wood to the palace in the final act. But neither set of sounds is explicitly attributed to him, possibly leaving many in the audience guessing.

Philostrate is dropped from the opera, dispensing with a cast member and avoiding a doubling of parts. His first function in the play, to "stir up the Athenian youths to merriments" (21; 1.1.12), becomes redundant with the deferral of Theseus's appearance. His second duty, to offer Theseus a choice of "abridgement" after the marriage supper (78; 5.1.36), becomes superfluous when the players' Prologue simply hands the single playbill to Hippolyta. In the opera score, as in the play text, the other court servants are mentioned only in the stage directions and are not referred to in the dramatis personae. It appears, however, from the casts of the first two performances as recorded in the score (vii), that a Master of Ceremonies, and Attendant, and two Pages, all silent, appeared on stage, at least one of whom, the Attendant (Jeremy Cullum, Britten's secretary), was there in recognition of services in making the opera (see the interview with Cullum, appendix C). A composer is liable to depart from the most carefully prepared score in a performance.

Shakespeare began and ended his play proper (which is followed by an epilogue) with the Athenian court actions; these subdivide into three plots (which it is important to distinguish), each derived from the court's social and political roles: the court nuptials plot, the court festivities plot, and the court juridical plot. The first plot comprises the ducal wedding announcement, Theseus and Hippolyta discussing their forthcoming wedding, four days off (21; 1.1.1), and the consummatory ordering to bed (89; 5.1.366). These events form a clear frame for the main action of the play. Although prominently displayed by Shakespeare, this plot by itself is unromantic, unexciting stuff, even, perhaps, for postwar devourers of glossy society magazines, especially as Shakespeare marries the ducal couple offstage.

In their major restructuring the librettists moved the wedding announcement to the final scene of the last act, causing problems in this plot. Theseus still, although belatedly, mentions his masculine nuptial desires, now to be delayed only a few minutes instead of the four days Shakespeare could impose. Theseus's reference to the old, slow-waning moon is delayed until a short time before the night of their solemnities, and perhaps this is why Hippolyta sings of the silver bow "*now* bent" in heaven, as in Q1 and F1, rather than "*new* bent," as in Harrison (21; 1.1.10 [emphasis added]). This change from "new bent" to "now bent" might be cited as one of the few indications that Britten and Pears, as Britten misleadingly said, "worked . . . principally from facsimiles of the First Folio and the First Quarto" (Palmer, 178): it certainly avoids a possibly confusing reference to a new moon and the old on the very same day. In the play, Theseus's ordering "lovers to bed" at midnight (89; 5.1.364) was no doubt intended to include not only the two young couples, Lysander with Hermia and Demetrius with Helena, but Hippolyta with himself. In the opera, there is a flaw in that the librettists failed to allow stage time in the revised structure for the ducal wedding to occur before bedtime. The lovers' nuptials are similarly preempted by the reshaping. Mervyn Cooke's discovery and analysis of these flaws is discussed later.

The court festivities plot comprises the civic festivities that Philostrate was to initiate (21; 1.1.12), probably with a proclamation that was understood by Shakespeare to prompt the tradesmen to offer their interlude. The play does not show any civic festivities, and the opera does not even mention them—appropriately, because it no longer portrays a clear excursion into and out of the kind of festive state identified in Barber's analysis of this and other Shakespearean comedies (11). Another much later court festivity, the hunt (72; 4.1.103), was eliminated, avoiding an expensive spectacle that would be disappointing without visible hounds, or probably chaotic or unwittingly comical with them. Possibly contemporary sensitivities about blood sports are spared. The hunt did not need to be eliminated to avoid moral censure: it could have been satirized—a nice touch for opera, "the extravagant art" of Lindenberger, to parody extravagance. But an acceptable performance time discouraged this. In the play, Theseus chooses an entertainment from four offered by Philostrate (78; 5.1.32), but this ritual was cut from the opera. The comedy's play-watching festivity (81; 5.1.108) was retained in the opera; indeed Britten extended the stage audience's participation by making the female lovers comment, enriching the musical sound and avoiding long silences for visible principals.

The play's court juridical plot begins with the upholding of patriarchy, when Hermia's father calls upon Theseus to confirm, in the presence of the parties concerned, that she must obediently marry not Lysander, her beloved, but Demetrius, the paternal choice of son-in-law (21; 1.1.41). Much later Theseus provides relief in equity, reversing his earlier adjudication (74; 4.1.179), and he orders the now properly paired lovers to be married. This event is generated by the actions of a different character group in another plot—Hermia had disobeyed her father before he took her and her suitors to court—and exists predominantly to reinforce the blocking of the lovers' aspirations. The librettists dispensed with the early adjudication scene, merely indicating that the sharp Athenian law that Lysander and Hermia are fleeing is one compelling her to marry with Demetrius. Theseus's characterization in the play as initially conservative but becoming liberal is lost.

Delaying Theseus's and Hippolyta's appearance, achieves a major simplification and, incidentally, makes the most substantial "abbreviation" of the play, which majestic Theseus himself would have resented. But in a play as well integrated as Shakespeare's *Dream,* no plot stands alone, and its importance often lies in its relations with other plots. When all the plots have been outlined, their links and the effects of changing their relative importance need to be examined.

The main characters in the lovers group are the two men, Lysander and Demetrius, both described by Harrison as in love with Hermia, and the two women, Hermia, daughter to Egeus, in love with Lysander, and Helena, in love with Demetrius. During the action Helena is referred to as "Nedar's daughter" (24; 1.1.107) and "old Nedar's Helena" (73; 4.1.130), familiarizing but unnecessary elaborations that were both omitted from the opera. Egeus belongs within the lovers' story and group. As Hermia's father, he is the character blocking true love and thus initiating the main action; he approaches the court in highly respectful terms as an outside subject, rather than as an inside member. The librettists were able to dispense with him and his lengthy introductory litigation, and thus to economize on another cast member.

A case can be made that the four young aristocrats are the only real lovers in the play: the wooing with a sword (21; 1.1.16) suggests that the Duke and the Amazon Queen are about to make a dynastic alliance, and the Fairy King and Queen are already married persons but alienated after a squabble over the custody of an adopted child. The designation "lovers" fits only the four young Athenians. Nevertheless, there are significant relations between the actual and the would-be married states in these three distinct character groups. In the opera, the lovers remain among the leading characters, their personalities, sometimes considered rather uniform in the play, further unified yet distinguished by musical patterns.

The lovers' nuptials plot, one remembers, is a single action: two young women, longtime friends, desire marriages with specific young men; these are blocked by one the women's father's different, enforceable wishes. The first portrayed event in the lovers' plot occurs early in the play's opening scene with Egeus's litigation; he recounts Hermia's disobedience, which she reaffirms (22; 1.1.41). A member of the play audience can hardly fail to understand the lovers' predicaments and may possibly identify with one or the other of them. The first scene of the play also introduces Helena, distressed by Demetrius's desertion of her for Hermia and for Egeus's love (26; 1.1.180), and it explicitly confirms the lovers' desired partnerships. In the next act, Demetrius pursues the elopers, chased by his formerly betrothed, ever-hopeful informant, Helena (38; 2.1.189). In the second scene of act 2, Lysander and Hermia are shown eloping (42; 2.2.35); Lysander is anointed with magic flower-juice (43; 2.2.78) and falls in love with Helena (44; 2.2.103). The long second scene of the third act shows Demetrius and Hermia quarreling (54; 3.2.43), Demetrius's anointment (56; 3.2.104), his falling violently in love with Helena (57; 3.2.137), their quarrel (146), Helena's and Hermia's falling out (59; 3.2.192), and Demetrius's and Lysander's preparation to duel to the death (64; 3.2.330). They all finally fall asleep (67; 3.2.418), and Lysander is anointed with an antidote (68; 3.2.451). Their next portrayed actions—in the last act—include attending the court festivities (78; 5.1.28), watching the play (81; 5.1.108), and going to bed (89; 5.1.366). This material should be welcome grist to any opera-maker's mill: a story of thwarted love in which the problems are aggravated before being solved, much emotion is paraded in raised voices, and personal relationships between and within the sexes change rapidly. To sweeten all, through dramatic irony, there is humor for the observers of the discomfited, overserious, immature lovers, who will obviously triumph in the end.

The librettists retained all the major events in this plot although some of its connections with the other plots were weakened, and some restructuring was required as a result of the court's deferral. There is not a word, for instance, in the opera of the severe punishment Hermia will suffer if she does not do as she is told. Further, since the Duke's hunt is not staged, the lovers' awakening must be otherwise contrived. They could have been allowed to awake with the lark heard by Puck (71; 4.1.94), but the libretto has a stage direction, "Distant horns," which, in the score, materializes as no less than eleven offstage horn duos, approaching and receding, but which are not explicitly associated with Theseus. The events take place in essentially the same order, although with different intervals between them. Viewed in this way, the opera is no simpler than the play. One should not forget that the librettists' compressed final scene precluded the celebration of the couples' decreed weddings before Theseus ordered "lovers to bed."

"Tradesmen" is perhaps the simplest label for the well-remembered character group who appear in the play. They are Quince, a carpenter; Snug, a joiner; Bottom, a weaver; Flute, a bellows-mender; Snout, a tinker; and Starveling, a tailor—names that suggest not only aspects of their trades but also their physical attributes. Recognizing Shakespeare's extraordinary gift for punning, one might conclude that Quince is not merely named for the carpenter's quoin; perhaps, conforming to his unlikely fruity-sounding patronymic, he is sour and pear-shaped. In the play, they are most commonly called the "rustics," Britten's preferred designation in his stage directions in the score (84; 1.53.3), but they are obviously not the country folk that term primarily denotes. In the play, Puck describes them as "hempen home-spuns" (48; 3.1.77), a "crew of patches," "rude mechanicals" (a term that appropriately anticipates a criterion for humor of Henri Bergson), and "that barren sort" (53; 3.2.9–13). The librettists dropped the last three labels as part of a speech by Puck containing a description of their panic on seeing Bottom translated, a narrative dispensable because the audience has already seen the actual event. The librettists retained the tag, "hard-handed men . . . which never labour'd in their minds till now" (80; 5.1.72-73), which, however, becomes less characteristically uttered when transferred from the abolished, snobbish Philostrate to the retained, gentle Hippolyta. They are the "clowns" in several stage directions in Q1, F1, Harrison, and *Riverside*. They are, once, "the rabble" in Q1 (and in *Riverside* [4.2.1]), but they are called neither of these things in the opera: by its time, the sensitivities of organized labor might have been offended.

All six men figure prominently in the opera, their characters further differentiated by their distinctive musical parts. In particular, the activities of Flute, the bellows-mender, are enhanced, perhaps because this role (appropriately tenor!) was intended to be played in the first performance by Peter Pears. Indeed, Howard notes, perhaps oversensitively, that the considerable impact of this very great singer on certain of Britten's operas was not always for their improvement (231–32). But it would be unreasonable to attribute any serious structural imbalance in the *Dream* to Flute's greater prominence in the opera than in the play.

The tradesmen's interlude plot, too, is extremely simple: to play an interlude before the Duke and Duchess on the night of their wedding day (29; 2.1.5). In the second scene of Shakespeare's first act, the six tradesmen meet to cast a play that seems to have been chosen by their self-appointed director and impresario, Peter Quince. In the third act, they rehearse (46; 3.1.1), but their leading man, Bottom, is translated, becoming ass-headed (49; 3.1.103). In the next act, he is restored (71; 4.1.81), wakes (75; 4.1.200), and, in the next scene, is reunited with the other players (76; 4.2.25). In the final act, they put on their play (81; 5.1.108), followed by their bergomask (88; 5.1.360). This material, a combination of situation comedy and of a display of verbal and histrionic ineptitude, is probably more suited to musical comedy than to opera. The plot, however, broadens the social spectrum portrayed, a positive feature in attracting audiences. In the lovers' plot, the audience sees persons of high social status making fools of themselves; in the tradesmen's plot, members of lower classes deviate ridiculously from their prosaic norms.

The librettists kept all essentials, and their opening the opera in the wood paid another dividend in the simplification of this action.

The early casting scene was transferred to the wood from the city, and Shakespeare's "*there* we may rehearse" was appropriately changed in the libretto to "*here* we may rehearse" (emphasis added). In the play, there has to be a change of scene between Bottom's awakening in the wood (75; 4.1.199) and his rejoining his colleagues in the city (76; 4.2.25). In the opera, they are reunited in the wood, and another scene change is avoided. It would have been better for Britten's audience had he also changed Quince's inquiry concerning Bottom's whereabouts, from "is he *come* home yet?" to "has he *gone* home yet?" If, however, Shakespeare's Theseus and later his guests could accept a play with "not one word apt" (79; 5.1.65), surely Britten's audience could tolerate one word inapt.

The principals in the fairies character group are Oberon, King of the Fairies, and Titania, Queen of the Fairies. He is assisted by Puck, or Robin Goodfellow, she by four named fairies—Peaseblossom, Cobweb, Moth, and Mustardseed—and by other fairies, sometimes differentiated as "First" or another such qualifier. The fairies are all kept in the opera, organized into performing subgroups with musical talents, functions, and traits that characterize them beyond their natures in the play. Their royal leaders are advanced into the foreground. Puck, a speaking part, becomes a boy acrobat, his tumbling neatly accentuating his mischievous nature. Britten specifically says in his *Observer* article that

> the fairies . . . are very different from the innocent nothings that often appear in productions of Shakespeare. I have always been struck by a kind of sharpness in Shakespeare's fairies, . . . they are the guards to Tytania: so they have, in places, martial music. (Palmer, 179)

Highlighted by the main reshaping, the fairies in the opera are far from "innocent nothings," despite the names of Tytania's attendants that suggest small or delicate things.

The librettists would have seen the fairies' activities as consisting of three separable plots: an earth beautification exercise following some serious ecological disruptions, a rift-mending between the King and Queen, and a matchmaking intrusion into the mortal world. Puck provides an epilogue to the play. The beautification plot has the fairies dispensing dew (32; 2.1.9), adding pearls to cowslips (32; 2.1.15), killing cankers in musk rose buds (41; 2.2.3). Titania describes "the mazed world" in a catalog of environmental disasters (35; 2.1.88), this progeny of environmental evils, the negative of beautification, coming from the royal dissension (36;

2.1.115). At the conclusion of the final act, the Fairy King orders blessings on the bedded lovers (90; 5.1.404) and proscribes the despised "blots of Nature's hand" from the children-to-be (90; 5.1.409). The material in the beautification plot is incidental to the main story, but is the subject of many of the songlike passages in the play, which, in the opera, become musical occasions.

The fairies' rift-repairing plot opens with a described and demonstrated rift between the King and the Queen (34; 2.1.60), his demand for a remedy (36; 2.1.120), and her reasoned rejection of the terms (36; 2.1.122). In the next scene, the King anoints the Queen's eyes (42; 2.2.27) so that in the following act she loves Bottom who has been transformed into an ass (50; 3.1.141). An act later still, she continues loving him (68; 4.1.1). In the same scene the audience learns that she has met the King's demand (70; 4.1.60), and he disenchants her (71; 4.1.70). The rift is healed (71; 4.1.87). The royal marriage estrangement is prominent, and the mutual abuse is excellent operatic material, for the same reason as the lovers' quarreling. The ass-nolled Bottom should be regarded as temporarily part of this plot, an unwitting agent. The librettists keep all essentials, making a structural simplification and avoiding scene changes by joining the two Titania-Bottom love scenes in Shakespeare's act 3, scene 1, and act 4, scene 1.

The fairies' matchmaking plot is their third action. The mortal matchmaking begins as an impetuous act on Oberon's part, profeminist in contrast to Egeus's patriarchal will. Excusable lack of certainty in Oberon's orders leads to a comic aggravation of the problem, later to be compounded, but ultimately easily remedied by super-supernatural powers. Oberon will help Helena (40; 2.1.245), and, on his orders, initially disruptive spells are cast upon the male lovers (43; 2.2.78, 56; 3.2.104, and 68; 4.1.450). There is a symmetry in the order of Shakespeare's anointings: they are of Titania, Lysander, Demetrius, Lysander, and Titania, an A B C B A form, such as will appear also in the order of his settings. Britten, as a result of consolidating other scenes, reversed the order of the first two anointings—encountering no difficulty since the incidents are independent, and causing no structural problem since the play's symmetry is expendable in this case.

There is an epilogue, independent of the plots. Oberon's servant, regarded as Robin Goodfellow rather than Puck, is a mortal from folklore rather than a true fairy, and is thus better qualified as intermediary to end the play with an appeal to the human theater audience for applause (91; 5.1.423). The librettists kept the epilogue. It might well have been omitted to save time and leave a

clearer faery frame, but, apparently, authenticity and acknowledgment of the theater audience prevailed, rounding out an overall
progression from magic wood to normality and explicitly announcing the therapeutic possibilities of sleep and dream.

A few general points should be noted about the plots executed
by character groups, elements of the play that the librettists must
have regarded as naturally manipulable units. Fairy-tale opera
flourished in the early part of this century, and any of the material
in the fairies' plots could stand alone as a brief story with "operatic" elements of the kinds found in other congenial comedy plots:
a love interest and quarrel, situation comedy, verbal bravado, and
the revelation of basic human animality by an ass in more senses
than one. The librettists kept all the fairy plots, which they simplified by running on scenes that are separated in the play. The librettists retained all the character groups, while making a significant
saving in cast requirements and avoiding some possible confusion
from sheer numbers of active performers. Opera can handle
crowds, as choruses, better than plays can, but it, too, can profit
from simplification—the thing Britten initially stipulated—by including fewer players for the audience to comprehend. Each of the
eight plots was retained by the librettists, a remarkable feat in an
exercise of this kind—a prominent aspect of the "almost formidable authenticity" that Peter Evans notes (236). The libretto for
Verdi's *Otello* is another of the few highly praised Shakespearean
adaptations; Boito had a much simpler story to reshape, and he,
too, chose a different starting point from Shakespeare's, a storm-
threatened hero's arrival in Cyprus that the composer could portray in intense music. In Britten's *Dream*, the court's roles were
abridged, a simplification, but the other character groups' actions
were presented entire in their essentials with the fairies' roles enhanced. This preserves for the opera audience's entertainment the
diverse antics with which it is probably familiar. But, to anticipate
later discussion, some may feel deprived of the lost philosophical
content: admirers of down-to-earth Theseus, who loses the opportunity to express his disbelief in the imagination of the lunatic, the
lover, and the poet, and disciples of understanding Hippolyta, who
is not called upon in the opera to rebut her conqueror and see
beyond fancy's images to something of great constancy (77–78;
5.1.2–26).

Shakespeare's settings of place and time are other elements that
invited the librettists' attention for reshaping. They responded ag-
gressively, first with the locales of the play. The earlier expressed
opinion that the enchanted wood near Athens struck Britten as

the best opening locale for the opera calls for elaboration, and it implies that the night of the three rendezvous there—of the fairies, the lovers, and the tradesmen—was the optimum time to begin. Harrison's edition of the play confines its stage directions to the names of characters entering and exiting, but, following contemporary practice required by the neutral stage without specific scenery and with minimum properties, either the speeches indicate the locales or they are self-evident from the action.

Theseus onstage opens the play, and Egeus's apparently premeditated approach to him, seeking a judgment, strongly suggests that the first scene is in Theseus's palace-cum-court. Lysander's and Hermia's lamentations and vows—and their confiding in Helena—also apparently take place there. In the next scene, the tradesmen would not be in the palace with their secret preparations, and they explicitly have yet to go to the wood (32; 1.2.100): thus they are probably where editors indicate, in Quince's house in Athens. Opening the second act, the third scene clearly shows the fairies to be in the wood, although it is somewhat late in the text before Oberon asks Titania, "How long within this wood intend you stay" (36; 2.1.138). Numerous references confirm that all the main characters, including Theseus a-hunting, are in the wood until the penultimate scene (76; 4.2.1–45). After that, in Quince's inquiry whether Bottom is "come home yet" (76; 4.2.1), the word "come" suggests that the other tradesmen are back in the city, which is soon confirmed because Snug, entering, has only just seen that the Duke "is coming" from the Temple. The final scene clearly reverts to the Duke's palace, where Theseus refers to "this long age . . . between our after-supper and bedtime" (78; 5.1.33–34), and the tradesmen play their interlude. The pattern of the locales is symmetrical: Theseus's palace in Athens, Quince's house there, the wood near the city, Quince's house again, and Theseus's palace once more, another A B C B A form, a sequence presenting no staging problem in Shakespeare's day.

Britten and Pears were making a work for the simple stage of the small, 316-seat Aldeburgh Jubilee Hall. Shakespeare's varied sequence would have meant procuring scenery for three sets and making four changes after the initial setup. This could be done with painted drop curtains—perhaps with acoustical disadvantages—but the requirement to establish five distinct locales by changes in the deployment of operatic stage resources might well appear something to avoid as costly, time-consuming, and even potentially inimical to simplicity and overall unity. Shakespeare's is a neat, symmetrical form of movement of the kind involving

Frye's "Green World" or Barber's festivities. But it had to go, and a new, progressive development replaced it.

Timings of events in the play, too, invited restructuring changes. In the play's second line, Theseus states that his wedding is four days away. Further timings are indicated by other statements: Lysander's "steal forth . . . tomorrow night" (26; 1.1.164), Helena's "O long and tedious night" (67; 3.2.431), Theseus's "vaward of the day," indicating the following morning (72; 4.1.105), and his ordering the lovers' weddings "by and by with us" (74; 4.1.180). But a day seems to have been lost. A three- or four-day time span, although not the most compact unity, would probably not have deterred the librettists had they decided to retain Shakespeare's plan. But they had other ideas, and in order to procure Britten's opening musical advantage, the librettists had to introduce the lovers in the wood, whence they had to exit the following day to attend the final ceremonies, thus making a severe temporal curtailment. They left more flaws than Shakespeare did with his lost day.

The librettists restructured the settings of both kinds, locations and timings. Britten, according to Dean's criticism of the *Dream* (in Hartnoll, 118), was an operatic composer with the "capacity of genius": he insisted on full compositional license. He could not tolerate constraints caused by complexity, including scene shifting and time breaks; he demanded freedom to present a musical opening that immediately seized the audience's whole attention and that could also be used to build a tonal form spanning and unifying a full operatic act. The overwhelming influence of Britten's preconceived music not only disqualified Shakespeare's point of departure, it precluded the choice of a later incident capable of dramatic musical treatment (such as the climax of the lovers' quarreling) that might have attracted another devotee of starting in medias res.

A drama consists not only of a number of stories involving character groups in their own actions and settings, but also, even essentially, in interfaces between these stories. When Britten expressed his excitement over the "quite separate groups" of characters in the play, he continued that they "nevertheless interact" (Palmer, 177). With the character groups and plots examined separately, the many links between them call for attention, as they must have exercised the librettists. Viewed as obvious causes and effects, the connections produce a tightly unified plot network, vulnerable to a drastic reshaping.

The nature of a link governs its expendability. The most thoroughgoing and generally indispensable kind of link is the joint presence on stage of two or more character groups, each openly taking part in a joint action and thus aware of each other. A looser kind of link—but necessary for such results as dramatic irony—is found when only one group is aware of the other—as happens when Oberon, through Puck, operates on the lovers and they continue to believe themselves rational—for the audience's greater delight. A third kind of link is made by explicit narration, as when, in the play, the tradesmen say they are rehearsing to perform at the Duke's wedding (29; 1.2.6). This device is less dramatic and may be easily dropped by a simple excision; a librettist may well be tempted to omit the words, trusting the composer to substitute a musical association. If a narrated linkage is cut out, the result may be either unwanted confusion or to create welcome, imaginative, link-forging speculations on the part of the audience. There is thus the possibility that a simple juxtaposition or a musical conjoining of events in different plots may suggest more numerous and more meaningful associations than a narrated logical connection that tends to limit speculation.

Some links are initiated by the court. In the opening of the play, the court nuptials immediately lead to the court festivities, through a decree for civic rejoicing and Theseus's plan to wed Hippolyta with reveling (21; 1.1.13 and 19). As the tradesmen acknowledge in their casting session (29; 1.2.1), the impending court festivities generate the secretly prepared theatricals. The court nuptials are also the reason for the Fairy Queen's presence in the neighborhood (36; 2.1.139), and the court festivities become a milieu wherein the royal fairy couple will dance, a balletic activity Shakespeare's Oberon orders when announcing his final song (90; 5.1.394). The deferral of the court's appearance in the opera causes the librettists to eliminate early reference to the civic and court festivities, the occasions responsible for the tradesmen's preparing their interlude and Titania's reveling when she did. A courtly hunting party in the play awakens the four lovers in the wood (73; 4.1.138); it is dropped from the opera. Also, the court in festive mood selects as entertainment, from an otherwise uninspiring list, the play on which the tradesmen have gambled so much (79; 5.1.32). In the opera, the competition is suppressed.

In the play, when Demetrius is again betrothed to Helena, Theseus addresses a still vengeful father; "Egeus, I will overbear your will" (74; 4.1.179). Egeus is excluded from the opera, and Theseus, on stage at long last, announces his judgment in equity directly to Hermia. Without the details given in the play of the original blocking action and judgment in favor of Egeus against Hermia, this first reference to her father's will at such a late stage is potentially puzzling. Theseus orders the lovers' weddings alongside his own nuptials (74; 4.1.180), but the librettists allow no time for the ceremonies before the entertainment and the climactic iron tongue of midnight. A multiple, court-initiated link occurs when the court dignitaries and the lovers (and perhaps the fairies) witness the tradesmen's tedious brief scene of tragical mirth. During the ensuing bergomask all have the chance to contemplate the tragic consequences of unameliorated paternal domination over a daughter.

Other interplot links are initiated by the lovers. Theseus's verdict and clarification of Hermia's prospective penalty early in the play is better regarded as a link with the court that is initiated by the lovers, especially in that it is her disobedience that invokes Theseus's intervention, with consequences that immediately affect the lovers. The suppression of Theseus's early appearance precluded announcing on the opera stage the common law of patriarchal supremacy that Theseus is called upon to uphold in the play (23; 1.1.65). The librettists had to find another means of explaining Demetrius's right to court Hermia and had to give a reason for Lysander's and Hermia's elopement and lamenting the rough course of true love chosen by another's eyes (25; 1.1.140). As to Demetrius's courting of Hermia, in the play he has her father's blessing, and there is an overtone that the dowry and her potential inheritance are attractions. In the opera, he appears simply to be enamoured, and the loss of the parental blessing and the material things is acceptable in 1960. As to the elopement, the librettists added a line that makes Lysander say in his elopement proposal to Hermia that the "sharp Athenian Law" (26; 1.1.162) is one "compelling thee to marry with Demetrius." Britten seems to have been satisfied (Palmer, 178), but, compared with the play's detailed, reiterated edict of Theseus, which the librettists cannot stage because of his deferred entrance, this operatic explanation is perfunctory indeed. Jan Morris Bach, in his 1971 doctoral dissertation entitled "An Analysis of Britten's 'A Midsummer Night's Dream'" says, "the lovers' verbal recollection of their predicament has none of the dramatic power of witnessing the plight itself" (20). As Howard notes, opera is "a blunt instrument [which] tends to simplify rather than compress" (164) and which, unkind to words, does not thrive well on the narrations that a play could use to avoid lacunae. The links initiated by the lovers are few, relatively unimportant, and readily dispensable: the librettists retain them and add a minor enrichment by having the women as well as the men deride *Pyramus and Thisby,* perhaps a postwar recognition of equal sexual opportunity as well as an effective musical deployment of an expensive vocal cast, each with expectant fans.

With regard to interplot connection involving the tradesmen, their interlude is regarded as initiated by the court. When the depleted cast of tradesmen is reassembled in Quince's house in Athens in the play, they mention again the long-planned ducal nuptials and give news that additional aristocratic weddings have taken place (76; 4.2.16). The audience also learns their views on the requirements for a cast's effective relations with their audience, including uncut fingernails for the lion and gastronomic restraint for all (77; 4.2.35). The rounding-out bergomask, which the tradesmen offer and Theseus accepts (88; 5.1.360), is notable among the many set forms with musical associations in the play. All the forms of this kind were retained in the opera and are welcome according to operatic conventions (Bach, 15). The other tradesmen's plot connections were all retained in the libretto, with a notable exception: Snug does not mention, as he does in the play, that "there is two or three Lords and Ladies more married." This is understandable, because, at that time, Theseus has not been introduced to order the weddings.

Several links are initiated by the fairies. In the play, the results of the fairies' beautification plot are ignored by the mortals. But at the very end, midnight struck, Theseus notes, "'tis almost fairy time" (90; 5.1.404). The mortals are unaware that they receive the blessings of the fairy world. It is possible that the setting to music will widen the separation between the mortals and the supernaturals, for, although the text retained in the libretto comes unaltered from the play, Britten "used a different kind of texture and orchestral 'colour' for each section" (Palmer, 177). After Puck has introduced the fairy rift-repairing plot, the Fairy Queen and King make mutual accusations of past amatory involvements, probably extramarital, with the mortal ducal pair about to be wed (34; 2.1.70 and 76). The librettists omitted these accusations, and, in view of the restructuring, the opera audience must wait until after Oberon and Titania have become reconciled and ready to "dance in Duke Theseus's house . . . and bless it" to hear of the fairy court's connection with the mortal court (71; 4.1.89).

The impact of the fairies' rift-repairing plot on the tradesmen's plot, as Oberon unclearly orders Titania's punishment, is decisive. Their lead man is translated (3.1.103), loved by the enchanted Fairy Queen (3.1.141 and 4.1.60), and loathed by her when she is released from the "hateful imperfection of her eyes" (70; 4.1.63). This is the last case to be cured by medication in an ocular epidemic, first diagnosed in her father by Hermia when she was ordered to "choose love by another's eyes" (25; 1.1.140). Although most of the first scene in the play is cut, these words are kept in a climactic duet in the opera (51; 1.28.1), and the theme of false versus true seeing is preserved. Through the fairies' matchmaking plot, the lovers, unaware of the cause, are much affected by the anointings (performed by the Fairy King or pursuant to his instructions, sometimes vague and bungled) of Lysander (43; 2.2.78), Demetrius (56; 3.2.104), and Lysander again (68; 3.2.451). Again through his agent Puck, the King thwarts the male lovers' impending duel over Helena (64; 3.2.355). As a final link, though "fools these mortals be" (56; 3.2.115), the Puck-Robin solicits applause at the final curtain, extending the fairy-human connection beyond the players to the theater audience (91; 5.1.327). The librettists kept all the fairy-mortal associations portrayed in the play, but some narrated connections are dropped out.

The librettists' restructuring compeled them to drop some of the expressed links between plots. In particular, the ones in the early parts of the play were necessarily sacrificed as a result of the suppression of the play's opening Athenian court scene. Most of the omissions are covered by other circumstances and devices, but there are residuary problems.

3
Reshaping the Libretto

Once [Britten] decides that he loves a text, whether it needs adaptation or not, he regards it as his duty to take the kind of binding step which, in our relations to people rather than to texts, has been firmly formalized: before he puts pen to paper, or (on his composing walks) musical thought to words, he inwardly declares himself to be married to his text, with all the implications of faithful service and, yes, mastery which an engagement ineluctably carries.

—Hans Keller,
"Operatic Music and Britten"

In order to clarify the possibilities for reshaping, the several kinds of manipulable elements of the play have been introduced, with some mention of the librettists' adaptations and the sometimes awkward reverberations. Next, to focus on the reshaping process in its totality, the rough synopsis of the opera made by one of the librettists should be examined, and a collation and further analysis of a dozen items of restructuring should be attempted, dealing first with those having the greatest impact.

The first visible evidence of the restructuring of the play to make the opera is a rough scenario of the libretto, in Pears's hand, which appears on a blank page after the text in his Penguin edition (if numbered the page would be 108). It is untidy, containing corrections and adjustments. The order of two events in this rough scenario is reversed in the working libretto, and Pears spells the Fairy Queen "Titania" whereas Britten's final decision was to spell it "Tytania" to indicate a long first syllable. Thus Cooke is probably correct in assuming that this represents part of the reshaping process preparatory to the detailed writing of the libretto, rather than a summary made afterwards. He gives a facsimile of the scenario in his plate I. A typescript is given in table 3.1 below. Pears's page numbers refer to the Penguin edition. As will become apparent

Table 3.1 Rough Preliminary Scenario of Benjamin Britten's Opera, *A Midsummer Night's Dream,* by Peter Pears; in His Hand, in His Penguin Edition of Shakespeare's Comedy. (The continuous arrows [——>] are part of the original synopsis. The dotted arrows [– – –>] have been added to show the order of entries in the finished libretto and the lovers' entry in the final scene, omitted by Pears.)

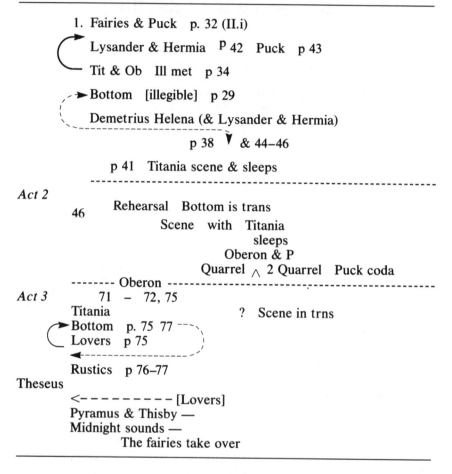

from tables 3.2 and 3.3, the added dotted arrows (– – –>) indicate the changes made in the order of entries in the finished libretto and show the lovers' entry in the final scene, omitted by Pears. The scenario shows that the librettists probably blocked out the opera before putting their pencils to Shakespeare's text itself.

The opera opens in the wood near Athens, rather than in Theseus's court. The curtain rises after a brief but remarkable orchestral prelude, which in itself is sufficient warning not to expect an appearance of Theseus's no-nonsense court. The words "mysterious" and "other-worldly" come to mind to describe the wood, empty, at deepening twilight. The slow pulse of strange sound, sliding upwards and downwards, readily suggests not only breathing in sleep (which has been sensed by such critics as White [224] and Peter Evans [239]) and sighing and spellbinding (Kennedy, 220), but also portrays "in the night . . . some fear" such as Theseus, in the play, associated with strong imagination (78; 5.1.19–22). Christina J. Burridge senses the wood as a living character (151). The ducal court could have been announced and characterized at curtain-up with a variety of courtly music. But, for it to be recognized as such, the music would probably have needed to be far less original and striking than Britten's wood music. In fact *"l'innovatore"* was almost literally *silenzioso* at first, and the extremely quiet, slow initial notes are more remarkable than the conventional loud horn passages that probably would have accompanied a stage-front Theseus. Alexandra Browning "had never heard music like that" when she, as a member of the English Opera Group, played Helena in a later production (interview, 1 October 1989). Britten could afford to dispense with a loud, attention-getting overture and go straight to whatever he saw as the heart of the matter.

Although, in the play, the fairies are the last characters on stage, in the opera, they are the first. They appear before any mortals are seen, although humans are mentioned as Puck's homely English victims and Tytania's oriental changeling boy. The music that accompanies the fairies reflects their supernaturalness, and, in this expository stage of the work, it follows the passage of otherworldly wood music more appropriately than would a sharply contrasted kind of accompaniment necessary for a mortal character. Apart from making a smoother musical juxtaposition, the promotion of the fairies to openers turns their world into the frame of the work, structurally important as a standard against which to set the human universe. The fairies are also made prominent in concluding the opera's acts 1 and 2, leaving fresh memories of the supernatural to operate on the audience's minds during the intervals.

In the opera, the court's entry is drastically deferred. Any advancement naturally entails a deferral, which may be a simple reversal of the original order or something more drastic. Britten's advancement of the enchanted wood setting and other decisions necessitated by it had a nearly devastating effect on the role of the court and its characters. He presumably did not want to introduce the court unless he could show it on stage, and to have done that in the beginning or the middle of the opera would have meant a disruptive change of scene from the wood. He therefore deferred the physical entry of Theseus and Hipployta until his last scene, when they were essential to legalize the lovers' happy new arrangement and to host them witnessing the tradesmen's presentation of yet another termination to the path of true love that never did run smooth. In the opera, the ducal nuptials and the resulting festivities still represent adult love triumphant over territorial strife, but they are no longer a structural frame providing an exemplum to set against the troubled youthful amours of the lovers. The change reflects different mores of the mid-twentieth century. The court, instead of being a typical point of departure for Frye's "Green World" of the wood near Athens and a predictable point of return after the remedial adventures there, becomes the unexpected destination of a misadventure-filled quest by immature lovers.

The tradesmen's operatic entry is deferred less extremely. In the play, the appearances are: court with lovers, tradesmen, fairies; in the opera: fairies, lovers, tradesmen. As stations in his main progression from city to wood to city, Shakespeare inserted scenes at Quince's house (the natural meeting place for the tradesmen) between city and wood on the outward journey and between wood and city on the return. He thus constructed a multilink symmetrical chain of locales: Theseus's palace, a subject's house, everyone's wood, the subject's house again, and back to the Duke's palace, now containing and accommodating all. Shakespeare would no doubt have thought of the wood as the sovereign's domain where everyone was graciously allowed access, and thus all his locales reflect the authority of Theseus. The Athenian law probably extended to the wood, a league without the city, but not to Lysander's aunt's house, seven leagues away. In the opera, the political status of the wood is vague. With Shakespeare's courtly pattern precluded in the opera by the opening in the wood, the tradesmen could be introduced at virtually any later stage in the exposition, in particular either before or after the fairies. But, with the best entrance time for the fairies and their etherial music decided as immediately after the supernatural wood music, the tradesmen's appearance had to be after that. Britten did this without difficulty, and one hopes that he appreciated the men's accommodating nature in this matter of precedence as much as Theseus did their simpleness and duty in offering their interlude.

The librettists had to bring the lovers into the opera in a place and manner notably different from their initial staging in court in the play, a further result of the fairies-in-the-wood opening and its effect on the court. Early in the play, Hermia and both her suitors are summoned before Theseus in court, and it is there that she and Lysander, left alone, lament their predicament, meet Helena, and unwisely entrust her with a dangerous confidence. In the opera, the court is excluded until the denouement, but the lovers are still central as situation-comedy material and must be made to appear in the wood without undue delay. Lysander and Hermia meet there without reference to any prearrangement or, indeed, for any stated reason, and decide to be patient, but he proposes instead going to his rich aunt's house. They exchange vows, she apparently consenting to go. As in the play, Demetrius and Helena are first shown together in the wood on their own, but, in the opera, they immediately follow the appearance of their peers, without the tradesmen's casting and the royal fairies' quarrel intervening. The result is a simplifying concentration of an important character group's staging and their actions.

As a result of the foregoing shuffles, the opera's first act now has a distinctive new shape. Table 3.2 shows in outline the structures of the expositions of the opera and the play by reference to the appearances of character groups as they introduce their problems and interactions. It summarizes the foregoing items of major restructuring, confirming the enhancement of the role of the fairies, whose dominating presence is left in the audience's minds during the first interval.

There are no grounds to argue that the lovers or the tradesmen, as a result of their rearrangement, have changed absolute or relative importance. But there is a tidying up in that Helena's "I am your spaniel" episode (38; 2.1.188–244), isolated in the play, is made to follow the Lysander-Hermia vows in the opera, thus saving scene changes. More importantly, table 3.2 highlights a new symmetry in the opera: its act 1 presents, in order: fairies, lovers, tradesmen, lovers, fairies. The tradesmen are seen by Cooke (in his table 2, p. 36) as a centrally placed mirror reversing the order of the objects in the image. There is no such symmetry in the corresponding Shakespearean introductory scenes in the play's first two acts. For his first act Britten, prospective composer, has moulded a balanced A B C B A shape based on a changed importance of the character groups, thus replacing Shakespeare's construct based on a journey from city to wood. If Britten and his audience saw themselves mainly within the social class of the lovers, there is another new symmetry evident in the operatic posi-

Table 3.2 Comparative Outline of the Structure of Act 1 of Britten's Opera, *A Midsummer Night's Dream,* and the Corresponding acts 1 and 2 of Shakespeare's Comedy, by Reference to Character Groups. ("www" represents Britten's wood music.)

Opera	Play
Act 1	**Act 1.1**
www	Court
Fairies	Lovers
www	**Act 1.2**
Lovers	Tradesmen
www	**Act 2.1**
Tradesmen	Fairies
www	Lovers
Lovers	Fairies
www	**Act 2.2**
Fairies	Fairies
www	Lovers

tioning—on two occasions—of the lovers' familiar world between two strange, contrasted other domains: those of the intangible fairies and of the socially unacceptable rabble.

The preconceived wood music that initiated the reshaping, represented in table 3.2 by "www," continues to participate in the structuring by reappearing in the form of ritornelli, punctuating the character group appearances and accompanying the second fairies episode. These passages insist repeatedly on the mystery and power of the wood, their sonic similarity setting a relatively static musical shape against a developmental dramatic pattern. The functional significance of returning musical themes will be examined more fully later.

In the opera, Tytania's enchantment is made into a single scene. In the play, Titania's falling in love with Bottom and her instruction to members of her train to attend on him (50–52; 3.1.137–201) are separated from the satisfying of his unromantic cravings, his "exposition of sleep," and her embracing him (68–70; 4.1.1–45) by the long quarrel among the lovers and their falling asleep (54–68; 3.2.41–463). Bringing together Shakespeare's two distinct scenes in the opera is structurally significant as a unification, an elimination of scene changes, and a simplification. Further as Peter Evans notes, the music is afforded more time in one continuous episode than in two separate ones to create and hold the mood (218). But the long suspense in the play over the impending but unresolved love scene between beauty and the beast is lost.

Also, the tradesmen's reunion is made one scene. The librettists, almost willy-nilly, make another consolidation when they deal with the episodes in the play in which Bottom awakes (75–76; 4.1.200–19) and when he rejoins his colleagues (76–77; 4.2.1–45). In the opera, the second of these episodes is transferred to the wood, where Bottom, without his ass-head, marvels at his dream. Bottom simply exits; Quince, Flute, Snout, and Starveling enter to be joined shortly by Snug, and Bottom reenters. This avoidance of a scene change has similar advantages to those arising from Tytania's new one-scene enchantment, although the impact is less this time.

The initial appearances of Puck and the fairies are transposed in the opera. In the play, Puck precedes and introduces the wandering fairies, by whom he is characterized as a mischief-maker, after he has explained Oberon's wrath. In the opera, the fairies begin with their "Over hill, over dale" song, a smoother continuation of the initial wood music and a more operatic opening than Puck's speaking voice. It is a more logical sequence for the fairies to identify him before he gives his account of the royal rift, which can then be staged immediately in the "ill met by moonlight" encounter. This new, natural sequence increases the dramatic pace, a welcome change in opera in which singing retards the utterance.

Oberon's beastly spells are modified. In the play, Oberon takes several lines to explain to Puck the power of the flower, love-in-idleness (37; 2.1.169–74), and he lists the beasts that might become his Queen's beloved (38; 2.1.176–85) by uttering parenthetically "(Be it on lion, bear, or wolf, or bull, / On meddling monkey, or on busy ape)" (180–1). Britten cut some lines and moved the list of beasts forward in the speech, where it makes equal sense. In the play, this planning of the trick on Titania occurs just before Oberon makes himself invisible to spy on Helena pursuing Demetrius onto the stage (38; 2.1.186).

Something different happens, however, in the operatic reshaping: instead of Helena pursuing Demetrius at this point, Lysander and Hermia enter, meet, lament, plot elopement, and exchange vows. Therefore, so that Oberon can remain unaware of Lysander and assume that Demetrius is the only Athenian present whom Puck could anoint, Oberon must disappear rather than simply become invisible and still seeing. So, immediately after Lysander's and Hermia's vows, when Demetrius and Helena do enter and complete the first lovers' scene, Oberon must be brought on again, in plain view, in order that he, although present, may make himself invisible, witness the spurning, decide on remedial matchmaking, and order Puck to anoint the eyes of the disdainful man in Athenian garments. Britten made Oberon accompany his own reappearance and precede his announcement of invisibility with a repetition of the parenthetical bestiary. Why? Cooke suggests two reasons for the repetition: "Oberon's total preoccupation with the charm"—in which case one must believe he said it twice, separately—and "[Britten's suggesting] that both lovers' scenes occur simultaneously—in which case the audience must believe he said it only once (4). The second interpretation appears more likely—an ingenious extrication, but perhaps easily overlooked during performance.

The order of Titania's falling asleep to "You spotted snakes" and the lovers' early adventures in the wood (including the misdirected anointing of Lysander and Hermia's nightmarish awakening) is reversed in the opera. Tytania's falling asleep is postponed, leaving only Oberon to anoint her and utter a supplementary and mainly different bestiary before the curtain falls. This reversal brings the fairies, who began the act, to their prominent end-of-act position and completes the dramatic symmetry shown in table 3.2.

In the opera, the "gentle concord" among the lovers is explained later. Deferring the court's appearance in the opera necessitated transferring the early events in the lovers' nuptial plot from the palace into the wood: excluding Theseus's hunt necessitates a transfer in the reverse direction, from the wood into the palace, of Lysander's and Demetrius's explanation of their excursion and proper pairing. Early in the play, when Theseus pleads pressure of business for having failed to reprimand Demetrius for jilting Helena, one perhaps suspects that he was not much interested and that courtship adjustments were low on his agenda. Late in the opera, this suspicion is confirmed by a different incident in the restructured sequence of events. Not even waiting for Demetrius to announce his renewed love for Helena as part of the lovers' explanation of their new gentle accord, Theseus interrupts, regally: "We more will hear anon," whereupon he legalizes and orders the additional temple weddings. These impatient and hasty orders, arising from the librettists' compression of events, emphasize the negative side of Theseus's character.

Harrison's acts and scenes, as divisions of the play text, provide convenient labels to describe the reshaping in broad terms, but their loss in the opera is of no significance. They are editorial and are likely to be continuous in production, possibly providing just two intervals for the audience, as in the opera.

The restructurings appear mainly in the opera's first act, derived from the first two of the play's five acts. The opera's second act derives from the whole of Shakespeare's third act and part of his fourth to form a simple two-part operatic structure of set pieces, the first enacted by the tradesmen and the fairies (the Tytania-Bottom affair) and the second by the lovers, their sleep rounded by a fairy lullaby. The opera's third and last act is split into two scenes. The first (from the rest of Shakespeare's fourth act) shows the fairies, the lovers, and the tradesmen still in the wood early next morning; the second (from Shakespeare's fifth act, preceded by his very opening incident) presents all these character groups— and Theseus and Hippolyta for the first time—transferred to the palace. Britten's almost complete retention of the plots and their interconnections requires a very similar sequence of events in the opera to Shakespeare's, once the interactions intensify. Thus, except for the changes already examined, the librettists' reshapings of the middle and the end of the play are minor and do not call for close attention. The action of the play as a whole is very substantially preserved, far more than is customary in making a libretto from a full-length play. This is yet another aspect of the opera's formidable authenticity.

Table 3.3 gives a comparative outline of the structures of the scenes of complication and the denouement in the opera and the play, confirming that by these later stages the reshaping is minimal. Earlier, in table 3.2, which compared the expositions, it was indicated that, in the opera's act 1, a distinctive musical passage, the "wood music," worked with the dramatic structure. The opera's second act is also formally assisted by a distinctive musical structure, the "sleep music" (represented in table 3.3 by "sss") which appears at the opening and closing of the act and between the separate set pieces, forming a passacaglia. More on this later.

Before evaluating the reshaping which Britten and Pears did in the libretto, it is helpful to collect and review the already described results that are arguably flaws, albeit unintended, in the opera and to add a few more that have not yet been mentioned. All the dozen major and minor flaws about to be mentioned, although they occur in six different plots, can be traced to the deferring of the court's appearance, which in turn arose from the opening in the wood.

The most serious flaw, a structural defect, is Theseus's ordering the lovers, and indeed Hippolyta and himself, to bed unmarried. This fault was apparently unnoticed by all the commentators quoted, except Cooke, whose keen observation first perceived it. He aptly criticizes: "Since there is no conceivable moment between Theseus' declaration [' . . . in the Temple, by and by with us, / These couples shall eternally be knit' (libretto, 43.10–11)] and

Table 3.3 Comparative Outline of the Structures of acts 2 and 3 of Britten's Opera, *A Midsummer Night's Dream,* and the Corresponding acts 3, 4, and 5 of Shakespeare's Comedy, by Reference to Character Groups. ("sss" represents Britten's sleep music.)

Opera	Play
Act 2	**Act 3.1**
sss	
Tradesmen	Tradesmen
Fairies	Fairies
sss	**Act 3.2**
Lovers	Lovers
sss	
Fairies	Fairies
sss	
Act 3, part 1	**Act 4.1**
Fairies	Fairies
	Court
Lovers	Lovers
Tradesmen	Tradesmen
	Act 4.2
Tradesmen	Tradesmen
Act 3, part 2	**Act 1.1**
Court	Court
	Act 5.1
	Court
Lovers	Lovers
Tradesmen	Tradesmen
Court	Court
Fairies	Fairies
Epilogue	**Epilogue**
Puck	Puck

the end of the opera in which the lovers may legally be united, it is evident that they go to bed unmarried and the fairies bless pleasures which are in fact illicit!" (8). The lack of possible marriage opportunity is clear from the libretto and scores. Having decreed the weddings and invoked joy and love, Theseus goes right on to demand entertainment "to while away this long age of three hours"[1] between after supper and bedtime. The intervening two bars of music and the change from orchestral to harpsichordal accompaniment are insufficient to suggest a time lapse long enough to accommodate the weddings before the entertainment. The tradesmen's bergomask and their exit overlap the sounding of midnight. Cooke continues his criticism: "Genuine oversights are extremely rare in Britten's operas" (8), and it seems very likely that, indeed, the librettists—particularly Britten, the perfectionist—were unaware of the absence of marriages. It is probable, too, that the audience, not noticing the lacuna, assumes that the marriages took place. Hippolyta and the lovers, even Hermia who had insisted that Lysander lie further off yet in the wood, do not protest when ordered to bed, and it took several years for a critic to draw attention to the difficulty. Also, still in the lovers' nuptial plot, the explanation of Hermia's predicament may appear perfunctory, leading to confusion, and the expected Shakespearean romantic comedy pattern, wherein the blocking character acquires self-knowledge, is destroyed and may be missed.

The librettists' marring of the court nuptials plot by crowding the events in the final scene is compounded by Theseus's unwarranted berating of the moon for lingering his desires. Cooke pertinently comments: "Theseus has but twenty minutes of stage time to endure before the attainment of conjugal bliss and his impatience, designed by Shakespeare to reflect the agony of four days' waiting, seems hyperbolic in the extreme in Britten's context" (7).

The very late appearance of Theseus and Hippolyta also demands two things that Shakespeare's audience was spared: a long scene break in the denouement that the operatic music may not clearly explain, and accommodation to two new, powerful characters, "entirely unknown and inevitably stiff" as Peter Evans sees them (238).

In the surviving court festivities, the replacement of the hunt by offstage horn passages may be unclear. The residual, abbreviated court judgment plot is marred, first, by Theseus's unprepared announcement of Hermia's father's intransigence and, second, by an unjustified negative change to his characterization. In the play, it was proper for him to tell Egeus that "*these* couples" shall be married (74; 4.1.180), but, in the opera, having just spoken graciously to Hermia, he should surely have continued "*you* couples" shall be knit (empahsis added).

The failure in the opera to express early the purpose of the tradesmen's interlude and to make only a passing reference to the Duke and the Ladies when the casting is almost finished is realistic. Discounting the need for a full operatic reproduction of Shakespeare's meticulous linkage, the loss of the tradesmen's early reference to the ducal wedding is arguably not a flaw at all.

In the fairies' beautification plot, the opera's neglect to state the purpose of the Fairy Queen's presence—also to celebrate the ducal wedding—deserves the same tolerance as the silence in the tradesmen's introduction. But, in the matchmaking plot, Oberon's repetition of the list of beasts may well puzzle most members of the audience and appear too ingenious by half if explained as Cooke or this study sees it. Restructuring is a potentially dangerous thing, threatening the playwright's carefully planned cogency.

Certain features of the original play may be seen as structural flaws: the "tedious brief scene, . . . very tragical mirth" (79; 5.1.56–57) of *Pyramus and Thisbe* may appear as something just tacked on rather than a play-within-a-play, and Puck's epilogue may seem even more dispensable. Since these views are controversial, the librettists' retention of these features cannot definitively be labeled as lapses on their part.

Apparently at some stage during the writing of the libretto, Britten or Pears, like Bottom, realized that "there are things in this Comedy that will never please" (46; 3.1.9–10). The audience finds itself in a sylvan setting, a locale brilliantly portrayed by music that, in the score, bears the expression mark "mysterious." With only a single added non-Shakespearean line to explain Hermia's predicament, the audience, like Demetrius, would be "wode within this wood" (38; 2.1.192). Seeking "a device to make all well," Britten called upon his tried librettist, Myfanwy Piper, to emulate Quince: "Write me a prologue!" (46–47; 3.1.16–17).[2] She complied. Two heralds announce the Theseus-Hippolyta wedding, call for celebrations, explain Hermia's defiance and the Athenian law, and proclaim the option given her by Theseus that is to remain open until his nuptial day. This prologue is a neat summary of the main initial events in the play (21–25; 1.1.1–121), and it says "*tomorrow* [emphasis added] shall the moon . . . behold the night of their solemnities," indicating that the writer was aware of an abbreviated time scheme, presumably caused by the different starting place in the wood.

The foregoing interchange between Britten and Piper is indicated by a note in Britten's hand at the front of an already typed draft of the libretto, outlining a prologue and adding "(not yet written)." He also wrote on Piper's manuscript, when it had been supplied, "not used," and reasons are not hard to guess. Even though a prologue would have clarified the background and balanced Puck's epilogue, there are snags: Hermia's permitted time for decision, described as "till his [Lord Theseus's] nuptial day," is, in fact, merely overnight; the prologue was not Shakespeare; and, worst of all, it would have preempted the all-important wood music.

Cooke deserves further credit for tracing "four bars of music labelled 'Prologue' on a discarded page of the composer's composition sketch," and it is agreed that "it is highly unlikely that these would have been written before work on the libretto had reached its final stages" (8 and plate 7). But, despite Cooke's statement—immediately after citing several flaws including the lovers' illicit pleasures—that "striking evidence that Britten and Pears were very much aware of these problems and took steps to remedy them survives in a . . . Prologue to the *Dream*" (9), it seems preferable to think that "these problems" of which "Britten and Pears were very much aware" excluded the impossible marriages. It is unlikely that a perfectionist such as Britten would knowingly have let such slips pass, relying on the probability that in performance they would go unnoticed. Perhaps it was a deliberate concession to modern "common-law" marriages? No. With Britten's record of editing out defects, stressed in Strode's "Working for Benjamin Britten (II)" (Palmer, 55) and exemplified in his revision of *Billy Budd* in 1960 (White, 91), it is more likely that, had he been aware of the flaws, he would have been diligent, like Puck, "to sweep the dust behind the door" (89; 5.1.390) and leave a cleaner, revised version of a work that promised so many future performances. Deadlines for composing and other preparations were fast approaching. With Britten under pressure, and "quite ill, . . . not at all well with 'flu'" when writing the third act (Palmer, 179), the quality of the work may occasionally have suffered more than he realized. Probably the flaws were unnoticed.[3] The possibly confusing operatic opening warranted consideration of a prologue, but it would not have removed the structural flaws, notably the unwed ducal and lovers' beddings, and nothing is found to be convincing as indications that all the flaws in act 3 were recognized by the librettists and tolerated. The opening wood music, fortunately, survived.

A central criterion in evaluating the restructuring is the quality that Britten himself, in his *Observer* article, regarded as of prime importance, simplicity. If one regards the unobtrusive structural flaws as noncomplicating and concentrates on the broad sweep of events, the action has been made easier to understand by the shorter, simpler movement from enchanted wood to entertaining palace. Recognizing that the opera will require approximately the same performance time as the play, with the simplification goes a slowing of the dramatic pace, affording the music the time it needs. Further detailed specific items of simplification are the run-on scenes for the lovers, Tytania, and the tradesmen. The greater logic in the order of the fairies' introduction, although minor, is similarly an improvement. Production requirements are simpler too because fewer scene changes and characters are needed.

The librettists have avoided excessive simplicity that would make the story undramatic or artless: all Shakespeare's action is preserved, and, if anything, its artificiality has been increased through the increased prominence of the fairies. Manageable shape, in the sense of a new structure of character groups, settings, and plots, has been achieved in the libretto. The campaign for manageable size is the topic of the next chapter.

Notes

1. This line reveals textual problems which the author does not seek to solve. It appears in the vocal and full scores. It reads "To wear away . . . . " in *Q*1, *F*1, Harrison, and all other earlier (and later) editions consulted. There is no such line typed in the working libretto. The author does not know if it was added there in manuscript or if it appears in the composition sketches. Neither the Boosey & Hawkes libretto nor Herbert's collection of Britten opera librettos contains it.

2. Myfanwy Piper was Britten's librettist for *The Turn of the Screw* (1954). According to Mitchell's "Mapreading" in Palmer (91), Britten said that he had had to restructure that opera in midcomposition from the normal three-act form to a series of variations.

3. Concerning the overcompressed second scene of the opera's third act, Britten's copy of the Penguin text, page 77, has a note in his hand, "Transformation scene to Temple," between 4.2 and 5.1, which appears as a direction in the typed working libretto. Cooke rightly sees this as "indicative of some confusion at this point" (32).

4

Cutting the Text and Other Adjustments: Options and Decisions

> I believe passionately in the intelligibility of the words—opera being a fusion of music, acting, painting and poetry, of which the last-named demands to be understood.
> —Benjamin Britten,
> "On Writing English Opera"

Britten's first task with the libretto for his Dream, was, it should be remembered, "to get it into manageable shape, . . . simplifying and cutting an extremely complex story." His problem can be imagined: "Shall I 'hold or cut,' not Bottom's enigmatic bowstrings (32; 1.2.111), but, as he said, Shakespeare's 'great poetry'" (Palmer, 178). His simplification through restructuring was examined in the preceding chapters; cutting will be examined in this and the next chapter. It is a distinct process, depending on the opera maker's question: "Is the libretto to contain or not to contain all or some of this and that passage of text from the play?" Other textual adjustments in making the libretto not treated as structural in the foregoing chapters are discussed here. If they are sometimes called "amendments" or "emendations," this does not impute any error to Shakespeare, but implies that something else was better for the libretto. Occasionally a musical device receives advance mention here when it is closely associated with a textual adjustment.

Several influences doubtless pervaded the librettists' thoughts when adjusting specific passages of text. They would consider operatic conventions and follow their self-imposed, restrictive or liberating guidelines. According to Britten, the librettists "stuck faithfully to Shakespeare's words," implying an aim to make a minimum of alterations, even in the face of difficulties, and their "adding only one line" (Palmer, 178) implies no addition of textual material except in the most demanding circumstances. This devotion to the text is forcefully confirmed in the epigraph to chapter 3 (Keller, xxviii). The libretto was to consist only of Shakespeare's words, lovingly harvested and made ready for putting into music, where they would be reshaped by singing and enriched by accompanying orchestral sound.

The textual adjustments are of many kinds. If, as seems apparent, the Harrison Penguin edition is the true source text, the modernized spelling and punctuation in the libretto are not really changes made from Britten's declared chief sources, the First Quarto and the First Folio. But two spelling reversions by the librettists should be noted: "revennew" to indicate the archaic accentuation of the second syllable, and "Tytania" to preserve the old pronunciation. The librettists appear to have used Harrison's punctuation (he following $F1$ except where it seemed obviously wrong [18]), but, after all, any choice is of minor importance since the final sung articulation depends on added musical rhythms. The operagoer heeds sound, not spelling.

The excision of a group of words is the most prominent kind of textual amendment by the librettists, and, although it may be prompted by a reshaping, it must have a valid, independent reason related to the nature or context of the passage. It is incorrect to assume that the opening part of Shakespeare's first scene, revolving around Theseus (21–25; 1.1.1–127), has all been cut from the opera just because his physical presence there is restricted to the denouement. The whole action in the court had to be examined by the librettists to see whether, in their opinion, any statement was vital to their new structure, and, if so, whether it needed amendment. They retained the play's opening exchange between Theseus and Hippolyta concerning their nuptials (21; 1.1.1) for inclusion in the opera's final act, albeit with drastically modified timings. They encountered the clear promulgation of the "Law of Athens" (which Theseus might by no means extenuate), yielding Hermia to her death or to a vow of single life if she did not fit her fancies to her father's will (24; 1.1.118). They probably decided that it would be tedious to bring this law in after the elopement had been staged, but that some replacement was necessary. Their one added line, "(Compelling thee to marry with Demetrius)," elucidating Lysander's reference to "the sharp Athenian Law," is essentially a replacement of Theseus's judicial summary, in a perhaps oversimplified paraphrase (9.16).

Because Theseus does not appear in the opera until the final court scene, his speeches during the hunt had to be disposed of. Those on his hounds (72; 4.1.106) and those on the supposed nymphs observing the rite of May are excised; the speeches on the lovers' amorous realignments (72; 4.1.127) are reduced and deferred until the evening festivities. It seems, however, that Britten could not ignore Theseus completely before the court appearance for he inserted eleven offstage horn passages (at first "very distant," then "very near," finally "very distant") ostensibly to indicate Theseus's presence in the background, hunting and awakening the lovers on stage in the wood (341–53). The opera audience would probably need to recall the play in order to understand this winding of horns as it occurs, and, even if they do, there is no suggestion that they should reinstate Theseus as the Shakespearean model of stability, critically framing the amorous vicissitudes just resolved. Similarly, because the tradesmen open in the wood there is no need, as there is in the play, to explain a move there from the city, and the librettists drop the explanation that rehearsals in the city would have caused them to be "dogg'd with company" and their devices to be known" (32; 1.2.102). Indeed, the whole play had to be critically reviewed independently of the reshaping to ensure that what was retained was complete in essentials, free from redundancy, and in appropriate form for setting to music. Harrison's almost seventy pages of text had to be reduced to material that would have filled some thirty-five pages in similar format, a drastic sacrifice. But Britten did "not feel in the least guilty at having cut the play in half," saying "the original Shakespeare will survive" (Palmer, 178). Britten had, like Jonathan Miller, found an artifact, and he made clear that he was not about to deface it; he had the necessary mastery over the text that Keller identified. But, in keeping Shakespeare's diction, albeit modernized, he rejected a significant part of the librettist's freedom to rework the source advocated by Smith when discussing the strengths of librettists Quinault, Scribe, and Boito (55, 213, and 342).

Apart from excisions, other kinds of textual adjustments are obviously necessary, such as redefined times and locations of events stemming directly from the reshaping. In the opera, Hippolyta sees "this day" rather than "four days" quickly passing (21; 1.1.7), and Quince requires the company to rehearse "tonight" and "here" in the wood, instead of "tomorrow night" and "there" (32; 1.2.100).

Another kind of minor textual change made is the reversing of the order of short, related statements. These moves appear optional, and, when there is no obvious reason, they tend to erode the claim of having stuck faithfully to Shakespeare's words, as when the lines are reversed in Shakespeare's fairy's words, "Those that Hobgoblin call you, and sweet Puck, / You do their work, and they shall have good luck" (33; 2.1.40). (After the reversal, "Those" is grammatically altered to "They," to match that pronoun in the new leading line.) Britten also puzzlingly reordered Oberon's "Hast thou the flower there? Welcome wanderer," as found in $Q1$, $F1$, and Harrison (40; 2.1.247), to "Welcome wanderer. Hast thou the flower there?"—an arrangement found only in a 1964 reprint of Sir Arthur Quiller-Couch's and J. Dover Wilson's 1924 edition, which the librettists do not seem to have consulted (22). The original sequence is as natural as Britten's; indeed, with the question uttered abruptly first, as in Harrison, the drama is tauter and Oberon's businesslike traits are more evident.

Locutions may be switched to different characters in the opera. This happens frequently when the court and the lovers are ridiculing the tradesmen players, and almost all of Puck's "Now the hungry lion roars" speech (89; 5.1.371) is distributed among individual and grouped fairies.

Harrison indicates no simultaneous utterances (editors of old plays seldom do), whereas nine are shown in the Boosey & Hawkes libretto, bracketed in the left margin. Eight of these groupings combine different words, as when Oberon and Tytania, having sung "Ill met by moonlight" together, proceed with superposed "Proud Tytania" and "Jealous Oberon" (6.13–17). This kind of change is musically inspired, often producing a sung vocal set form of great antiquity where the precise timing of the conflicting words is carefully controlled by the score. A play producer who uses the device must either rely on a pattern worked out and learned in rehearsal or accept an aleatoric jumble of words, both meaningful in their respective ways.

A multiple textual movement, assembling couplets that are dispersed in the play to form the text of a musical ensemble, occurs during the lovers' quarreling. Two of Helena's lines, "You are both rivals, and love Hermia; / And now both rivals to mock Helena," from a seventeen-line speech (58; 3.2.155), and two lines from Demetrius's later four-line speech, "Lysander, keep thy Hermia, I will none: / If e'er I lov'd her, all that love is gone" (58; 3.2.169), were relocated after many other lines of other retained text. At the same time, Hermia complains, "What, can you do me greater harm than hate? / . . . Am not I Hermia? Are not you Lysander?" (62; 3.2.271), and Lysander, in considerably fewer words than in the play, swears, "Ay by my life: / . . . Be certain, . . . 'tis no jest, / That I do hate thee and love Helena" (62; 3.2.277). The four couplets, brought together and bracketed in the libretto (32.16–27), are sung *forte* in canon in which the staggered entries and a repetition of each couplet to a common melody fittingly produce several tritones, the *diabolus in musica,* wonderfully enriching the shouting match between individuals unaware of the ridiculous immaturity they share and portray.

To go into detail, the assembled couplets are noted on the typed working libretto in ink manuscript in Britten's hand (56). Act 2, where they appear, does not appear to have had a final "clean" typing before Britten "accepted" it and began writing the music; it contains both ink and pencil emendations. Britten wrote his composition sketches in pencil and probably continued to use a pencil when changing the libretto as he composed. The ink emendations, including the relocation of the couplets, may therefore well have been made earlier.

Repetitions of text, immediate restatements of a word or phrase from the play, are legion in the score, but they rarely appear in the libretto. On the other hand, returns of text, recurrences of a phrase after intervening material, are few and are shown there. The structurally significant return of Oberon's bestiary has been mentioned. An instance of an added decorative return is where Flute, practising in the background, sings "('Ah Pyramus lover dear, thy Thisby dear, and Lady dear')," (13.32), a line sung by Bottom three speeches earlier. A repeat of a portion of text, its immediate restatement, usually generates tension, whereas its return, its restatement after intervening material, usually brings release. Corresponding sensations normally accompany repeats and returns of musical themes and, to a lesser degree, musical figures.

The many kinds of textual adjustments are interrelated in different ways. The following examples illustrate the complexity and constitute a general warning against overcertainty in analysing changes when reasons for them may be plural—or even conflicting.

A reason may be obvious or obscure. In the play, Theseus's comment on Snout as Wall is, "Would you desire lime and hair to speak better?" (83; 5.1.165); in the opera, "speak" obviously becomes "sing." But the composer added a twist, and perhaps a grateful dig at Schoenberg's invention, for Wall's "singing" is *Sprechstimme,* in which each pitch is only approximated in a half-sung, half-spoken style and is probably abandoned by an immediate rising or falling. The substituted critic, Hermia, is expressly instructed to sing her comment sweetly. It is by no means obvious , however, why, in the libretto, Bottom, having desired more acquaintance of Mustardseed, should get a new line to address to Moth, "Your name, sir?" and the fairy should reply "M . . . " (25.27–29). According to Strode, Britten did not want the boy-actor playing Moth to feel inferior to his young colleagues, and, to this end the composer inserted the lines, and, later, a further line from Bottom: "Where's Mounsieur Moth?" to which the fairy aspirates "H . . . " (26.26).

Sometimes reasons are plural and supportive. In the play and the opera, when the fairies meet Puck for the first time, they charge him with six kinds of mischief—more than enough, surely. His admission to three more kinds was cut from the opera, and with it went unwanted obscurities: his comment "and tailor cries," which still puzzles some editors, and the reference to a roasted crab, possibly particularly misleading in the North Sea fishing village of Aldeburgh, venue of the first performance (34; 2.1.54).

More interesting is the librettists' different treatment of similar candidates for excision. Two jokes irresistable to Renaissance dramatists concern "the French disease," syphilis, causing baldness and the cuckolded man's rack of antlers. Both are in Shakespeare's play. Bottom's proposal of alternative beard colors draws Quince's retort, "Some of your French crowns have no hair at all" (31; 1.2.93), and Demetrius alleges Moon "should have worn the horns on his head" (85; 5.1.241). Both are bawdy, and one senses that Britten and Pears would rather not perpetuate such off-color jokes. But one also senses that few in Britten's audience would take the point of these quips, and one asks: "Can a thing be condemned as bawdy if it is not understood?" Either way, blue or obscure, both remarks invited the librettists' excision. The librettists cut the first, but left the second—and one is left wondering why. Perhaps they were merely avoiding a possible charge of anti-French racism. These are possibly two of the situations that caused Britten's remark that Pears and he "had endless trouble with the references" (Palmer, 178).

Another kind of conflict arises when a duplication or a mere comment that ought to go is very interesting or striking. When Puck describes the tradesmen's flight on seeing Bottom's ass's noll, he uses an epic simile of wild geese and russet-pated choughs taking off, noisily and madly sweeping the sky, on seeing the fowler and hearing the report of his gun (53; 3.2.20). It must have cost the nature-loving composer a pang to excise this image, which could have remained, quite at home in, say, a song.

It would be guesswork to attempt to explain why the pronouns "you" and "thee" at the end of three of Helena's lines differ in the score from the sources and the libretto. In *Q*1, *F*1, Harrison, and the libretto, she says to Demetrius: "give me leave . . . to follow you" (H39; 2.1.207, L10.35) and "I am sick when I look not on you" (H39; 2.1.206, L11.5). The score has "thee" instead of "you" in both places. Shortly afterwards, in the same texts, she vows, "I'll follow thee. . . ." (H40; 2.1.243, L11.11); in the score, this surprisingly becomes "I'll . . . follow you." Ralph Berry comments on the overtones of "you" and "thee" used by different social classes in Shakespeare's day and in his plays, where "nuances are regularly observed" (xvii). Berry states that in *Much Ado about Nothing* (4.1), Benedick risks an occasional "thou" to Beatrice, inviting her to reciprocate his loving feelings. But she invariably addresses him as "you," keeping him at a distance. Britten's first two changes from "you" to "thee" might be constructed as making Helena more friendly, but, if so, why were they not made in the libretto? His third, reverse change is puzzling in this context. Vocal acoustics might supply a rational answer.

The nature of the content of a passage of text, whether, for example, it advances the action or digresses into ornament, furnishes some general reasons for the specific textual changes the librettists made. But inconsistencies abound. One important textual characteristic in the reject-or-inject debate is the eventfulness of the content—whether the words describe something happening or whether they comment on that happening and perhaps its cause or the resulting situation. Titania's refusal to hand over the changeling boy (36; 2.1.122) is an event—a horizontal movement within a plot—whereas her amusing description of his pregnant mother's miming in the spiced Indian air on Neptune's yellow sands is comment as far as the *Dream* is concerned. In the opera, the event stays, but the comment was cut. The three anointings of the male lovers' eyes are events—with vertical interplot connections—for which the text is kept despite the fact that the event is obvious from the seen actions. In these scenes the ancillary comments of Puck and Oberon were kept too, but for a different, formal reason: they are in a distinctive verse pattern. The implications of seen action and verse pattern will be discussed further below. Why the librettists keep or reject comments is sometimes unclear. Hermia's and Lysander's analyses of mismatches accoring to blood, years, or the choice of friends (25; 1.1.135) are kept and foregrounded—to use a helpful neologism, worthy of a place in the dictionary. Their observations on the future perils of war, death, or sickness (25; 1.1.142) are, however, omitted from the opera, possibly because the former represent the reality of the lovers' situation and have outstanding musical possibilities, whereas the latter are mere prospects.

Another criterion applicable to a statement in the playtext is uniqueness, whether it is uttered once or more than once. Shakespeare is not commonly judged a repetitive writer, but, in subtle ways, he often drives his point home by a reminder. The fact that Hermia's and Helena's friendship, including quarrels, is of long standing, although inessential, is indicated five times: Hermia mentions they were "wont to lie" on primrose beds, emptying their bosoms (28; 1.1.215), and Helena's "dear expense" for splitting to Demetrius probably confirms this (29; 1.1.249). In the major quarrel, Helena elaborates on the past in mixed images of making one sampler, a double cherry, and heraldry (59; 3.2.199), pleads "I evermore did love you" (63; 3.2.307), and later recalls "she [Hermia] was a vixen when she went to school" (63; 3.2.324). The opera keeps only the sampler, double cherry, and vixen passages, adequately, although belatedly, retaining the point drummed in by Shakespeare. Shakespeare also explicitly indicates Demetrius's former love of Helena. Lysander mentions it to Theseus (24; 1.1.111), and, perhaps, Helena suggests it when she self-pityingly says she "did never . . . deserve a sweet look" from him (43; 2.2.126). She does not mention the old love when the anointed Demetrius, waking, extravagantly finds her "goddess" and much more (57; 3.2.137), but he does: his "heart . . . to Helen home return'd" (58; 3.2.172). The relation is recapitulated in the hunt scene when Demetrius admits to Theseus, "to her . . . was I betroth'd, ere I see Hermia" (74; 4.1.171). In the opera, one is never told of the old flame. Of these six passages, the opera keeps only the "goddess" apostrophe, which is silent about the past; all the others, perhaps because they are repetitive and retrospective, were excised. By contrast, the uniqueness of a comment is no guarantee of its survival in the opera. Titania and Oberon accuse each other only once of previous amatory involvements with Hippolyta and Theseus (34; 2.1.70), but Britten seemingly had no inclination to set such mythical references to music, even to preserve an interplot link.

Duplication in presentation takes many forms, often involving more than one medium, and, if unwanted, can be eliminated or reduced in different ways. A verbal description of something that will be seen occurs in the play when Titania says to Bottom, "I'll give thee Fairies to attend on thee," and the text continues with particulars: fetching jewels, singing, and purging mortal grossness (51; 3.1.157). These described details are a duplication in advance of what is to be acted out before the audience—all the sooner in the opera, where there is no scene break, they are not missed when excised. An unwanted overlap of simultaneous speech and action can usually be eliminated or reduced by cutting all or part of the speech, saving time if the action is performed quickly. In the play, when offering entertainments to Theseus, Philostrate makes a short speech, "there is a brief how many sports are ripe" (79; 5.1.42): in the opera, there is a simple stage direction "[Enter Quince with play bill. He hands it to Hippolyta and bows]."

Prose and verse receive somewhat different treatment in the librettists' excisions from the *Dream*.[1] The main users of prose are the tradesmen in their theatrical preparations; its secondary users are the court and the lovers in criticizing *Pyramus and Thisby*. About one-third of this prose was omitted from the libretto, compared to the overall fraction of one-half—the considerably lower excision rate probably due to its relative lack of disposable verbal embellishments and the librettists' desire to retain the immediate verbal humor concentrated there. Of the verse lines in Shakespeare's text, approximately one-eighth are shorter than the predominant pentameters. In the main, they are contrastingly trochaic, and virtually all are uttered by the fairies in special, ceremonial circumstances. These short lines are mainly in the "eight and eight" Bottom desired, but in his own bravado song, "The woosell cock," he becomes a balladeer and adopts Quince's suggested "eight and six" (50; 3.1.125). Oberon's three charms and Puck's two are kept almost uncut, recognizing several things: opera's conventional love of ritual, the importance of speech-acts even in a multi-medium presentation, and the inadquacy of merely demonstrating otherworldly climactic events. Puck is the most consistent user of short lines, mostly retained in the opera, the severest curtailments are in his heroic couplets relating Titania's and the tradesmen's discomfitures, which the audience has already seen (53; 3.2.6). It makes little difference to the fraction retained whether the play's predominant iambic pentameter is in rhymed couplets (mainly during intensification of the lovers' conversations) or blank verse.

Passages in the play probably performed as songs become even more prominent in the opera, highlighted by distinctive music. A song, even more than an aria, is detachable from the main action in an opera, but, because of opera audiences' ineradicable admiration of vocalists' exhibitionism, a favorite song omitted is likely to be regretfully missed. Harrison, relying partly on stage directions and characters' announced intentions of singing, distinguishes with italics: "You spotted snakes . . . " (41; 2.2.9), "Be as thou was wont to be; . . . " (71; 4.1.71), and "Now until the break of day, . . . " (90; 5.1.401). But a more accurate song catalog might include only the first of these with the addition of the fairies' "Over hill, over dale, . . . " (32; 2.1.2) and Oberon's "I know a bank . . . " (40; 2.1.249), especially if popular later settings of these words are acknowledged, as they probably would be by Britten's audience. In the opera, these last three are all kept intact, the two fairies' songs considerably redistributed among changing fairy ensembles, consistent with opera's conventional love of set forms. "Be as thou was wont to be; . . . " is short and kept intact as one of the charms; but "Now until the break of day, . . . " loses six of its twenty-two lines—the proscribed negative "blots of Nature's hand, . . . " rather than the desired positive blessings—and Oberon is given assistance from a fairy chorus.

Irony in a play's spoken dialogue is generally conveyed by distinctive audible tones developed during rehearsal; in opera, it can also be crystallized in the setting of the sung melody and emphasized by instrumental accompaniment or interjections. What little irony appears in Shakespeare's play is generally blatant: crude humour when Demetrius quips "Well roar'd Lion" and the others add similar false praise to Thisby and Moon (86; 5.1.265), but bitter sarcasm when Hermia comments "O brave touch" on Demetrius's supposed slaying of Lysander (55; 3.2.70), or Helena dubs the men's love of her "a trim exploit, a manly enterprise" (58; 3.2.157). In the libretto, the quips were retained, the sarcastic remarks were cut.

At first sight, the Shakespearean authorship might have a bearing on textual changes. Britten, mainly as composer but inevitably as librettist too, admitted to "the tremendous challenge of those Shakespearean words, . . . such great poetry" (Palmer, 178); the audience would respect passages that might evoke an admiring "That's our Shakespeare!" Dean believes that great poetry can be successfully set to music "only by a composer who is not afraid to impose his own personality on the text," and he says, "It can be done, as Britten has shown." This develops the "mastery" concept in the epigraph to chapter 3. Dean adds, "The fact that most foreign composers have set Shakespeare in translation must have been a help rather than a hindrance" (95). While the Shakespearean aura induced the librettists to stick faithfully to his words, however, it indicates few clear influences on the excision or retention of specific passages of text. One might distinguish pithy thoughts and catchy forms kept in the opera. Of the former, there are a few passages in Shakespeare's *Dream,* such as "the course of true love never did run smooth" (25; 1.1.134), familiar enough to be regarded as indispensable Shakespeare, but not on the scale of the well-known quotations from other plays such as *Hamlet.* As to the catchy forms, particularly the songs or songlike passages, Shakespeare provided the quality, but it is more appropriate to esteem them and recognize their retention as attractive verse ready-made for operatic presentation.

Apart from the nature of textual material, its context affects its liability to a librettists' change. The immediate context of a statement is its location within other text, and it is probably true to say that some excisions that would have been made for good reason were resisted because the unwanted word or phrase was inextricably embedded in a passage that must stay. The "Carthage Queen" and the "false Troyan" (26; 1.1.169) would probably be inexplicable to many of the audience, but, to preserve four balanced, complementary couplets for Hermia and Lysander in a formal duet expressing mutual vows of love, they were irremovable— probably to the delight of Britten who admired Purcell and had realized (with Imogen Holst) his 1689 opera *Dido and Aeneas* (1951).

A passage of text has a wider context, within other media than words. The librettists' made cuts on the understanding that the complete work would be performed with the assistance of elements that Shakespeare did not employ that can effectively substitute for the spoken word, even outdoing it in clarity of meaning or economy of expression. The gallant-occupied neutral stage of one of Shakespeare's public theatres, the open-to-all plebian innyard, and the exclusive patrician great hall were locales that, in themselves, suggested no specific place or one quite unlike the setting of the play. By contrast, an operatic stage, with its elaborate sets, can tolerate, even encourage, the loss of an orientation sentence such as Quince's converting an imaginary green spot and a hawthorn brake into a stage and tiring house (46; 3.1.4).

Besides expressive scenery, other additional elements available in opera can render speech superfluous. In the play, Oberon orders Puck to thwart the testy rivals, Lysander and Demetrius, by two physical obscurities: "overcast the night" and "the starry welkin cover . . . with drooping fog as black as Acheron" (64; 3.2.355), both of which must be imagined on an open-air, daylight Renaissance stage. In Britten's *Dream,* played in an opera house with artificial lighting and stage darkness realizable, the fog is not specified—an economy, if the producer is satisfied with the duellists' remaining confusion. The excision of speech, as in the preceding examples of Philostrate, Quince, and Oberon, affords the music an unencumbered or a less encumbered use of the sonic communication channel.

In citing the foregoing examples of the influences of verbal, scenic, and musical considerations on the retention or cutting of text found in the source, the opera was perceived mainly as an aesthetic event, its composition seen as Britten pursuing his goal of writing music for the theater that is dramatically effective. But, like any drama, like any art, opera is a part of culture (with a small "c" as well as a large one!), and it thus operates within other kinds of cultural pressures than the aesthetic, such as the philosophic, moral, and economic, each set of forces forming a distinct context establishing criteria for the opera. Considering only one character group, for instance, the court principals, some of Shakespeare's actions for it can be shown to operate in each of these distinct fields, but subject to the limited accommodation possible between the "laws" of the "discipline" and the conventions of opera.

In the play, after Hippolyta expresses fears of audience embarrassment at the tradesmen's probable "wretchedness o'ercharged," Theseus lectures her on the greater kindness of giving thanks for nothing (80; 5.1.89). Philosophical in nature, this exchange explicitly broadens the interprepation of the action and rounds out the characterizations, affecting him differently from her—but it is commentative rather than dramatic and is cut from the opera.

Moral issues meant much to Britten, a pacifist and conscientious objector in World War II; he satirized militarism in his next opera, *Owen Wingrave* (1970). "Politicians are so ghastly, aren't they? . . . I disbelieve profoundly in power and violence," Britten told Murray Schafer in 1963 (117). He possibly enjoyed downgrading the role of warrior Theseus while retaining the reparations to Hippolyta, woo'd with the sword, but to be wed with reveling (21; 1.1.16).

Economics is a prominent factor in opera, always dependent on sponsorship, and Lindengerger's label, "the extravagant art," refers not only to aesthetic matters. By 1960, many of Britten's compositions were commissioned, and any new work by him was likely to receive many performances rather than languish in score. But, as his Aspen Award speech testifies, he was acutely aware of practicalities, and the economies from reshaping, such as cutting the hunt scene, were no doubt deliberate. Chamber opera, able to be staged more economically, was in public demand, and Britten admitted that the *Dream* was small in scale (Palmer, 179). Peter Evans agrees, with a reservation: "On every count except that of economic practicability, the *Dream* must be reckoned among the chamber operas" (256). Nevertheless, the opera has an impressive record of many fully staged performances, probably due not only to the more refined aesthetic expression resulting from Britten's restrained use of the limited resources, but also to the economic advantages of the reduced production requirements.

Each of the librettists' excisions, retentions, and other minor textual changes was, naturally, an objective, based, if not on a firm, obvious need to excise or keep a passage, at least on a tendency either to do without it or to build with it, according to its capacity to function well with other operatic elements to produce an aesthetically successful opera. The items requied to be altered comprise things in the play rendered wrong by the reshaping and those that would be unntelligible or unacceptable in a mid-twentieth-century opera. Items required to be preserved comprise essential action needing explicit statement. There is a tendency, short of an absolute necessity, to cut digressive or merely ornamental commentary and to eliminate duplication, and an opposite tendency to retain popular features such as familiar song. Despite the uncertainties and complexities concerning textual changes mentioned earlier, the objectives of the librettists in their decisions can usefully be classified, albeit roughly, for analysis and further illustration. First, there are textual decisions related to the relatively unambiguous criteria of proper length, intelligibility, and inoffensiveness. Next, there are librettists' textual choices where more subjective judgment is required to determine whether the crucial attribute, be it drama, simplicity, or clarity, is sufficiently present— neither too little nor too much of it. Finally, there are the librettists' excisions made apparently in the light of a general goal of "attractiveness," dependent on a proper balance of the foregoing spectrum of criteria.

The three cardinal requirements—proper length, intelligibility, and attractiveness—demanding different things of the librettists, react on each other through a desirable density of content in the opera. Assuming length to be satisfactory, for instance, too much content will not be intelligible, and, if the audience realizes it is missing things projected too fast to be assimilated, the work will be unattractive. This required balance accounts for the excision of substantial parts of plots or subplots from some plays to allow a slower dramatic pace, as in the highly praised libretti for *Otello* and *Falstaff* by Boito for Verdi. Britten said that Pears and he "had endless trouble with . . . the proportions of the play" (Palmer, 178), and a desired balance probably induced them to seize the opportunity to reduce the court plots following the new opening in the wood.

The opera promised by Britten to the Aldeburgh Festival authorities was to be "full-length," which meant it would by itself provide a full evening's entertainment for an adult audience containing many experienced operagoers. After mentioning cutting, Britten said: "Since the sung word takes so much longer than the spoken word, to have done the complete *A Midsummer Night's Dream* would have produced an opera as long as the *Ring*" (Palmer, 178). He was probably attacking not only Wagner's plan of a four-night marathon of listening, but also the frequent dramatic tedium in the composer's "music-drama," the "anti-opera" concept, which failed to become the artwork of the future. By 1959, when he began work on his *Dream*, Britten had composed seven operatic works: *Paul Bunyan* (1941), *Peter Grimes* (1945), *The Rape of Lucretia* (1946), *Albert Herring* (1947), *Billy Budd* (1951), *Gloriana* (1953), and *The Turn of the Screw* (1954). In Herbert's edition of the librettos of the operas to 1960, Britten's *Dream* ranks third of eight in ascending order of length.[2] In published scores, among performance times, presumably of the premieres, the *Dream*, at 144 minutes, ranks fifth of seven.[3] These nearly midpoint rankings confirm that the opera was "full-length" by the standards of an internationally established composer. Britten's statement that he cut the play in half—severe surgery indeed (Palmer, 178)—is confirmed by word counts.[4] An implication of the required full-length standard is that the excision must not be overdone; all possible cutting is not necessarily good, and reasons for cutting other than to abbreviate are of prime importance.

Intelligibility to an aesthethically sympathetic but critical operagoer is a central, indispensable quality of a good libretto, without which the opera cannot be attractive. The epigraph to this chapter is not the only record of his insisting on the intelligibility of words in opera. In his 1964 speech accepting the First Aspen Award—disclosing a model approach to the audience—he effectively declared that his goal was to be intelligible: "When I am asked to compose a work for an occasion, great or small, I want to know . . . the kind of people who will hear it, and what language they will understand; . . . it is insulting to address anyone in a language which they do not understand" (12). Furthermore, Britten wanted operagoers to expect intelligibility: "I must say one hoped, after the war, that audiences would revolt at seeing opera performed . . . in a foreign language (Palmer, 180).

Britten's words suggest a definition of intelligibility applicable to all aspects of an operatic performance: the linguistic and other symbols heard and seen must have denotations for the audience. For the libretto, the symbols are words in context; for the other media—music, mime, and scenery—they are sounds, movements, colors, forms, and so forth, all working together. In this sense, a foreign tongue is unintelligible, along with references to things once but no longer familiar, such as many persons, places, things, and events from Shakespeare's day, classical antiquity, myth, and folklore. The librettists' retention of Shakespeare's own familiar words, in modern spelling for modern pronunciation, generally purged of archaic references, is a major factor in achieving intelligibility.

This limited definition of intelligibility may be clarified by a comment on its relation to symbolism beyond denotation and to other attributes that might appear to affect it or derive from it. The opera maker, as creator, has a duty to make his work apprehensible to operagoers, who, in their turn, are responsible for connotations of the symbols and for comprehension. Certainty of connotation is beyond the responsibility of the maker. The audience welcomes imagery and punning. Moreover, the content may be made deliberately unclear, as when the listener or eyewitness is meant to be challenged. Pyramus, in the interest of tragedy, misunderstands Thisbe's blood-stained mantle (86; 5.1.282), and Puck, in his epilogue, invites the theater audience itself to doubt its own state of consciousness (91; 5.1.424). Oberon's instructions to Puck to anoint the eyes of the man in Athenian garments are absolutely intelligible, and, to Puck, they are clear, defining a chore (40; 2.1.264), but, to the audience, through dramatic irony, they are unclear and even pregnant with drama.

Also threatening apprehension, the content may necessarily and intentionally not be simple. In citing the obscure references excised to ensure intelligibility, resulting simplifications are mentioned. But, while the combined reshaping and the textual adjustments reduce the extreme complexity Britten saw, his keeping the essence of all the actions ensures that the libretto cannot be termed simple in an absolute, deprecatory sense.

From Britten's emphatic words it is reasonable to expect, as a counsel of perfection, that anything in the source unintelligible in 1960 would be excluded from the opera. In practice, there is an obstacle to discovering how far the librettists and the composer achieved this goal: whether or not the words have sufficiently precise denotations to enough audience members is necessarily a subjective judgment. The librettists had specific intelligibility problems: "Peter Pears . . . and I had endless trouble with the references" (Palmer, 178)—no wonder, after more than three-and-a-half centuries of cultural change. Notably, 1960 audiences were drastically less acquainted with figures from classical antiquity, mythology, and folklore. It is easy to understand the cutting of references to characters and things that are now much less familiar, such as Perigenia, Aegles, and Antiopa (35; 2.1.78), Aurora's harbinger (65; 3.2.380), a "brow of Egypt" (78; 5.1.11), and even "the sisters three" (88; 5.1.336). The first three of these are dispensable also as parts of unwanted longer passages containing comment on the past, largely forgotten folklore, or philosophy. Double obscurity is a compelling reason for excluding two single lines by Pyramus in which esoteric references are bungled: Limander, Shafalus, and Procrus (84; 5.1.196). In these examples, whether the reason for excision is simple or compound, the effect is an increase in intelligibility.

Obscure mythical matters retained are treated differently, for distinct reasons. The roles of Theseus and Hippolyta are simplified by flattening their characters during briefer appearances and by cutting Theseus's philosophizing. The opposite happens to the characters Pyramus and Thisbe, whose credibility is enhanced by the excision of Philostrate's contemptuous preview (79; 5.1.65), and Ovid's tragic lovers' contemporary unfamiliarity is soon remedied by largely retained prologues (82: 5.1.129). Over and above this, they are characterized more richly in the opera by parodic music, not to all critics' liking. In the play, when Puck mentions "we Fairies, that do run, / By the triple Hecate's team" (89; 5.1.383), he not only usurps fairy status, he drags in recondite mythology. The reference is inextricably embedded in rhythmically distinctive, alternately rhymed lines that Britten kept and highlighted in an important musical number; while he cannot avoid the obscure image, he can and does make it appear credible by having not Puck but the four named fairies sing the lines.

Shakespeare's play is rich in botanical and zoological references leavened with myth, which, in context, are soon if not immediately intelligible. The librettists treated these references in an intriguing variety of ways, not always governed by the criterion of intelligibility. As to the flowers, in the play love-in-idleness is meticulously introduced (37; 2.1.166); its antidote, Dian's bud (71; 4.1.73), is clearly another, different flower, and the six floral species Oberon identifies lulling Titania (40; 2.1.149) would still cause no problem in 1960. In Oberon's aria in the opera, "I know a bank . . . " (40, 2.1.249), the straightforward references to the six specific wild-flowers are kept, and perhaps the librettists thought this was enough, for the very label "love-in-idleness" was cut with Oberon's recollection of its mythical, metamorphic origin. This excision is an immediate simplification; the audience does not have to appre-hend a mythical tale. Later, in the play, when Oberon anoints De-metrius's eyes, his chant, "Flower of this purple dye," easily clarifies the vision of the charm, but "hit with Cupid's archery" (56; 3.2.102) incompletely and probably confusingly resurrects the myth. The magic object itself is kept in the opera, simplified as "the herb" (37; 2.1.169) and referred to as "this charm" (43; 2.2.79) and "love-juice" (54; 3.2.37 and 55; 3.2.89). The availability of an antidote was cavalierly treated, probably to create audience sus-pense, when Oberon, in the opera, loses his line that he is able to remove the charm on his Queen with another herb (38; 2.1.184), later on, he simply gives Puck "this herb" to release Lysander (65; 3.2.366). On the other hand, "Dian's bud, o'er Cupid's flower" stays in the opera as a short-lined incantation when Oberon restores Tytania's sight—and the audience can at least be thankful for a cryptic lesson in horticultural myth.

Shakespeare's zoological references are, with a couple of excep-tions, obviously to dangerous or unpleasant animals (38; 2.1.180 and 42; 2.2.30). Thanks to zoos and the listing of the animals to-gether, there are no intelligibility problems despite the disappear-ance from England of many of the species long before Britten's day. The librettists kept the collections—even bringing back the bestiary in Oberon's spell on Tytania—except Puck's menagerie of disguises when misleading the tradesmen frightened at Bottom's translation (49; 3.1.108). The long-suffering spaniel and the lovable ass are universally intelligible, accordingly, in the libretto, Helena, following Demetrius, still pleads for maltreatment (10.32), and Bot-tom, awakening from his dream, accordingly alters his reference to man from "but a patch'd fool" to "but an ass" (40.12).

Some references are treated inconsistently; occurring more than once in the play, they are left untouched in one context and cut in another. Of these, Venus and Cupid were and still are familiar fig-ures, and India had become topical by recently acquiring its politi-cal independence. A changeling, however, would confuse Britten's audience more than Shakespeare's. This group of inconsistently edited references suggests no rationale for the selection made or declined.

Not all the references that probably troubled the librettists were to pre-Shakespearean material. Scholars have detected Elizabethan topical allusions in the play, including: to foul weather during the mid-1590s in Titania's catalog of the "mazed world" (35; 2.1.88); to Queen Elizabeth I in Oberon's reference to "a fair Vestal, throned by the west . . . the imperial Votaress" (37; 2.1.158 and 163); to an incident at the Scottish court in the tradesmen's concern over "the Ladies afear'd of the Lion" (47; 3.1.27); and to the sordid end of University Wit Robert Greene in "the death of Learning, late deceased in beggary" (79; 5.1.53). The mock-lion absurdity can stand without past associations, and it is kept as a prelude to Snug's funnier, illusion-breaking precautionary explanation. Bottom's "fearful wild fowl" comment does not fly in the opera. Weather, fair or foul, never ceases to be topical, and samples of the environmental damage from Titania's lament are retained, the performance shared with Oberon and introducing an operatic duet, an apt set piece admitting their parenthood of the altered seasons. The historical personal references were fittingly excised.

The librettists' varied treatment of such references illustrates the complexity of the excision process. Fortunately, a decision to keep a passage of original text that is now inimical to intelligibility can be tolerated, even excused, as preserving the atmosphere of the well-read master, Shakespeare, whose penetrating references continue to provide food for thought.

The third relatively objective criterion for attractiveness is best described through the negative attribute inoffensiveness. There are few things in the play that might be sufficiently objectionable to need excision in order to keep the opera attractive; there is no evidence that Britten and Pears attempted to bowdlerize the play. Eric Partridge regards it as Shakespeare's most bawdy-free (45); sexual and other physical references are relatively mild and too plentiful to sacrifice with impunity—and many operagoers, covertly at least, would wish them retained as adult entertainment. The inconsistent treatment of capital baldness and cornuting has been mentioned. Is it possible that Pears, who was to play Flute, did not wish to perpetrate the paramour-paragon malapropism (76; 4.2.11), when he penciled it out? Titania's order to "pluck the wings from painted butterflies" (52; 3.1.172) was probably dropped as unnecessary, cruel aggression.

The changes made in the libretto regarding hereditary class distinctions—ever strong in Britain, satirized by Britten in *Albert Herring* (1947), and regarded with increased misgivings in 1960— are few but reactionary. In the opera, to have gentle Hippolyta rather than snobbish Philostrate refer disparagingly to manual laborers (80; 5.1.72) makes her condescending, and the failure to have Theseus reprove her by decrying "the rattling tongue / Of saucy and audacious eloquence" in favor of tongue-tied simplicity (81; 5.1.102) makes him an accomplice in the snobbery.

A displeasing thing can be retained in order to be satirized, the exercise as a whole then becoming inoffensive, indeed attractive. The opera retains from the play the "hammiest" tragedy—even featuring an ingenue kissing the hole of a human wall (84; 5.1.201)—but, in the libretto, there is nothing to suggest that it is offensive, and members of the stage audience praise it good-humoredly among themselves. It becomes clear to all later that Britten's setting to music mercilessly satirizes the tradesmen's performance techniques, but it remains an open, subjective opinion whether Ovid's content is satirized.

One should also consider a group of qualities needed for a stage work's attractiveness, involving more subjective judgment, but whose degree of presence should be a happy mean. First, "drama," denoting a content that is psychologically plausible or excitingly eventful rather than a generic form, a distinction emphasized by Conrad (*Romantic Opera,* 2). Granted sufficient exciting events within a conventional performance timespan, an obvious corollary is the absence of descriptive passages that impede plot development by delaying incidents. Verbal accounts of past or anticipated events are duplications of acted incidents seen or to be seen, while descriptions of things external to the plot are digressions or philosophy. Opera, in particular, must avoid most comment of this nature, the events themselves are slowed down by the singing of their text, and interjecting more than an essential minimum of sung comment makes the performance insufficiently dramatic. Moreover, opera can rely on music to furnish much of the comment on the action, and simultaneous comment by other media requires careful handling. If music and words signify the same thing there is a risk of mutual interference or undesirable duplication—even unwanted humor. Ironic musical comment on the text, however, can be dramatically effective, but not if overdone.

The dramatic nature of an opera's action is first revealed in the libretto: beginning with a source, incidents required for the operatic plot must be segreated from commentary and preserved. In this opera, when Oberon would find out how the spell on his Queen is working, the libretto need not have him "wonder if Titania be awak'd" or what she saw (53; 3.2.1), but he must still inquire of Puck "what night-rule now?" Of Puck's twenty-nine-line reply in the play, summarizing what happened to translated Bottom, enchanted Titania, and the haunted tradesmen, only the first line is kept: "my Mistress with a monster is in love" (53; 3.2.6); it is sufficient to inform Oberon. For good measure, the libretto neatly precedes this line of Puck's with an added "See" (27.19), which, for better measure, the composer has him utter twice, causing Oberon and the audience to look as well as listen and thus be sure of what happens.

Similarly, Shakespeare considers it necessary to allow Oberon twenty-five lines to recount to Puck how Titania had relented (70; 4.1.46) and to order Bottom's release. The opera gets by successfully with four lines, indicating Tytania's dotage and allowing Oberon to explain and predict: "now I have the boy, I will undo / This hateful imperfection of her eyes." This introduces his next, disenchanting quatrain, "Be as thou was wont to be." Duplication, as well as comment, can dilute drama and is readily dispensable. Only Oberon's second-time instruction in the play, "Robin, take off his head," is kept in the libretto (38.24), and thus Bottom, despite the cutting of the first order, is clearly ordered normalized.

Much of the small-scale philosophic theorizing suffers the same dismissal as the longer lectures. The opera audience is not advised that "a surfeit of the sweetest things / The deepest loathing to the stomach brings" (45; 2.2.137) or that "dark night, that from the eye his function takes, / The ear more quick of apprehension makes" (58; 3.2.177). Even Bottom's "reason and love keep little company together, now-a-days" (51; 3.1.144) goes. The verbal love versus reason debate is virtually purged. Helena's "love looks not with the eyes, but with the mind, . . . nor hath Love's mind of any judgement taste" (28; 1.1.234) had been cut out with the rest of her early self-pitying speech, and, later, Theseus's association of the poet with the madman and the lover (78; 5.1.10) is also cut. Sometimes specific points in the debate are selectively excised, as when, in the opera, bewitched Lysander does not tell his new love, Helena, when he sees her as a dove for a raven, that "the will of man is by his reason swayed; / And reason says you are the worthier maid" (45; 2.2.115). But, later, he does say, "I had no judgement, when to [Hermia] I swore" (57; 3.2.134). The operagoers are substantially spared the play's formal rhetoric on the rationality of the love theme and are left to make their own analysis of its truth from the staged action and musical comment in the lovers' querulous comedy and the tradesmen's parodied tragedy. To prove the rule that opera and philosophy do not mix well, one might note that Britten used Shakespeare's meditative Sonnet 43, "When most I wink, then do mine eyes best see," for the concluding text of his

Nocturne (1958). That work is widely regarded as a precursor of his *Dream* in a sequence of compositions exploring aspects of night, sleep, and dreaming, but *Nocturne* is a song cycle, a genre better able than opera to accommodate philosophical matter.

For "drama" to be satisfying it must be cogent—forcible and convincing—a quality depending much on continuity and unity of action and, in opera, requiring the integration of an additional, potentially uncooperative element, music. Shakespeare's comedy is cogent to a remarkable degree, largely through stated explanations of cause and effect within plots and indications of links between actions. The librettists generally managed to preserve cogency in their reshaped text by more economical means. In the play, when Puck has brought Helena near the sleeping, newly anointed Demetrius, Oberon says: "stand aside: the noise they [approaching Lysander and Helena] make, / Will cause Demetrius to wake," and Puck promptly sees that "then will two at once woo one" and provide welcome sport (56; 3.2.116). Although Puck's prognostic exchange is cut from the opera, the audience grasps the continuity that the ensuing enacted events reveal.

Part of the organic unity of the play springs from the initially announced ducal post-nuptial festivity that is finally to provide Barber's "release through clarification," as everyone witnesses the lamentable comedy of *Pyramus and Thisbe*. In the play, when Theseus abandons his selfish hunting to return to Athens where he and the lovers will "hold a feast in great solemnity" (74; 4.1.183), he makes and explains an interplot link vital to the festive comedy. In the reshaped libretto, Theseus does not return to civic responsibility from private pleasure, but the entertainment is featured in full, and the audience can probably ultimately deduce the antecedents. To notice the continuity and the unity differently evident in the opera, however, the audience is required to think harder, rather than listen to explanatory words.

An appropriate degree of simplicity is another criterion of attractiveness that can be achieved by minor textual adjustments as well as the reshaping. When Puck thinks he has found the man in "weeds of Athens" whom he has been ordered to charm (43; 2.2.74), there is a reference in the play to "the maiden sleeping sound" but not near the apparent "lack-love . . . kill-courtesy." The maiden is not mentioned in the opera, simplifying the logic in Puck's soliloquy, but robbing him of circumstantial support for his act. Shakespeare again makes Puck mention this maiden, whom he excusably assumed to be Helena spurned by Demetrius, when first reporting to Oberon (54; 3.2.39); the librettists again neglect her. Even the playwright surprisingly fails to have Puck cite her as defensive corroboration when later pleading "I mistook" to Oberon, by then irate (64; 3.2.350). At that stage, the librettists go further in curtailing Puck's defense by stopping him from mentioning even the "Athenian garments he had on." This simplification appropriately accelerates the dramatic tempo at a point when Oberon must explain at some length his new orders to Puck to lead the testy rivals astray. The lovers' quarrel is simplified when, following Hermia's question, "Why unkindly did you leave me so?" (59; 3.2.183), Lysander's answer and the ensuing debate are cut out, and the plot switches immediately to Helena's "injurious Hermia" accusation. This leaves a loose end, but that is how quarrels go in practice, and the resulting touch of realism cannot be faulted. Peter Evans points out a simplification of Bottom's asininity while he enjoys the fairies' courtesies, ultimately leading to greater intelligibility in the musical context: "his more cloddish witticisms are omitted lest they disrupt the sublime musical poise between sensuousness and irony" (238).

Clarity was distinguished from intelligibility in the above examples when the merits of a degree of obscurity in the interests of suspense and challenge for the audience were illustrated. For the moment, let it be noted, without full discussion, a general aspect of the librettists' search for the best degree of clarity after excising. They no doubt recognized in the play, Shakespeare's hypotactic style—how he carefully explains what goes on and gives complete, explicit data for interpreting sequences of happenings. They substituted the different, common, contemporary paratactic style, relying on simple juxtapositions of events, situations, and characters, designed to generate unlimited, creative interpretive speculations. The opera, particularly its libretto, is decidedly more paratactic than the play, but an examination of music's role is required to study this difference properly.

Attractiveness required for Britten's projected opera performance can now perhaps be understood as a combination of proper duration for the main event in a major annual music festival, intelligibility to the pilgrims to that event and later audiences, and acceptability, without offensiveness, of material kept as essential to the meaning of the work. Attractiveness further required the librettists to create, from Shakespeare's words, by excisions and adjustments, a text with adequate drama—not dull—with developable simplicity—not naive—and with challenging clarity—not tediously explained. The examples just discussed individually in the light of goals for excision illustrate these attributes, provisionally suggesting attractiveness itself to a limited degree. In the next chapter a reexamination of the cuts with a broader field of view, newly organized according to the play's actions and their interactions and specifying further details, will reveal whether Britten and Pears really made the libretto attractive as a whole.

Notes

1. In Spevack's *Concordance* the word counts of 3,288 for prose and 12,859 for verse show that prose accounts for almost exactly one-fifth of Shakespeare's text (632).

2. In Herbert's edition of the librettos, in whole number of columns, the libretto lengths are, in ascending order: *Screw* 23; *Lucretia,* 26; *Dream,* 29; *Gloriana,* 34; *Bunyan,* 34; *Grimes,* 36; *Budd,* 37; and *Herring,* 48, for an average of 34 columns. Later works are comparable: *Owen Wingrave* (1971), 32, and *Death in Venice* (1973), 30.

3. In the vocal or full score, the cited performance times are, in minutes: *Screw,* 106; *Lucretia,* 107; *Bunyan,* 120; *Herring,* 137; *Dream,* 144; *Grimes,* 151; and *Budd,* 158; giving an average of 130 minutes. Of the later operas, *Wingrave* is timed at 106 minutes, and *Death* at 145.

4. From the counted number of words to be uttered in Herbert's published libretto, 7,748, and Spevack's *Concordance,* 16,087, Britten's "cut in half" is very close.

5

The Effects of Changes in the Libretto on the Actions

Polonius: What do you read, my lord?
Hamlet: Words, words, words.
—*Hamlet* (2.2.195)

The substantial reshaping of the court plots necessitated many textual changes beyond simple excisions, not all of which were made. The court nuptials plot is essentially simple, and the initial textual change has the effect of putting a shorter waiting period before his wedding into bridegroom Theseus's speeches. Conveniently Shakespeare refers not to the approaching nuptial day but to the nuptial hour, a reference that can stand in the compressed time scale of the opera. But, immediately after supper, before the choice of entertainment, the ducal pair and the lovers are still to be knit, and, from that time on, all are confined to the court watching the lamentable comedy until midnight, when Theseus orders everyone to bed. Shakespeare's reference to a four-day wait was adjusted by the librettists to indicate nuptials on "this happy day"; Theseus says "I wed thee" instead of "I will wed thee," and Hippolyta's reference to the moon's phase is rationalized. Her revised line, "this day will quickly steep itself in night," implies that darkness is yet to descend, which is probably true on a long midsummer evening. But, rejecting the improbable idea that the triple temple wedding was to be a confirmation of earlier civil contracts, the fornication, because it includes the Duke and his Amazon Queen, is even more widespread than Cooke indicated. There is no musically imposed break in which the weddings could take place; the mere two bars between Theseus wishing the newly arrived lovers well (409) and calling for entertainment (410) is taken up with lovers' embracing. The hunt and Theseus's and Hippolyta's admiration of canine cries producing "musical confusion / Of hounds and echo in conjunction," "musical discord," and "sweet thunder" (72; 4.1.110) are excised, precluding the occasion for a composer's representational tour de force, a challenge Britten might well have scorned to accept. It also brings about a loss of folklore: Saint Valentine would have been understood, but the idea of woodbirds' coupling on his day could have been educational—an amusing glimpse of sex for the audience—but something perhaps not sought by the librettists.

The changes in the court plots from reshaping the libretto and other adjustments make them more intelligible, particularly through the loss of classical references in the hunt scene, and simpler because the court loses its framing function. On the one hand, the drama within the plots is reduced, since Theseus is not shown desirously waiting throughout four acts, and he does not appear as a character jointly blocking young love. On the other hand, Theseus's frequent philosophizing, arresting the plots, is largely eliminated. The attribute most drastically affected is clarity: the opportunity for the ducal pair's wedding to take place "in the Temple, by and by" (74; 4.1.180) is worse than obscured, it is lost in the reshaping and the consequent adjustments.

The characters of both Theseus and Hippolyta lose a dimension when their formal philosophizing is lost from the libretto. He remains a figure of respect and stability, but less rational in not expounding the power of imagination and less noble by not treating tongue-tied social inferiors graciously. She becomes shallower through not debating Theseus's ideas and less gracious in assuming the role of the excised Master of Revels and condemning the tradesmen's offering, a disinterested subjects' duty on their part—aside from their hopes for Bottom's sixpence a day.

By this stage, the libretto completed, the reduced status in the opera of the head of state can already be seen as Britten and Pears reflection of historical developments. Theseus's court no longer applies the law of the land since he simply overbears Hermia's father's will (43.9), using the good influence expected of one who still reigns though, perhaps, no longer rules. Royal compassion for the afflicted is an expected personal trait; in the opera, there is no need for Philostrate's or Egeus's presence portraying the court as a focus of power. The court wedding in the opera is a contemporary social event rather than a dynastic marriage with political advantages warranting public festivities. By 1960, the common man and woman had attained a form of permanent release through another process, enfranchisement.

Do the librettists' character changes for Theseus and Hippolyta reflect new concepts of class in society? The couple remain true aristocrats, members of the small, highest class, outstandingly "gentle" according to the ideas of birth, education, wealth, behavior, and values, which Ralph Berry suggests roughly define a Renaissance gentleman (xii). Marwick, however, viewing British society since 1945, comments that quiet speech was "definitely not an upper-class characteristic" in Britten's day and that it indicates not aristocratic but upper-middle-class status (45). Two related speeches in the play might reflect relative voice dynamics among interacting upper social classes. When Pyramus approaches the well, Theseus, apparently addressing the last speaker, Demetrius, calls for silence (5.1.169); when Thisby first approaches the tomb, Demetrius, checking Hippolyta, Theseus, and Lysander, again calls for silence (5.1.261). Shakespeare does not here suggest that true, ruling aristocrats speak any louder or softer than members of the next lower stratum.

In the libretto, on the first of these occasions, as a result of the reassignment of speeches, Theseus addresses Lysander and Hermia (45.28), and no class switch is involved. On the second occasion, "All" are to sing, apparently to each other, for silence (48.10); this generalization does not suggest any specific change in interclass tones of voice. The librettists seem to follow Shakespeare.

In the score, however, the composer is obliged to make the vocal dynamics plain. In the first incident, although Hermia and Lysander comment on the wall quietly, Theseus, seeing Pyramus, demands silence loudly and accentedly (427): authority is weaker, thus noisier, perhaps. In Britten's setting of the second incident, however, after Hippolyta had quietly wished for a moon-change, the score lumps together the four lovers and Theseus, each singing "silence" *piano* (445). If Britten had wanted to reflect consistently Marwick's view of relatively loudmouthed aristocracy, he could have made Hippolyta, with Theseus, dismiss Wall's "silliest stuff" at the top of their voices, only to be silenced, gently, by the lovers. One can only guess at the many possible reasons why Britten did not thus round out his downgrading of the ducal couple and at the same time emphasize the distinct interacting groups he welcomed. Perhaps it should be left that Theseus and Hippolyta were definitely "U" according to Nancy Mitford's 1955 article (Marwick, 45) and thus vulnerable to satirical reverberations.

The first change in the libretto for the tradesmen's interlude plot, occurring immediately after Quince's opening, "Is all our company here?" is an addition, "*All:* Ay, Ay," allowing the five others the opportunity to build successively a musical dissonance as they try to achieve harmony (12.7). Balancing these opening "Ays," the librettists close the casting session with ensemble "Adieus," to be similarly "harmonized" (15.16). When the tradesmen meet again to open the opera's second act, Shakespeare's "Pat, Pat" is retained (20.8): it may have suggested the earlier, added, "ays" and "adieus." Their musical, trade-unionistic "solidarity for ever" might strike another chord in 1960.

In the play, when the tradesmen first gather to cast their interlude, Quince very early says it is to be played before the Duke on his wedding night (29; 1.2.5), an interplot link presumably generated by the announcement of court festivities that Philostrate was to make offstage (21; 1.1.12). In the opera, Quince's failure to name the occasion can be rationalized because the court activities have not been mentioned, and it is a common dramatic device to stage disjunct actions that members of the audience, trusting the dramatist, can pleasurably attempt to associate in one or more ways. Or, congratulating themselves, the audience can call on memories of the source. Later in the operatic scene, however, after Quince's short-lived hope that "here is a play fitted," Bottom boasts of receiving an encore from the Duke for the leonine roaring he wished to make; whereupon Flute (not Quince as in the play) visualizes "the Duchess and the Ladies" shrieking from fright (14.24). So, the tradesmen are obviously going to play before the Duke, Duchess, and some ladies—but the audience must guess the occasion. The ladies are mentioned twice again in the opera's rehearsal scene, and the Duke three times in the reunion after Bottom's dream, when he also concludes with an exhortation "to the Palace away." The reference to the Ladies, whom the tragedy and the lion might offend, must remain in the casting scene or the valuable humor from the players' aesthetic misconceptions of dramatic illusion would be lost. Although Quince's opening statement of intention is cut, no less than nine other pointers are retained, and one can commend the librettists for both initially arousing one's curiosity and progressively clarifying how the plots are unified.

The textual changes to the tradesmen's action are numerous, varied, and generally insubstantial. In the libretto, one is not told that only the tradesmen, in all Athens, are fit to play in the interlude, or that Bottom would "let the audience look to their eyes." His repetition of Quince's statement that they would be hanged for frightening the Ladies is omitted. After the casting and Quince's urgent entreaty to con the parts, they still agree to meet at the Duke's oak to rehearse, but, consequent on the reshaping, it is now "tonight" and "here," and they need not fear being plagued with unwanted company as might happen in the city. The tradesmen's lamentable comedy's title need not be repeated at the rehearsal. Bottom's speeches insisting on telling the actors' real names for Pyramus and Lion are drastically reduced, while his idea of an open casement to admit real moonshine and his desired plaster, loam, or roughcast for Wall is not mentioned. When the tradesmen meet again, the only thing cut is Bottom's refusal, twice, to tell his dream. In the opera, it is not Bottom but "All [except Bottom]" who describe necessary last-minute preparations for properties and costumes and exhort abstentions from nail-paring and garlic.

In the palace entertainment, their competition—from Hercules and the Centaurs, tipsy Baccanals, and three mourning Muses—obscure but humorously incongruous, is omitted from the opera; Quince's prologue is pruned of its revelation of the tragic end, suspense being more important than a comical, plosive singing of how Pyramus, "with bloody blameful blade, / . . . bravely broach'd his boiling bloody breast" (82; 5.1.46). In *Pyramus and Thisby*, the only losses are some bungled mythical references, a few of Lion's threats, Pyramus's thanks to the Moon for revealing Thisby, a repetitive "that left pap, where heart do hop," and other, mythical references, one by Thisby to the "Sisters Three." In the play, Bottom offers a bergomask dance "between two of our company," but the limitation is removed in the opera to allow them all to perform in a musical set number, a survival of the ballet conventionally interjected into opera. The librettists enhance intelligibility by omitting Bottom's troublesome "hold, or cut bow-strings." The exclusion of the paramour-paragon quip and the joke about the colored beards and hairless French heads were noted earlier as possible examples of bawdy or racism avoided in order to be inoffensive. All in all, these assorted excisions hardly affect the drama, and the loss of detail only slightly increases simplicity and decreases clarity. The tradesmen's interlude plot is equally attractive in the play and the libretto: its culmination, the performance of *Pyramus and Thisby* as an opera-within-an-opera is, arguably, the thing most modified—by the music, as will be seen.

Shakespeare presents Quince and company as "hard-handed men that work . . . / Which never laboured in their minds till now" (80: 5.1.72), saying nothing to characterize their individual, named trades, but placing them, as manual workers, squarely in the lowest social class Sir Thomas Smith deemed worth mentioning (Ralph Berry, xi). This is exactly what was required for the play to indicate a harmonious working relationship between the social classes. Britten wisely leaves well alone—his forbearance in not reintroducing $Q1$'s and $F1$'s colorful label, "rabble," has been noted. As will appear when the setting is examined, however, Britten makes striking changes to their dramatic talents, when, after rehearsing as the incompetent amateurs Shakespeare characterized, they put on their show as, in the eyes of one critic, a clever team of spoofers.

The textual changes made to the stage audience's critical comments on the drama-within-the-drama are minimal. The court's and the lovers' witticisms are similar in their mocking spirit, and the librettists easily switch nine of the interjections to different characters, notably from Theseus to the middle-class women, Hermia and Helena. An interesting example of aleatoric superposition of all six stage audience parts occurs following the mispunctuated prologue, clearly described in the score, but only partly revealed in the printed libretto by redistributed speeches without the customary marginal bracket. The librettists preserve Shakespeare's switch from blank verse to prose for the court and the lovers, complementing the thespian tradesmen's reverse switch, a distinction that setting to music can illuminate. Theseus continues to say the play needs no epilogue, but his positive though double-edged judgment, "this palpable gross play hath well beguiled / The heavy gait of night" (89: 5.1.367), is cut, along with the renewed promise of a fortnight's nightly revels.

The librettists probably noted, as did Ralph Berry, with emphasis, that "the courtiers' running commentary is . . . *to one another,* semi-private, and not hurled at the actors" (36–37). Britten and Pears could gratefully and realistically carry this deadly audience courtesy over into the modern opera house, treating the court and the lovers to a performance that misfires, satirizing the tense drama and fine singing of its bel canto models.

A review of the opening of the lovers' nuptials plot in Shakespeare's first scene was forced upon the librettists by their deferral of the appearances by the court and the lovers. Their amendments were drastic. Theseus's articulate judgment and sentence was cut out, together with the comprehensive picture of the pattern of the characters' personal loves and hates, some long-standing. Hermia and Lysander retain their protestations and vows, but lose their pessimistic prognosis of achieved true love. They are deprived of the chance to plan their elopement on stage and to confide in Helena, who in turn cannot confess the "dear expense" in mitigation of the treachery she still obviously commits offstage. The retimed entrances of the pairs of lovers into the wood have been discussed: excisions include comments on Helena's wish to be Demetrius's

dog, much of the recrimination over his past and impending aban-
donments, and Helena's now antifeminist requirement, "we should
be woo'd" (40; 2.1.242). When Lysander and Hermia appear in the
wood (in the opera, before the other lovers), his arguments for "one
bed" and her refusal, in which she, too, "riddles very prettily," are
omitted. Some elaborating words but no sense is lost, both when
"transparent Helena" is unexpectedly demanded by the waking,
bewitched Lysander and, later, when Hermia wakes from her
serpent-infested nightmare.

The excisions in the long lovers' quarrel scene in the play (some
400 lines), illustrated by the following examples, are typical of the
kinds of cuts throughout the libretto. When Hermia chides Demetrius for pursuing her, she uses an astro-geological metaphor, the
unlikely event of the moon creeping through the center of the earth,
to convince herself that Lysander would not desert her; laughably
strange, this is omitted. Helena in the play chides the men at length
for conspiring and pretending to love her for merriment; this is
cut, probably because it could be tedious. Hermia's irate question
to Lysander about his desertion goes unanswered in the opera,
and Helena's attack on Hermia for joining in the supposed mocking
is stripped of her convoluted reasoning designed to prove her case.
Some repetition in the play is cut, as when Lysander reiterates
"Helen, I love thee" (61; 3.2.251) and when the women keep accus-
ing each other of immodesty. A highlight is created in the opera
when a couplet by each quarreling lover is assembled as text for
a fiery vocal quartet.

The connection with the fairies' matchmaking plot when Oberon
tells Puck "still thou mistak'st" (64; 3.2.345) is reduced to its essentials when the librettists eliminate Oberon's details of how to set
things right, maintaining suspense. The opera also loses Puck's
folklore about ghosts retiring at dawn, and with this gone, Oberon
need not contradict Puck with a boast: "but we are spirits of another sort" (65; 3.2.388).

In the opera, the lovers awake to offstage horn passages rather
than Theseus's hunt—with no reference to the Duke, to his orders
for the lovers to be wed, or to Hermia's father; instead they sing
a musical quartet of reconciliation. It has already been noted that,
in the opera, Snug does not mention that "there is two or three
Lords and Ladies more married" (76; 4.2.16), because, through the
librettists' reshaping and oversight, there were not. Part of what
Theseus said in the play to the lovers during his hunt he says in
the opera at the palace while ordering the extra weddings, but the

edict does not now appear as a reversal of his former judgment or bring the lovers to court to witness the tradesmen's entertainment.

There is little, if anything, unintelligible in the play that needed the librettists' attention. The outdated male-to-female sexist sentiments are unobjectionable in the immature young characters; indeed those attitudes and the obsessive patriarchy are necessarily there to be overcome as the target of the overall romantic movement. The initial drama of Theseus's judgment in the play is lost with his deferred appearance, and Hermia's threatened fates are never mentioned in the opera. No significant simplification is needed or made in the central and minor quarrel scenes, in which complexity, especially if not completely grasped at the time, contributes to the ridiculous effect. The libretto experiences some loss of clarity when the reasons for the elopement and Demetrius's pursuit are deferred and abbreviated. On balance, however, the lovers' text for setting is as attractive as Shakespeare's, especially to those who welcome realism and a challenge to understand. The characters of the lovers in the libretto are little altered from those in the play.

The librettists undoubtedly reflect 1960 society when Hermia is not threatened with the cloister. They keep out the explicit blocking patriarchy and paternalism so prominent in the play, inserting only a passing, inconspicuous reference to a sharp law. Richard Levin argues convincingly that Renaissance parental authority was only half the story and that "there was another idea of the time, affirmed in many proverbs, that love cannot be compelled, and that it will find a way, despite . . . obstacles set up by the anti-romantic older generation" (133). Shakespeare could rely on his audience knowing this; so could Britten, with the postwar crop of social frustrations and Marwick's "great release from older restraints and controls" (16) providing further credibility.

The beautification plot of the fairies is unessential dramatically, but important for atmosphere and characterization. As expected, nothing is cut from the song "Over hill, over dale," detailing the bedewing and the making of the spring flowers fit for the Queen, although Shakespeare's solo fairy part is taken over by all the fairies in interacting groups. Again, rather than the single fairy in the play, several fairies charge Puck with mischief in the opera. His own supplementary catalog of pranks is excised, and, comparing the nature of the peccadillos on the two lists, the omission makes him more acceptable socially.

Many of the specific disasters resulting from the royal quarrel are omitted, but a report on the altered seasons is retained. As in the play, the mortals in the opera do not notice the progeny of environmental evils: in 1960, hostile weather was still regarded as an act of God. Today, one might comment on the upset climate, but do so with scientific explanations, beginning to place the blame on our mortal selves. The fairies' lullaby includes protection for Titania, showing that some potentially nasty terrestrial creatures can be restrained to advantage; again the opera makes much of every word of a musical verse form. At the end of the play, Puck, characteristically, has the chance to threaten everyone with the horrors of the night, citing lion, wolf, screech owl, sprites from gaping graves, and then, as one of "we Fairies," to take credit because "not a mouse shall disturb the hallow'd house" (89; 5.1.387). In the opera, he must be silent on the sidelines and not inject his speaking voice into the fairies' choral singing; he must be content with a claim to be sweeping dust. Oberon, too, must share with a fairy chorus his "Now until the break of day" song of blessing, without mentioning the moles, harelips, and scars to be prevented, his countertenor voice retreating into the boys' treble voices. The function of the attendant fairies in this beautification plot and their role in the opera is greatly augmented, probably to help realize the country-loving composer's emphasis on the wood and its bewitching powers.

The plot portraying the rift between Oberon and Titania and its healing by his tormenting her with human asininity was notably foregrounded by the librettists' reshaping; it is extensively purged of dispensable explanation, comment, and ornament in their excising. The initial cuts consist in not narrating but simply showing that the royal revels are imminent and in removing allusions to Theseus and Hippolyta and their forthcoming wedding. Details of Titania's joy over the changeling, of his mother's service, and of the persistent royal "squaring" are left out of the opera. So is Titania's conciliatory invitation to Oberon to "patiently dance in our round" (3; 2.1.140), but his unreasonable demand for the boy, made twice over, and her emphatic refusals, the genesis of the plot, are retained and stressed, first, in clear, unaccompanied recitatives and, second, in an emphatic, combative duet. Oberon's colorfully imaged recollections of the metamorphosis of the milk-white pansy with the topical allusions are let go, leaving the bare description of its magical powers and his orders to Puck to fetch it. He still waits until Puck has departed to announce his intentions, but, in the opera, he adds a touch of suspense by failing to announce how he can remove the charm.

In the libretto, when Puck stumbles across the tradesmen's rehearsal, he refrains from unnecessarily saying he will listen and intervene (48; 3.1.79), and he leaves out the details of the animal disguises he will use to lead them around (49; 3.1.108). The Tytania-Bottom scenes of the rift-repairing plot are relieved of a few lines of repetition, lunar mythology, philosophy, and Bottom's cryptic ability to "gleek upon occasion." Since the play's scenes are consolidated in the opera, there is no need for Tytania to order Bottom brought to her bower. Finally, Oberon can see, without Puck's tedious report, how things fall out better than he could devise. In a musical drama, Bottom's "reasonable good ear in music" could not be left unsatisfied, and the opera features an amusing performance. But Bottom does have to forgo his "bottle of hay," perhaps because that archaic measure of quantity, comically misunderstood, would make him seem more cloddish and interrupt the music's balancing of moods. The cut removes any possible need for staging and cleaning up after a repast the actor might well decline.

The rift plot ends when Tytania is disenchanted so that Oberon and she are "new in amity" and ready to dance and bless at Theseus's house—in the opera, at "this very" midnight rather than tomorrow's. The opera belatedly mentions this reconciliation without Oberon's long account of his triumph in acquiring the boy or Tytania's request to be told how it all happened. As a coda to the plot, Bottom tells of his most rare vision and dream, but, in the opera, he does not claim visionary powers. Two statements of man's wise restraint from explaining a vision of the supernatural are conflated, the ambiguous designation "a patch'd fool" yielding to the more intelligible "an ass."

The simple matchmaking plot is the most important link between character groups and actions in the play, and the three anointings of the mortal men's eyes are, of necessity, retained—but with an economy of words. In the opera, when Puck returns with the flower, it is handed over wordlessly. Oberon does not tell Puck to do his job carefully so that the vaguely defined "he" may "prove more fond" (an unexpectedly apt word) on "her"; they do not agree to meet "ere the first cock crow." The confirmatory mention of the maiden sleeping nearby, and Puck's glee at the potential disruptive prospect of anointing the real Demetrius's eyes, dropped from the opera, have been discussed. When Puck distracts Lysander and Demetrius from their duel, the opera again does without some mythology and philosophizing. The final disenchantment of Demetrius is spoken by Puck in the play: it is he who performs the ocular application in the opera, but it is the fairies (who can sing, whereas Puck cannot) who deliver the incantation, changing "I'll apply . . . remedy" to "he'll apply . . . remedy."

In the opera, as in the play, Oberon predicts, "There shall the pairs of faithful lovers be / Wedded, with Theseus, all in jollity" (71; 4.1.91), but "there" clearly means in Theseus's house, not in the temple. Perhaps Shakespeare lapsed a little, as the librettists did in their reshaping; perhaps no writer can escape infection when writing about confusion. When Puck has received his order to lead the testy rivals astray, he advises Oberon of imminent dawn with a folkloric warning against wandering ghosts homeward bound for churchyards and damned spirits of suicides already in their wormy beds (65; 3.2.381). At the play's end, still in character, Puck states that it is night, depicting the spirits venturing forth from gaping graves (89; 5.1.380). Why the librettists excised the first spooky reference and kept the second is perhaps best explained in the light of several operatic conventions. Proclaiming the ghosts' retirement would have indicated their recent activities during the night so troublesome for the lovers and the tradesmen, clinching its weirdness. But to have narrated their hauntings would have been undramatic and to have staged them would have overcrowded the cast. Above all, the music could unaided forcibly portray the supernatural presences simultaneously with the mortals' discomfitures: hence the omission. Retaining the later reference, the librettists respected a distinctive, singable verse form, and, transferring it from Puck to fairy ensembles, they ensured it would be sung rather than spoken. Again they involved the fairies in not-so-nice goings-on, validating Britten's observation that they are "very different from the innocent nothings that often appear in productions of Shakespeare" (Palmer, 179).

In the operatic version of the fairies there is a gain in intelligibility from the excision of classical, mythical, folkloric, and archaic references. Their only piece of nastiness, the mutilation of butterflies, is excluded. The dramatic incidents in the rift-repairing and the matchmaking plots are retained, but a good deal of the verbal commentary—predictions and reports of action—is omitted, allowing the duration of each actual event, when sung, to be extended without making the whole too long. The fairies' actions, kept virtually intact, are as simple and clear as in the play, and the excision of many verbal explanations of seen actions causes no problems for an attentive audience. Having these dispensable words sung would have obscured some of them anyway. In the libretto, Oberon's decisiveness is accentuated by the excision of the elaborations of his orders, which, combined with his foregrounding by the reshaping, moves him further ahead of down-graded Theseus as a force in the opera.

The greater prominence of the fairies in the opera has been attributed to musical opportunities seen by Britten; and he, at Aspen, referred to

> the something which emerges from [music] but transcends it, which cannot be analyzed because it is not *in* it, but *of* it. . . . I quite simply call it—magic: a quality which would appear to be by no means unacknowledged by scientists. (17–18)

This does not establish any definitive 1960 audience attitude toward the supernatural, however. There were both continuities and changes from the beliefs of Shakespeare's day. Pilots in World War II had still experienced gremlins "on the stick," spoiling their flying, and the welfare state was to many a new fairy godmother: altered seasons, on the other hand, were generally explained by random variability of natural forces; it was too early for widespread self-accusation. Fairy-tale opera had experienced a wave of popularity, and, at least, Britten can be said to recognize the fashion.

One of the librettists' most significant textual decisions was to retain the epilogue, as much a reshaping declined as an excision resisted. It is not required to make the preceding actions intelligible, dramatic, simple, or clear, but the opera, thereby, preserves attractive, half-whimsical, half-serious features of the play—an apology for nonexistent offense and involvement of the audience in the awake-asleep ambiguity. Britten's featuring this conclusion is not surprising in view of his interest in night, sleep, and dreams.

Before leaving this examination of the making of the libretto, significant points concerning restructuring and textual excisions can be discovered in the Verdi connections, both backwards to Shakespeare and forwards to Britten, by looking at another Verdi work, *Macbetto* (1847), his fourteenth opera, written some forty years before *Otello*. Schmidgall convincingly argues that Shakespeare and Verdi as true men of the theater, eclectic innovators who never theorized about their arts, were birds of a fine feather (*Literature*, 214–15). Surely Britten is a worthy successor in that intriguing kind, as is exemplified by Verdi's and his similar expectations for adapting Shakespeare's plays to make acceptable librettos.

Concerning *Macbetto*, Verdi wrote to his librettist, Piave: "I've got the general character and color of the opera into my head just as if the libretto were already written" (translation in Schmidgall, *Literature*, 188). How like Britten with his describable, precompositional musical ideas! Both composers depend on a pervasive mood, eloquently portrayed at the outset, to validate their operas. Verdi blasts in the explosive tone of *Otello* by opening with the storm at sea as the hero arrives in Cyprus; Britten evokes the mysterious aura of the *Dream* by opening with extraordinary noises as the fairies materialize in the wood near Athens. Both scenes are dramatic moments, identified by the composers as necessary for the effective, early creation of the essential atmosphere—and, here is the point: if the right dramatic moment is not at the beginning of the source text, a reconstruction must be made to put it at the operatic curtain-up.

A less extensive but structurally similar revision occurs in *Macbetto*. Shakespeare provided two witches scenes in his opening act, but in the first, the weird sisters perform no deeds, merely announcing that they will meet again upon the heath to greet Macbeth. Then the King's party are staged, essentially to receive a narrated battle situation report. Soon, however, in the play's second witches scene the hags begin to describe their nasty, killing rites, and they hail a trembling Macbeth "that shalt be King hereafter." It is at this sinister, dramatic encounter that the opera is made to open, introducing the supernaturals and the hero. Schmidgall terms *Macbetto* "a far more faithful setting than has been realized before" (182), but one should not overlook Verdi's vital reshaping to create without delay a dynamic, potent impact on the audience. Compared with *Otello*, this work was a failure because (Schmidgall, 183) in it Verdi was urging the end of popular bel canto and pioneering the rise of verismo.

If this Verdi-Britten comparison can be indulged a moment longer by turning to look at the reasons for keeping or cutting text in *Macbetto*, it is clear that Verdi does much as Britten does. Schmidgall again explains: "a librettist, . . . fashioning his text from a literary source, will naturally gravitate away from passages of discursive complexity and toward those that issue in psychological or physical action." Macbetto's early great monologue on the implications of assassination, when nothing happens (1.7.1), is cut; his later soliloquy, the famous dagger speech, brimful of mental and bodily action (2.1.33), "inspired one of Verdi's finest accompanied recitatives,"—including, incidentally, an admonition to librettists generally: "Words to the heat of deeds too cold breath gives" (15–16).

It is time to summarize and become evaluative—provisionally—
of a few points. By the excisions and the other textual adjustments
made in the light of the reshaping, the librettists have prepared a
text of appropriate length for the composer to set to music, the
words more or less fixed and Shakespeare's extremely complex
story simplified and cut as Britten wanted. Some musical influences have already had effect. The excisions did more than the
reshaping to make the libretto intelligible, and but a few audience
members would lament the loss of now unsharable curiosities the
excision of which was as much a reflection of changes in post-
Renaissance school curricula as of operatic conventions. A few
possibly unpleasant passages have disappeared from the opera,
also perhaps partly to respect different mores. The simplification
from reshaping was carried further as the librettists excised detail,
including some of Shakespeare's precautions against missed
events, indications of sequences in the actions, and interplot links.
The opera audience is left less to apprehend, but, by virtue of the
same deletions, initial, immediate clarity is somewhat less. The
work is not yet realized, however, and the fashionable, more paratactic ordering of the essential dramatic material preserved from
the source, when infused with musical associations, may well turn
out to be at least as attractive as the play's closely knit structure
if both are viewed—as they must be for valid comparison—in the
modern time frame. Any required amendments to the settings of
place and time were made in the reshaping, but not without residuary problems. The composer and a future producer are faced with
a considerably more important and prominent Oberon. Britten's
daring musical solutions will be examined next.

6

Implications of the Use of Music

I . . . take note of the human circumstances of music, of its
environment and conventions; . . . I try to write dramatically
effective music for the theatre.

—Benjamin Britten,
*On Receiving the First
Aspen Award*

With the play restructured and cut, the libretto ready, "the words
more or less fixed," Britten, turned composer, could concentrate
on writing "dramatically effective music for the theatre," on creating *dramma per musica*. Mitchell's "silent innovator" never explained his music; one must seek its meaning in the music itself
within its operatic context.

Peter Evans, in 1979, sought "to study the musical processes of
each of Britten's works and to offer the results in the form of a
commentary, . . . commonly chronological, . . . [setting] out from
a strong, but *essentially intuitive, response* to [his] music, . . . directed towards identifying the compositional grounds for the nature
of the response, the causes that have ensured the composer's effects." He argues, convincingly, for the necessary use of "technical
terms of a reasonably unambiguous nature." He describes Britten's
mastery of the art of composition: "a mastery of tonal and harmonic structures, of thematic cast, cross-reference and transformation, of resourceful textural variety and of imaginative
deployment of voices and instruments." He indirectly but rightly
claims to show, for the operas, "the uniquely fitting relationship of
each of these to verbal and dramatic contingencies" (4–5, emphasis added).

Commenting on Bottom's first appearance with the ass-head,
Evans finds a snigger in Puck's trumpet's quiet trill followed by a
loud upward glissando octave scale and a braying in the trombone's
fortissimo pedal tone, low B♭, descending still lower during its

thrice three intrusions. The meaning of these virtual sound effects is clear, as is the symbolization of Snug's slow-wittedness by augmentation of the values of the notes he sings (245). It is less obvious, however, why an "apparently rootless diatonicism" in the orchestral prelude to act 3 should establish a different mood from those of the "shifting yet solidly rooted tonalities of the [preceding] wood ritornelli and the Sleep ground." Moreover, just before the curtain-up of act 3, music that "floats in . . . thin air," even if so sensed, can hardly by itself make one see specifically the wood "in the clarity of early morning" (250); indeed, the "cool, imperturbable motion" can symbolize not one but many different things.

Bach's doctoral dissertation contains a detailed technical musical analysis of the opera, particularly of the first act, profusely illustrated by annotated score extracts and concentrating on the internal musical relationships. He shows that "Britten's music displays evidences of deeper thought processes in addition to its most immediately accessible values" (221), and he frequently associates musical processes and structures with dramatic situations. His response is, apparently, like Evans's, essentially intuitive.

Acknowledging debts to Evans and Bach, the approach here is to study the *process* of making the opera rather than to analyze the *result*, although that is necessary to apprehend the work. There is an attempt to provide specific descriptions of Britten's compositional procedures and musical structures, striving to identify bases for their denotations and functionality, and, sometimes, recognizing different, equally tenable responses. The analyses often focus on the multiple, small-scale constructs in Britten's music, which, it is believed, are as important for its functionality as the larger-scale features usually identified. Rather than chronologically, musical examples are selected as required to illustrate the ordered theoretical topics. The implications of many of Britten's musical events are wider than those propounded by many critics, thus interpretations are sometimes offered that might appear off-center. The general defense (if any is needed) is that these interpretations fall within the range of the powerful ambivalence Britten has incorporated into his panoramic and penetrating vision. The composer's eclecticism, too, prompts certain observations that might appear peripheral.

In two earlier chapters Britten's and Pears's libretto-making procedures—restructuring and excising—were studied; in this, the first of four chapters on Britten's musical procedures, different but complementary concepts—those involving musical meaning—are examined and illustrated. Susanne K. Langer's concept of "significant form," a term that she gratefully acknowledges was coined by Clive Bell, is the point of departure. It springs from her brief recapitulation of her theory of music, cited in the epigraph to the next chapter (*Feeling*, 27), and it underlies the other theories of meaning in music that are discussed. Britten invokes these forms in opera, focusing on the particular musical element or elements that provide potential for rational or emotional implication and response.

In succeeding chapters, several matters of a more specific nature are examined: what Britten does in vocal passages of diverse kinds to ensure that words and music work together to discharge their respective and joint responsibilities most effectively; a look at the longer solely instrumental passages, some suggesting atmosphere, others action; and some aspects of Britten's opera in relation to "reality," including the opera-within-an-opera, *Pyramus and Thisby*. In conclusion, an evaluation of the complete work according to the criteria previously (provisionally) applied to the libretto, from initial intelligibility to final attractiveness will be considered.

The functionality of music has been recognized throughout its history. Peter Evans reasonably assumes that readers understand and accept his perceptions of certain musical attributes functioning in certain ways within the operatic context. Here, it is proposed that musical meanings have objective bases in musical processes, which Britten consciously knew and innovatively employed in reinterpreting and enhancing the stripped-down Shakespearean comedy.

Supporting this position, one might consider the work of Susanne K. Langer, a philosopher of art and music, Aaron Copland, an eminent composer who, like Britten, composed many film scores, thereby acquiring experience valuable for an opera composer, and Leonard B. Meyer and Wallace Berry, music theorists, whose concepts depend on inherent musical features as objective bases for meanings. These persons have different approaches, but their views are reconcilable and appear to underlie the opinions of many scholars and critics commenting on, even explaining, Britten's *Dream*.

Langer identifies music as a symbol of special potency:

There are certain aspects of the so-called "inner life"—physical or mental—which have formal properties similar to those of music—pattern or motion and rest, of tension and release, of agreement and dis-

agreement, preparation, fulfilment, excitation, sudden change, etc.
(*Philosophy,* 227–28)

A simple example may suffice to demonstrate this; at the end of
act 1, Tytania, fallen asleep and protected by a sentinel, can expect
a period of peaceful, refreshing quiet, rounding out the day; thus
the enchanting wood music subsides to a simple *piano,* low G-B
major third harmonic interval in the double basses, the very sound
that began the act. But Oberon has just surreptitiously enchanted
her to fall in love with some vile thing on awakening, and, while
the G of the second basses fades, the B of the first basses swells
and throbs, causing a top-heavy imbalance in the interval and intensifying the sonority (156), thus suggesting that sleep can harbor
disturbing forces, as Britten knew from experience and admitted
to Mitchell ("Mapreading," 92). Langer states further: "The real
power of music lies in the fact that it can be 'true' to the life of
feeling in a way that language cannot; for its significant forms have
that *ambivalence* of content which words cannot have" (*Philosophy,* 243). Her idea of ambivalent content of musical forms can be
accepted, even if her contrast with words is rejected.

Copland, in his 1939 book (revised and enlarged in 1957) advises
"what to listen for in music" and states the ways (functions) in
which music serves the cinema screen, concentrating on the relation between musical influences and specific dramatic ingredients
such as settings, characters, and actions (154–55). His views raise
topics that must have concerned Britten during the period 1935 to
1939, when he composed music for some twenty documentary
films, mainly for the United Kingdom's General Post Office. Mitchell sees this experience as valuably formative and the resultant
skills as profitably carried over into Britten's career as operatic
composer:

> His work on the sound-track of *Night Mail* is typical of the way Britten
> would labour and labour to contrive, to devise, the particular sound
> for the particular context; and he could summon up these astonishingly
> graphic sonorities even when faced with the most improbable collec-
> tion of instruments.

Mitchell goes on:

> This meant the development by Britten of a quite singular descriptive
> gift . . . for mimicry in sound to the nth degree of imagination. He had
> . . . always had this marvellous, well-nigh photographic ear . . . and
> he continued to use it. . . . We hear it . . . in . . . his last opera, *Death*

in Venice, when the sound of the engines of the ship ferrying Aschen-bach back to Venice explodes into life.

Mitchell corrects a possible expectation of excessive onomato-poeia when he continues, citing a criterion of John Grierson, pio-neer documentary filmmaker: "'the creative treatment of actuality' might well serve as a very neat summing-up of one aspect of Brit-ten's treatment of sound" (*Britten and Auden,* 85–86).

Copland's first function for film music is "creating a more con-vincing atmosphere of time and place." Two different atmospheres of time, one realistic, the other supernatural, are portrayed near the end of the opera. While the double bases, harps, timpani, trom-bone, and a bell slowly toll midnight in G♯ and the court and the lovers complete their departure with a choral "to bed," the por-trayed ambient time is sensed as realistic (466–70). But, then, an-nouncing and accompanying the fairies as they appear chanting a catalog of the eerie sights and sounds of the night, Britten has various other instruments, notably from the percussion group, make some thirty twelve-note tintinabulations in widely different registers and at assorted speeds, dispersing the orderly, stable at-mosphere of the court, so that the portrayed chaos is sensed as the unrealistic temporal dimension of the supernatural world (471–80). A special atmosphere of place, of the magic-filled wood near Athens, depicted by the eerie sounds of Britten's opening music, has already been cited as his reason for drastically restructuring the play and starting the opera there.

Copland's next musical function is "underlining psychological refinements—the unspoken thoughts of a character or the unseen implications of a situation." Shakespeare implants unspoken thoughts, an imperfect recollection of Saint Paul's marveling, into astonished Bottom's words, "the eye of man hath not heard . . ." (75; 4.1.210). Britten injects an equally remarkable example of mu-sically expressed subconscious recollections when Bottom wakes, for his melodic line is an enriched echo of Tytania's distinctive, waltzlike aria of instructions to her attendants to serve him. Fea-turing melodic thirds while the flutes and clarinets repeat the short staccato scale they played in the love scene, Bottom's area is now embellished with scale fragments played by the earthier English horn and bassoon, portraying his own mental contribution to the revelation (361).

Britten's musical underlining of the unseen implications of a situ-ation is evident when the second pair of lovers, Demetrius pursued by Helena, enter for the first time. They are distinguished from

Lysander and Hermia, who appeared before, by contrasting dialogue and different musical motives. Lysander and Hermia had declared to each other," I swear to thee"; whereas Demetrius says "I love thee not" and Helena retorts "you hard-hearted adamant." The earlier couple had been accompanied by a soft, smooth flute and oboe figure G. F♯, D♯, E, shortly followed by its transposition, D, C♯, A♯, B (46); whereas the later duo enter with a loud, jerky figure in the strings (64). The verbal and musical media ostentatiously cooperate in defining the difference between the pairs. But Britten insinuates more into these passages, an ambivalence: when Demetrius and Helena are introduced, the soft, smooth figure in the woodwinds is added to their loud, jerky string accompaniment, suggesting that the separate pairs, canopied by the same tortuous motive, are destined to merge and behave similarly.

The lovers' G, F♯, D♯, E motive closely resembles a prominent Renaissance musical figure, the *cambiata,* wherein a stepwise descending melodic passage, like the *Urmotiv,* is prolonged by a downward leap of a third from one note (in this case, F♯) to an added, decorative, nonharmonic note (D♯) the *nota cambiata,* which is a step below the final (E) (see example 7.1[d]).

The third of Copland's functions for film music is "serving as a kind of background filler." As music is a full partner in opera rather than a conventional intruder, as in film, it cannot properly be regarded as a "filler," but there are obvious occasions when it should retreat into the background. Uneventful instrumental passages, as changes from busy accompaniments or as punctuations of the dialogue and action, provide welcome variety and tactical releases permitting strategic intensifications. Moreover, if a work is to be opera rather than musical comedy, dialogue that pushes the action forward must be sung in recitative rather than spoken. Recitative requires instrumental support, not merely to give the singer the note from time to time, but also to justify the unreality and the distancing effect of protracted utterances that are musically disciplined as to pitch, rhythm, and other qualities. At crucial moments, however, the instrumental support can profitably disappear altogether, allowing the dialogue or mime unencumbered freedom to deliver its message. When Britten introduces Lysander and Hermia, they lament at length the rough course of true love to a uniform, busy accompaniment in the woodwinds. But, when, next, Hermia suggests patience, the winds retreat into silence, simultaneously avoiding imminent monotony and leaving the sound channel unencumbered for important dialogue. The winds make *diminuendo* rising leaps between dominants and tonics of key D♭, a significant instrumental up-and-out form to be elaborated on later; the lower strings cease their sustained "filling," coming back briefly only on the name "Hermia," unimportant in its context, and between the singer's words. Consequently Lysander, unaccompanied, can propound the details of his dramatically important elopement plan without competition (52).

Opera does not depend on the cinema's "quick flashes of disconnected scenes," which Copland sees rescued from chaos by music's building a sense of continuity. But, in a multiplot work like the *Dream,* where interdependent actions must each be moved forward in rotation, the temporally detached segments of each story can be unified by musical devices, and development, as well as simple continuity, can be revealed. When Lysander and Hermia have become lost in the wood, Britten brings them back on stage accompanied by recognizably similar, mildly dissonant, agitated sonorities transferred to the higher pitched woodwind instruments. But the tempo is "a little slower than before" and the original rhythm (see example 7.2[c]) is in retrograde, the previous *accelerando* now a *rallentando,* thus revealing the same characters on the same exploit, but indicating that Hermia is now "faint with wandering" and both are ready to rest—Lysander agreeing, more readily than in Shakespeare, to "lie further off yet" (109).

Fifth, Copland mentions "underpinning the theatrical build-up of a scene, and rounding it off with a sense of finality." Britten uses this resource in the tradesmen's casting scene, where the main required dramatic development is getting the players into their unwelcome parts in an unlikely play. When Quince announces the comedy "of *Pyramus and Thisby,*" he does so in an unaccompanied cadential motive squarely in A♭: a downward-leaping, rhythmically distinctive, tonic to dominant to tonic melodic progression (see example 7.2[e]). (This may be designated the *Pyramus and Thisby* motive.) The others, except Bottom, immediately echo his words and rhythm in a snatch of traditional four-part singing, using his final tonic, A♭, as their initial mediant, G♯, and leaving their new melody poised expectantly on its new dominant, B. This harmonized fragment is conveniently labeled the "Grieg" motive—in recognition of its similarity to the first phrase of the piano's first subject in that composer's piano concerto (see example 7.2[f]).[1] The momentary finality of Quince's pronouncement is promptly converted, by a textual repetition, a developmental musical root shift, and a harmonization, into a tensing dramatic buildup (86).

The key to Meyer's system of functionality in music is stylistic abnormality—which he calls deviation—causing tension. In text-dominated situations, the musical procedures that constitute abnormality include, first of all, ornamentation. Britten progressively ornaments, ground by ground, the instrumental passacaglia at the beginning of act 2 in order to intensify sleep's as yet unexplained powers (157–64), and, in midact, to recharge the wood's spell before the next scene (236–42).

Meyer's idea of abnormality from chromaticism can perhaps best be illustrated by the effect of the use of its obverse, diatonicism, within Britten's generally twelve-tone sound. In the operatic performance of *Pyramus and Thisby,* Britten proffers the normal romantic diatonicism of early nineteenth-century Italian opera as artificial and passé, creating a pleasurable tension with his normal chromatic language. He parodies bel canto for amusement (413–60).

Another of Meyer's deviations is "the minor mode in Western music," as commonly used to depict sadness and suffering. But its irrelevance, indeed virtual unusabilty, in Britten's *Dream,* at least when the fairies are active, is an index of the distance his musical language has traveled from traditional Western practices. Britten's assimilation of elements of both tertian and nontertian harmony, functional and otherwise, and atonal, even serial procedures, frequently results in successions of sonorities that suggest the music in the opera is supernatural rather than Western, a foreign language to the human courtly and plebian characters, denizens of the major-minor aural kingdom. Thus the context necessary for Meyer's minor mode to function is removed. Moreover, Britten's concept of hierarchy among tones often includes a resurrection of the richer, if subtler, medieval spectrum of modes. Peter Evans notes, in the fairies' homage to Bottom, a "familiar Lydian/Mixolydian compound" (*Music,* 246; S212–14), and there are clear Phrygian passages in Oberon's and Tytania's duet "the seasons alter" (28, 32). Franz Schubert, admired by Britten, achieved startling dramatic effects by alternating between the major and minor modes; as the price of the eclectic tonality and atonality of his language, Britten relinquished this resource, but he could recall it to a limited degree in the "old-fashioned" musical language of *Pyramus and Thisby.*

A central idea in Meyer's system is that musical tension and release result from, respectively, the frustration and the fulfillment of implications contained in relationships between the musical components. The implications and consequent expectations may be for continuation, change, or closure: in particular, a process discontinued too soon or dragged out too long is tensing, and final completion, closure, with at least partial release, is hoped for. The relationships may be of similarity between or hierarchy among the musical elements of various kinds and the passages of various magnitudes; appropriately timed change is crucial for effective drama.

In the fourth scene of the opera's act 1, the lovers return for the first misdirected anointing. After a ritornello passage has boosted the spell of the wood, empty again, a retrograde rhythmic motive and the *cambiata* motive reappear, a device unifying segments in a multiplot work in which actions are interrupted (109). The effect of the returns is, on balance, a release: a break from the tradesmen's inanities and an assurance that the absent lovers have not been overlooked. These two motives now recur alternately more than ten times each—an ample number—despite many modifications, to begin to weary the audience and make it long for a change: Hippolyta, later, is far less patient watching Moon's repetitive self-introduction (444). Thus, when Lysander and Hermia have completed their decorous sleeping arrangements (114), Britten makes a manifold change, nevertheless maintaining links with earlier passages. The chordal accompaniment changes to a steady, tranquil rhythm, which, though in a $\frac{4}{4}$ meter, is reminiscent of the barcarolle with Helena's "I am your spaniel" aria; the horns and trombone carry on, with, however, the clarinets and bassoon replaced by the first harp. Above all, the lovers switch from recitative to a passage that is functionally an aria, singing a contemplative "Amen" several times, forming a canon from the *cambiata* motive and its transformations in doubled note values. The dissonant counterpoint and clashing words, supported by two solo cellos, eventually achieve unity as the tones in the overlapping parts of the two weary singers squeeze together by semitonal steps from a tritone, A over E♭, to a midpoint unison, F♯ (115). Change is prominent, both in the sung lines and the accompaniment, but the residual similarities with earlier versions of the motives confirm that the characters, in essence, have not changed.

A pattern succeeded by a modification of itself, as just described, demands, in turn, relief. Britten provides it by switching to different, though familiar, material as Puck enters to bewitch the man in "weeds of Athens" (115). Relief, however, is not abandonment, and, when Puck returns to Oberon, Britten makes Hermia, in her sleep, sing the "Amen" phrase again (119). She now sings solo, no others' words to obstruct hers, for anointed Lysander is necessarily asleep, and he must not awake to see Hermia or the plot complication would be frustrated. The differences Britten makes in the passage on bringing it back testify to his recognition of universal,

everlasting change: on the first "Amen" occasion (114), the writh-
ing cellos complement the clash of staggered words as Lysander
and Hermia fumble to give their thoughts a unified expression; on
the passage's return (119), the cellos, less distanced in their entries
but still contrapuntally dissonant, show something subtler and
more sinister, the disturbing elements of sleep. There is more.
Overviewing all the passages just discussed, one can see that Britten builds musical relations into a hierarchic A A^1 B A^2 structure,
unifying the Lysander-Hermia episode, the final A^2 segment making a progressive closure to the subscene, which can itself be set
among other compound units to make an organic whole.

Much later in the opera, when Lysander and Demetrius leave
the stage "to try whose right . . . is most in Helena" (285), Britten
reuses the *cambiata* motive in a striking frustration of musical
expectation to generate tension and subtly enrich a dramatic crisis.
Thus far in the plot, whenever two or more of the lovers sing
the *cambiata* theme together, whether in quarter-note or half-note
form, they begin at different pitches, in canon, and use mirror or
retrograde forms, producing more dissonance than consonance.
This gives the motive a connotation of animosity, open if the characters are enemies, hidden if they are friends—something to be
expected on future hearings. As the motive returns, accompanying
the duel-bent men, it is augmented and inverted, the contour of
the opening notes, G, A♭, C♭, B♭, perhaps by now suggesting a
distorted opening of the finale of Mozart's "Jupiter" symphony.
The motive is instantly recognized, and its past contexts and connotations are recalled. But, for the first time—surprisingly—Britten has it sung in unison, words together, with no contrapuntal or
textual dissonance in the vocal lines. Although the accompanying
woodwinds and brass, playing snatches of the motive, sound several semitonal clashes, the voice leading is extremely smooth, leading to a cadence in C major, high G over C, perfectly consonant,
even characterless. The music's relative blandness, because unexpected, is tensing, underpinning the men's intention to fight; but
one unanticipated musical implication may well herald another,
and, with Puck stage-managing the duel, anything might happen.
In this Lysander-Demetrius challenge, Britten's manifold musical
forms are, at once, tensing and releasing, simultaneously eliciting
different interpretations of the dramatic situation that may all be
valid. The different, now orderly vocal lines suggest that the men
are trying to resolve the senseless, bitter debate, making the first
move—constructive albeit potentially destructive, illegal albeit socially condoned in Shakespeare's day.[2] But the *cambiata* motive's

connotation of imperfect harmony and the labyrinthine accompaniment's dissonances suggest that beneath the surface of the men's short, unison declaration lies a more deadly antagonism than that in the longer, musically busier women's slangings. Britten's use of similar material in opposite musical styles in support of apparently similar, but subtly different, dramatic situations not only provides variety in unity, but also spotlights additional, equally valid meanings and is a further index of the skill and care he devoted to the work. Langer was impressed with the powerful ambivalence of music's significant forms, and, according to Mitchell in *L'innovatore,* Britten also exploited ambivalence musically at the fundamental level: "His nature as an artist, the modes of thinking and feeling which we find expressed in his individual operas, are often—and, I maintain, deliberately—ambiguous" (my translation, 45).[3]

Wallace Berry's concept of functionality in music, too, depends upon the tension and relaxation engendered in a listener by processes in the sonic variables, and, because of this agreement with Langer and Meyer, only his focus on change, rather than theirs on significant form and deviation, is examined here. Berry sees changes in musical variables as "element-actions," events or processes that are "progressive" and "recessive." He claims, for instance, that a move towards more frequent accents is tensing. The Lysander and Hermia *accelerando* motive (46) is a small-scale instance of this: the concluding of the tradesmen's bergomask ("quick, ♩. = 120") with a kind of instrumental cabaletta ("very quick, ♩ = 184"), containing many more sixteenth notes, is a larger-scale use of the same tensing device (463). It would seem, however, that Berry's idea of a "progressive" change in tempo requires expanding to the tensing effect of the opposite abnormality, a very slow rhythm, as when, in the passage following the bergomask ("slow, ♩ = 60"), the prominent midnight clock booms out only fifteen times a minute, suspensefully hinting, with Theseus's "lovers to bed," at exciting new experiences to follow (466).

Berry sees progression, recession, and stasis as three possibilities in musical passages of changing intensity, and he notes the prevalence or rarity of each in the basic formal processes of music: introduction, statement, restatement, transition and development, and cadence (7–10). These propositions are best tested against a passage of music not dominated by text, such as Britten's long instrumental interlude in act 3 (385). That passage, however, also illustrates the use of music to portray a change of scene, and the analysis is deferred until that topic is examined in chapter 9.

The persons just named write generally on aspects of musical functions that apply in opera. Others write more specifically, with different approaches: Grout, Kerman, Lindenberger, Cone, and Charles Rosen. One can agree with Grout that music in opera is probably like other music of the same period, but . . . often simpler, more popular, more tuneful, more obvious in rhythms, less contrapuntal, but more varied in instrumental color (5–6). These traits are, perhaps, to be expected, if music is not to violate its cooperative equality with other ingredients by obtruding or by retiring into insignificance. This comparison is not of concern here.

When Kerman cites three principal conventional ways that music can contribute to drama, other elements are involved: the characters, the action, and the environment (214–15). He gives instances of music turning "the pasteboard characters outlined by the librettos's words and plot into 'real' people." including Britten's eponymous character Peter Grimes, "who gains the audience's sympathy entirely by means of music reveling an inner life sharply at variance with an . . . unsympathetic exterior" (216). A musically revealed "real" person may also be a subversion of the apparent character (217–19).

Kerman goes on to say that music "generates" an action, explicitly using that verb in preference to "matches," "illustrates," or "supports," in order to indicate music's creativity and indispensability. Among other devices, he approves as effective the returns of musical passages at high points in the drama, bringing images to fulfill the attenuated scenario in the text. It may be noted that such returns might even replace narrative descriptions excised in making the libretto. The music must be adequate to this challenge or the action will be trivialized or nullified (Kerman, 219–23).

"A total drenching of the action by music of a particular sort" is Kerman's phrase for his third item of music's operatic roles: "music establishes a world." He instances a world of growing obsession in Britten's *The Turn of the Screw,* generated by "formal variations on a single twelve-note melody, which builds tension by its 'turn of the screw' upward movement as well as by saturation of the whole chromatic." Or, as is to be expected, unfitting music can demolish a world (223–26). Or, one might add, if not skillfully integrated, the orchestral background could evoke images of the wrong world, such as our own unoperatic everyday world of Muzak.

When Kerman asserts that music bears the ultimate responsibility for articulating drama (214), he implicitly recognizes, first, that they both function in the same dimension, time: second, that effective organization demands a locus of final authority; and, third, that music is charged with recognizing total form and not merely with providing sufficient striking individual "numbers." This stance ties in with Grout's point that, in opera, compared to spoken drama,"the entire dramatic tempo is slower, so as to allow time . . . for the deployment of the musical ideas" (5).

Lindenberger states that opera is able to create an illusion of inevitability with greater ease than spoken drama, largely through the "primacy of the musical flow" and its imposition of greater limits on a performer's freedom. He continues: "Opera's ability to impose inevitability on action is most discernible whenever a familiar dramatic text has been set to music" (54), a comment of particular interest in this study of an extremely well-known play with so many possible meanings. (It is endorsed later.)

The ability of a piece of music to work with drama—to articulate it—is perhaps because music is seen as a form of drama itself—exciting, unified, consummated. Two esteemed musicologists support this view. Edward T. Cone states that "a proper musical performance must . . . be a dramatic, even a theatrical event";[4] Charles Rosen found the classical style superior to the preceding Baroque style because "the movement towards the dominant," while common to both, is dramatized in the later music—it becomes "an event as well as a directional force."[5] Examples to be given will endorse these musicologists' opinions.

Notes

1. The author is indebted to Professor Robin Harrison of the University of Saskatchewan for pointing out the resemblance. Could Purcell be given the opportunity to perform Britten's score, he would probably follow seventeenth-century practice and extemporize an appogiatura C♯ in place of the penultimate B, making the passage even closer to Grieg's.

2. According to S. P. Zitner on dueling, the prospective duel is unlikely to have been widely condoned in Shakespeare's 1590s. The men's cause was flimsy—their rebuffed proposals are no seductions—and their motivation was misdirected. They were acting selfishly rather than as agents of God's justice (7–8).

3. The Italian text of Mitchell's article, p. 45, reads: "La complessità della sua natura d'artista, i modi di pensare e di sentire che troviamo espressi nelle sue singole opere sono spesso—e, ritengo, deliberatamente—ambugui."

4. Edward T. Cone, *Musical Form and Musical Performance* (New York: Norton, 1968), 13, quoted in Lindenberger, 62.

5. Charles Rosen, *The Classical Style: Haydn, Mozart, Beethoven* (1971, reprinted New York: Norton, 1972), 70, quoted in Lindenberger, 63.

7

Significant Forms in the Music

... forms of growth and of attenuation, flowing and stowing, conflict and resolution, speed, arrest, terrific excitement, calm, or subtle activation and dreamy lapses ... the greatness and brevity and eternal passing of everything vitally felt. Such is the pattern, or logical form, of sentience; and the pattern of music is that same form worked out in pure, measured sound and silence. Music is a tonal analogue of emotive life.
—Susanne K. Langer,
Feeling and Form

When Britten considered the musical resources at his disposal for setting the *Dream*'s libretto, he must have been aware of "significant form," although not necessarily of Langer's discussions of it. A form emerges from the content of an event, process, or situation, dependent upon spatial or temporal features, or both. It is perceived over the short, medium, or long term and suggests similarities with or differences from other forms. In artistic creation, original matter is presented, or previously offered matter is repeated or brought back, as it was or tellingly modified. Musical forms can be attributed to many components, which Jan La Rue classifies as sound, harmony, melody, rhythm, growth, and text influence, often operating together (10 and 148), sometimes producing a stereotype of shape, process, or even genre, such as a ritornello, a passacaglia, a fugal exposition or stretto, or a binary or ternary shape, each with its own secondary implications. The significance of a form, inherent or acquired as a work unfolds, depends upon the feelings of tension, release, or stasis, which different listeners experience in common, arising from the denotations and connotations of the apprehended shape. Certain general, value-charged sets of attributes are discernible in significant forms, including normality or abnormality, tradition or innovation, unity or variety, balance or imbalance, and fulfillment or frustration of implications. The composer's prime concern is that these forms be intelligible for they underlie a great deal of any "meaning" ascribed to music.

The concepts of theme and motive are a useful introduction to musical form; Britten's use of them provides a starting point for considering his treatment of significant forms, leading to the identification of certain musical passages that it is useful to recognize and have labeled at an early stage. In the *Dream,* as elsewhere, a musical idea becomes a theme—or, if short, a motive—from the way it is used rather than from its content or form. A theme inevitably has a recognizable form as a result of the distinctive shape of any musical element or elements, but that form's main significance springs from its subsequent appearances, perhaps modified and in different contexts. It becomes a distinctive building block in a larger structure, even in a whole composition. In a work with a program—either conveyed by words as in opera, or conveyed by musical, subjective images, as in a symphonic poem—the composer connects his musical themes and motives with characters, things, actions, or setting, the association working both ways. Apart from using different instrumental groups with their own expressive timbres to characterize collectively the members of the different social groups (Palmer, 177), Britten uses musical themes and motives to round out individual characters, chiefly to announce, accompany, and dismiss them. He rarely combines the themes to make a predominantly musical occasion, and the *Dream* has no symbolic object to warrant a leitmotiv.

Britten adds a dimension to the thematic concept by making several of his motives themselves originate in a single, simple musical progression that can conveniently be labeled the *Urmotiv.* It rarely appears as itself, but is the source of several thematic figures derived from it by rhythmic, harmonic, or melodic ornamentation, each clearly associated with a specific character. It is thus a powerful, economical source of musical variety in unity.

The *Urmotiv* is *mi, re, do*—the third, second, and first notes of the major scale, or the mediant, supertonic, and tonic degrees. It is shown in line (a) of example 7.1, in which are also brought together, for easy comparison, its derivatives and their labels. It might be associated with Heinrich Schenker's concept of a *Terzzug* (or *3–Zug,* a linear progression through a third), or even with a short *Urlinie* (the upper voice of a fundamental harmonic progression). So simple a motive has numerous guises: many will recollect

Example 7.1. *Urmotiv* and Related Motives in Britten's Opera *A Midsummer Night's Dream*

(a) *Urmotiv*

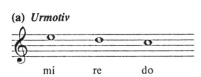

mi   re   do

(b) Fairies' Chorus Motive (5)

(c) Royal Fairies' Motive (20)

(d) Lovers' *Cambiata* Motive (46)

(e) Trademen's Trombone-Bassoon Motive (84)

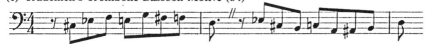

(f) Bottom's "Joy" Motive (88–89)

(g) Court Harpsichord Motive (394)

the opening *"Le-be-wohl"* of Beethoven's piano *sonate caractéris-tique,* op. 81a; everyone will recall "Three Blind Mice." Schenker's distinguished pupils, including Felix Salzer, have found that the master's analytical insights can be applied to compositions in later, postromantic musical languages, and, while the idea cannot be fully developed here, one of Britten's outstanding accomplishments is the integration of features of the language of the "common-practice" period, on which Schenker's models are based, and the methods and systems of later periods, including those based on twelve-tone and even "atonal" principles. Schenker's *Terzzug,* through the *Urmotiv,* is perhaps more central to Britten's musical procedures than at first appears.

It is impossible to say whether the concept of a definable *Urmotiv* generating specific thematic figures consciously motivated Britten: possibly the *Urmotiv* is only imagined because of the similarity of certain themes. The fact remains, however, that several of his themes can easily be seen as simple modifications of the *mi, re, do* sequence and, thus, as not merely devices differentiating characters, but, col-lectively, as a force unifying the opus. These are the fairies' chorus motive, the royal fairies' motive, the lovers' *cambiata* motive, the tradesmen's trombone-bassoon motive, Bottom's "Joy" motive, and the court harpsichord motive—all shown in example 7.1.

The very first sung sounds, in the striking timbre of the boy-fairies' treble voices, are the quarter-note tones F♯, E, D, descending in whole-tone steps, of the fairies' chorus motive (5). For good measure the pattern is reinforced in two ways: first, by a similarly constructed subjoined sung C♯, B, A (see example 7.1[b]), and, second, by the supportive harmonic lines played by the harps and harpsichord as major triads on each melodic degree. Britten's meticulously exact chromatic parallel part movement does more than Debussy's usually diatonic planing could do in driving home the *Terzzug* motive. By this planing in invariably major triads with doublings, Britten earns a double dividend: the simple directional motion is exactly replicated and emphasized, and the tonality is complicated, adding to the strangeness.

Peter Evans has commented on the frequent and developmental use of another figure that turns out to be a rhythmic version of the *Urmotiv,* the first note lengthened at the expense of the second, intro-duced as G♯, F♯, E, a dominant figure in an A major tonal region (20). It forms an accompaniment for Tytania and Oberon—the royal fairies' motive (see example 7.1[c]).

As cited earlier, before the first of the lovers, Lysander and Her-mia, enter in the next scene, the flutes and oboe announce, in quarter-note rhythm, a compact G, F♯, D♯, and E motive (see example 7.1[d]), and Lysander's first, soon-to-follow utterance is a matching subjoined motive, D, C♯, A♯ B (46). Acknowledging, perhaps, some license in that the G in the first sounding and the D in the second are anacrustic, the D♯ and the A♯ may be heard as ornaments (*nota cambiata*) to the *Urmotiv,* now in minor keys, E minor and B minor. This figure, already labeled the *cambiata* motive, persists when the other lovers, Demetrius and Helena, appear.

When the tradesmen assemble for their casting session, the trombone whispers two staccato eighth-note passages (84). The first divides into two sections: C♯ (= D♭), E♭, F, E, the *cambiata* motive inverted in a distorting mirror, and G, F♯, F, D, the *Urmotiv* compressed into semitonal steps with an added final. The second passage, two bars later, beginning on E♭ and ending eight notes later on D, is an exact inversion of the first, and thus a normal *cambiata* and an inverted, compressed *Urmotiv* (see example 7.1[e]). Britten brings the motive back, in part or in whole, during the rehearsal (165), generally modified and played by the bassoon or the trombone, to introduce characters. Later, the repeated figure on the solo English horn as four of the tradesmen enter before Bottom rejoins them, C, B♭, B, A, G♯, is essentially an *Urmotiv* with the short, staccato B and A forming a decorated approach to the final, enharmonic A♭ (368).

Returning to the casting session, when Bottom steps into his desired Ercles the Tyrant part (88), he sings "to make all split the raging rocks" to a figure that can readily be heard as a slight rhythmic elaboration of the royal fairies' motive or a melodic simplification of the lovers' *cambiata* motive. The theme begins on C, B♭, A, A, settling into a ¼ rhythm. He sings the four-note figure five times in a rising sequence (see example 7.1[f]), then, after pausing for breath, four and five more times. The woodwinds punctuate his song with a version of the motive in secundal harmony, their sequence descending. The figure recurs many times, copied by others than Bottom (95, 355, 364), a form significant not only in thematically unifying the characters and character group one with another, but also in displaying the tradesmen's lack of true artistry by overworking a phrase to the point of comical tedium. The source for Britten's figure and its modulating, ascending repetitions might well be a bridge passage among Beethoven's themes for setting Schiller's "Ode to Joy" in the finale of the choral symphony. Even if an apology is due for the burlesque double entendre in applying the label "Bottom's 'Joy' motive" for this exuberant outburst, no excuse is needed for suggesting that, by making Shakespeare's Bottom capable of composing a classical passage yet to be written, Britten was taking a sly dig at his illustrious German predecessor. Forgiveness is begged of any reader who is hereafter distracted by images of earthy Ludwig van Bottom when absorbed in listening to the sublime finale of Beethoven's Ninth!

So far, all three main character groups in the opera are introduced by and extensively use identifiable and distinguishable forms of the *Urmotiv*. What of the court, when it belatedly appears? Late in the long interlude, wood to palace, the orchestra cadences in a *tutti* A major, and the strings proclaim, *espressivo,* a majestic, rhythmic introduction in that key to Theseus's and Hippolyta's entrance with their court. The material seems new, but the leaping, down-down-up melody can be heard as the *cambiata* motive with freely expanded intervals. But, much more significantly, the harpsichord enters with spread, *fortissimo* complete major triads covering two octaves—successively, A major, G major, and F major—with the keynotes prominent in both the bass and the melody (see example 7.1[g]). The rhythm of this court harpsichord motive is an emphatic augmentation of the other regal motive, that of the fairies. This is, too, a remarkable echo, melodically and in the planing chordal support, of the opening motive of Tytania's fairies.

Victor Zuckerkandl, in his article on Schenker in the *Harvard Dictionary,* opines that the real value of Schenker's insight is not to prove that different compositions are similarly constructed, but to show how a few basic patterns unfold into the variety and broad, rich life of the actual composition. Surely Britten demonstrates not only how three Schenkerian "background" tones, skillfully associated in the "middle ground" and masterfully developed in the "foreground," can integrate the diverse strands and layers of a much-patterned fabric, but also how music can explicitly connect characters as outwardly different as Tytania's light fairies and Athens's heavy Theseus, who nevertheless both inwardly portray unrealities, faerie and myth.

A dramatic coda deserves a matching musical coda, and Britten does not disappoint. The fairies' disconcerting description of the denizens of the night after the mortals have retired to bed is accompanied by a final return of the *Urmotiv,* G♯, (as A♭), F♯ (as G♭), E, in the flutes and clarinets, with melismatic links between the main tones (473). The final E of the *Urmotiv* is approached ornamentally by way of D, E♭, and F, making the passage also a decorated return of the *cambiata* motive as the lovers are finally blessed. But the false relations in the chromatic distortions must be explained by something other than the fact that, through an unrealized librettists' oversight, in the opera the lovers are not married. This passage is discussed again later in a different context.

Britten uses several other motives not derived from the *Urmotiv* to introduce dramatis personae and to characterize them through a significant form or sound. They include Puck's trumpet motive, Oberon's celesta motive, Lysander's and Hermia's *accelerando* motive, Demetrius's and Helena's spluttering motive, the tradesmen's *Pyramus and Thisby* and "Grieg" motives (already labeled), and Hermia's nightmare motive, all shown in example 7.2.

Puck's entry is to be a surprise for the fairies, causing them to scatter to the side, so he "appears suddenly," and his trumpet motive comes in after him rather than before (15). Only the pitch, F♯, and the syncopated rhythm are revealed first on the solo trumpet and a tamburo in F♯ alto (see example 7.2[a]), but when his name has been guessed by the fairies, the trumpet bounds away on an up-and-down rhythmic arpeggio emphasizing D major, soon answered by an inversion. Britten, when he wrote, could still prescribe it "gay," calling for maximum brightness of tone, and, for good measure, he sharped several notes, literally introducing G♯ and A♯ and enharmonically bringing in C♯ and D♯ (17). Pucks trumpet motive—often with slight modification, frequently with tamburo—persists throughout the opera whenever he is present, about to appear, or to take front stage, as in the epilogue (491).

Britten associates Oberon with the celesta. Both possess high-pitched voices of unusual timbre, and, indeed Oberon often seems to be straining upwards with his supernatural countertenor into the tinkling-bell range of the higher voiced celesta. The motive is most remarkable for its even, mesmerizing repetition of four harmonic major seconds, E♭ with F, A♭ with B♭, G with A, and E with F♯ (see example 7.2[b]). The eight restless tones are imprisoned in a narrow perfect fifth range, but are capped with a similarly timbred, slow, also confined glockenspiel melody introducing C♭, C, C♯, and D to complete the twelve-tone alphabet (41). Britten later exploits the confined pitch range when constructing a bewitching incantation for Oberon from the eight celesta tones, their rhythm reminiscent of dripping-water torture, when he anoints Demetrius (251). By that time, the celesta can afford to simplify its rhythm from $\frac{6}{8}$ to $\frac{2}{4}$ to sound mostly in harmonic fourths and fifths, and to accept a partnership with the harp for additional unusual color.

Each pair of lovers has a motive of its own, not derived from the *Urmotiv,* and separate from the *cambiata* motive that they share. The distinguishing feature of the Lysander-Hermia figure is its rhythm, a written-out *accelerando* and *crescendo*. One hears a

Example 7.2. Motives Not Related to the *Urmotiv* in Britten's Opera *A Midsummer Night's Dream*

(a) Puck's Trumpet Motive (15)

(b) Oberon's Celesta Motive (41)

(c) Lysander's and Hermia's *accelerando* Motive (49)

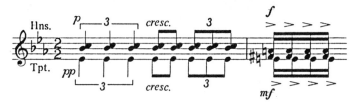

(d) Demetrius's and Helena's Spluttering Motive (64)

Fls. & Ob.

Vls. & Vla.

(e) Tradesmen's *Pyramus and Thisby* Motive (86)

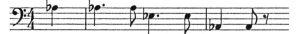

(f) Trademen's "Grieg" Motive (86)

(g) Hermia's Nightmare Motive (136)

dozen developing statements of a figure, usually in the horns and trombone or horns and trumpet, sounding different, mildly dissonant triads in polyrhythmic subdivisions of the main beat established by the smooth pulse of the interspersed *cambriata* motives (ninth version, example 7.2[c]). The polyrhythm, *accelerando, crescendo,* and changing harmonies portray the eloping lovers' agitation (49). As mentioned in discussing Copland, when these two return on stage a little later, lost, exhausted, ready to sleep, Britten brings the figure back, reversed in rhythm and dynamics, again sounding mild dissonances, now involving the higher woodwinds (109).

When Demetrius and Helena appear, she chasing him, Britten introduces them with a querulous, spluttering motive in the strings. Its significant features are a syncopated rhythm (of fourteen attacks in three bars, only three are on strong and medium beats), a unifying hint of the pitches of the *Urmotiv* (A, G, F, and then F, E, D♯) in the first two full statements, and a final big upward leap of a dissonant interval (64). It is generally played along with the diverse forms of the even-noted *cambiata* figure, the combined rhythms giving an attack on each eighth-note half-beat, producing a combative altercation between strings and winds as the "lovers," too, bicker (see example 7.2[d]). The figure comes back when these two return on stage (120).

The tradesmen's interlude, *Pyramus and Thisby,* has a motive, partially described above (see example 7.2[e]). The "Grieg" motive, which promptly follows, contains nothing less stable than first inversions of functional V/V and major triads, one with an added ninth (see example 7.2[f]). It is a rare display of classical choral discipline by the tradesmen, standing out in momentary striking contrast both to their recent, raggedly built dissonance on the "ay's" announcing their presence, and to their later barbershop vocal ensembles. Britten earlier used such a homophonic vocal interjection to vary the texture and to build up a musical number when the fairies temporarily abandon their "over hill . . ." scales to add a choral "and we serve the Fairy Queen" (9). In merely two parts, however, the fairies achieve sharper dissonances; they are less innocuous than the lovable tradesmen. The orchestra takes over this "interlude" motive, varying it, to show satisfaction when Bottom will undertake the Pyramus role, making the performance possible (105); when, at rehearsal, Pyramus must begin to act (177); when, later, they hear "our play is preferred" (376); and when they bow out after their bergomask (466). This last appearance rounds out the role of their "tragical mirth" as a comment on the lovers' misadventures and effects a double unification in that it is combined with the midnight striking of the clock.

To introduce Hermia's serpent-infested nightmare and her awakening, abandoned by Lysander, Britten uses a quiet, rapid, staccato quintuplet figure on the first beat of each $\frac{2}{4}$ measure, the bassoon's B forming a bass to the clarinets' F, a befuddling tritone above, and to the oboe's A♯, a stinging major seventh overhead (see example 7.2[g]). It recalls the agitation of the tail of the *accelerando* motive when she was eloping; on its later returns it shows both her terror of Demetrius when she accuses him of slaying Lysander (245) and her amazement at her long-time friend Helena's passionate words on joining the men in scorning her (267).

Britten eschews the pervasive use of representative motives, notably developed by Wagner in his later operas, where many figures are leitmotivs to be brought back consistently, modified, often almost beyond recognition, according to changing contexts. Although Britten associates musical figures with characters, it is not his fundamental method of composition, and to call a figure in the *Dream* a leitmotiv implies not so much that it is leading as that it is thematic.

Another of Britten's major uses of significant forms is his development and deployment of musical passages termed in this study "tonality sets." Their form depends principally, but not entirely, on the harmonic emphasizing, horizontally and vertically, of each of the twelve degrees of the chromatic scale in a distinctive order. Major complete sets occur as essential features in six passages, some of which are repeated or brought back several times: the wood music, the prelude to the royal fairies' entrance, Hermia's and Lysander's "I swear to thee" duet, the sleep music, the lovers' awakening quartet, and the wood-to-palace transition. Each is different, but effectively discharges a common responsibility: to distinguish and vitalize an important dramatic event or situation.

The term, "tonality set," distinguishes such a passage from a "tone row," the latter describing the melodic building element of Schoenberg's method of composition with twelve tones and later developments. Rather than using single pitch classes (sounds of definite pitches within any octave) as elements of a collection, Britten uses either tones, intervals (two different tones together), triads (three tones), or denser simultaneities, each with a more or less clear root, bass, and tonality. A dodecaphonic tone row requires the elements to be in a specific, precompositional order—often incorporating internal symmetries subject to manipulations—an order that, except for permitted permutations, is adhered to throughout many repetitions. Britten assembles his tonality elements for a specific dramatic occasion, a collection in which the emphasis is on the differences between the elements, thus generating stressful tonal changes as the passage unfolds, rather than on a particular progression or hierarchy. The tonalities of Britten's sets, as sonic events in time, necessarily have an order, and some elements may be repeated in his set, but the key significance of the pitch content of a tonality set of Britten's depends on its completeness within the twelve-tone repertory. In Britten's passages, generally of considerable length, his emphasis is on tonalities rather than single tones—on a harmonic set rather than a melodic row—hence the label "tonality set."

The tonality sets in the opera, designated (a) through (g), are located by page and briefly described in example 7.3. The central feature of each tonality set is the order of the twelve distinct tonalities, describable by reference to the roots of the sonorities establishing the tonalities. (Set [f] is later termed "monstrous," as it appears to be deliberately malformed.) The figure indicates these root successions. Set (b) will be analyzed in detail shortly. A comparative survey of the sets' root movements follows. The diversity of the root movements and their occasional repetitions are shown in the statistical analyses in appendix E, tables E.1 to E.5.

Of the tonality sets in Britten's *Dream*, the second is typical, rapidly building tension when the fairies and Puck have got acquainted and they warn each other: "here comes Oberon, . . . passing fell and wrath," and "here our mistress" (see example 7.3[b] and example 7.4). The twelve strongly functional tonalities of the set—numbered in the list below and in the examples—lie in major and minor triads, eleven sounding initially in first inversion and then moving to root position. The G♯-B-D triads—diminished, dissonant, vaguer in function—are regarded as temporary interruptions in the progression through the twelve clearly major or minor triads of the tonality set, and are unnumbered. The sonorities are: (1) A major, G♯ diminished, (2) E major, (3) G minor, (4) B minor, (5) D minor, (6) C♯ minor, (7) F minor, (8) G♯ minor, (9) C major, (10) E♭ major, (11) F♯ major, G♯ diminished, (12) B♭ major, and G♯ diminished. Apart from the simple

Example 7.3. Tonality Sets by Roots of Sonorities in Britten's Opera *A Midsummer Night's Dream* (Note: page numbers in the score are followed by measure numbers [in brackets] counted on the respective pages.)

(a) **Curtain-up: The Wood—deepening twilight (1[1]–2[6])**

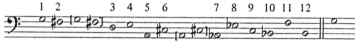

(b) **Puck and the Fairies Announce Oberon's and Tytania's Approaches and Entrances (20[1]–22[5])**

(c) **Hermia and Lysander: "I swear to thee" (55[3]–60[4])**

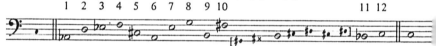

(d) **Curtain-up: The Wood; Tytania lying asleep (157[1–4])**

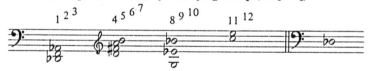

(e) **The Lovers Announce Their Reconciliation: "And I have found . . ." (346[7]–351[2])**

(f) **The Tradesmen Reunited: "our play is preferred" (376[4]–381[3])**

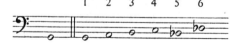

(g) Quick March: From wood to palace (385[3]–394[2])

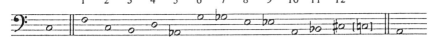

Key to note shapes: o   major tertian harmony

                           •   minor tertian harmony

                           o   single tone

                           ⊙   open fifth

                           x   diminished triad

Sonorities not counted in series of twelve:
    (o)   rootless   [o]   repeated
Notes outside double barlines are preceding and succeeding root tones.

presence of all twelve tonalities, the tonal variety in the passage is considerable: of the tonalities, six are major, six are minor (grouped in the interior of the passage), and three are diminished. The A major sonority beginning the set follows suddenly after a loud B♭ minor triad, a pattern echoed and varied when, completing the set, a B♭ major triad is succeeded by a shift to A major tonality for the "Ill met by moonlight" encounter.

As to the tonality of the complete passage, after the Neapolitan B♭-before-A introduction, Britten retains several other well-established traditional harmonic successions. These are the "classical" I to V progression at the outset (items 1 and 2), the two "romantic" ascending root progressions by chains of thirds, E to D (items 2 to 5), and, invoking enharmonic spellings, the longer C♯ to B♭ movement (items 6 to 12). These last root movements outline triadic chords, as did several of the tones in the row of Berg's violin concerto, another work reintegrating some of the diverse, divergent contemporary tonal experiments. There are two semitonal relations, features of the music of the whole opera, downwards in the D to C♯ half step (items 5 and 6) and upwards in the global A to B♭ movement (items 1 to 12), reversing the Neapolitan entry.

Most successions are intensifying through departures from a temporary tonic or through rising pitches. The set does not work alone in the field of tonality: along with it the melodic royal fairies' motive,

Example 7.4. Tonality Set, Preparing for Oberon's and Tytania's Entrances, in Britten's Opera, *A Midsummer Night's Dream* (20[1]–22[5])

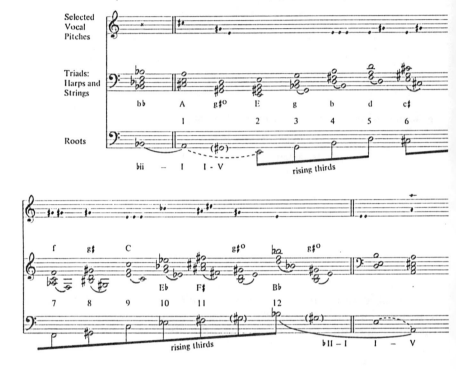

G♯, F♯, E, sounds eight times during the set, and the fairies' voices in recitative are harmonically integrated, consonant except for the occasional clash as when their repeated E persists along with the D minor triad on the key words "passing fell and wrath."

Britten provides other stylistic interests in this passage, such as its distinctive new timbres and texture and its fluctuating dynamics, but its main impact derives from the rapidly mounting musical tension in the tonality changes, integrated with the fairies' verbally expressed fear at Oberon's approach. Its tonal complexity stands out in marked contrast to the relative tonal simplicity and stability of the preceding and following sections. The first, when Puck and the fairies are forging a good-natured acquaintanceship, features a long D pedal point and innumerable F♯s; the second, when Oberon and Tytania "square" (as the excised Shakespeare text puts it), relies on the same dramatically contrasted A major and B♭ minor tonalities that began the set and immediately preceded it.

The other tonality sets in the *Dream* differ considerably from the one just described. The orders of the tonalities are different, and thus, while the overall effect of each is still intensification, the pattern of growth of that sensation is distinctive to each. Their lengths vary considerably. A comment on the main features of each will confirm Britten's fertility of inspiration within the different contexts.

The most striking feature of the first twelve-tone passage, solely instrumental, opening the opera, is the continual string *portamenti* that emphasize unstable tones that exist outside the twelve-tone vocabulary, suggesting the ominous unworldliness and mystery of the wood. Temporary dodecaphonic precise pitches provide respites from Britten's eerie exploitation of the wide pitch continuum available on the strings (see example 7.3[a]). Nine of the sonorities are major, the other three are single tones or open fifths (probably deemed major in context and indeed so harmonized in the repetition), so that the brighter mode contrasts with and heightens the tension. The initial G to F♯ and the internal A to C♯ progressions are repeated. The cycle is played twice for extended impact and the G to F♯ interchange is then continued several times as part of an intermittently bitonal accompaniment for the fairies in the next section. At the act level, the passage or a considerable part of it returns five times as a scene divider and a reminder that the empty wood remains influential as the different character groups succeed each other on stage. In its later uses, Britten cuts the cycle short in a key appropriate to lead into the section to follow. Finally the passage becomes an integrated accompaniment for sections of the closing number when Tytania calls for a roundel (140) and Oberon eventually disappears after anointing her eyes (156). Thus, in addition to establishing a potent atmosphere for the drama, the passage generates an overall musical form for the act, a ritornello, the balanced musical structure matching the symmetry of the character-groups' appearances in the act's A B C B A form. This could not have happened under Shakespeare's plan.

The tonalities of the set surrounding Lysander's and Hermia's duet "I swear to thee," a phrase that remains rhythmically unaltered in contrast to the changing harmony, are again mainly major, perhaps to symbolize confidence (see example 7.3[c]). Britten had to extend the passage to make it long enough to accompany the couplets he retained, which he did by repeating, and repeating again, the tonalities represented earlier. Also, he converted five later sonorities to the minor mode and one to a diminished spacing, making a climax of tension immediately before the end of the set so that, finally, the lovers go out on a triumphant C major triad that stabilizes itself into root position. The musical elements are integrated by using these lovers' *accelerando* figure at the required different pitches. As Cooke discovered, the printed full score is a testament to Britten's intention to construct a complete tonality set. In the dyeline proof, the passage originally began in C major, and the sequence had no A♭ section. On the proof the C major chord's Gs were made A♭s and its Es made E♭s to remedy the deficiency; a note in the engraver's hand suggests that Britten requested the alterations at that late stage.

Britten uses only one large tonality set in act 2, but it is repeated seventeen times as the ground of a passacaglia (see example 7.3[d]). The set with immediately following variations appears on three occasions, the first and second times as instrumental solos initially to imbue the wood with sleep and later to separate the act's two scenes, the third time as accompaniment when the fairies lullaby the sleepers to close the act. The set returns again in act 3, completing its macrostructural function, when Bottom is waking, reminding him of his fantastic dream experiences in the previous act. The twelve tones are grouped, both vertically and horizontally, into four sonorities: D♭, D major with an added sixth, E♭ in first inversion, and an E over C interval. The set symbolizes consonance, a satirical frame, contrasting with the tradesmen's rehearsal problems and the lovers' quarrel. Its narrow, convoluted, repetitive progression of remotely related chord roots, D♭, D, E♭, and C, significantly images unpredictability and the constricted ranges of the tradesmen's theatrical understanding and the lovers' pettiness.

Act 3 opens with the nondodecaphonic morning music, but, as the lovers awake, another tonality set intervenes (see example 7.3[e]). The aroused lovers, as well as being reconciled, become increasingly puzzled, all finally singing together, thrice, "mine own, and not mine own." The set has several prominent musical features, some distinguishing it from preceding sets: all sonorities are in the major mode and thus have fewer tensions in the overtones, the pace, with most entries spaced two bars apart, is slow, and the sound, consisting mainly of long, quiet notes alternately from strings and woodwinds, is calm. The set's soothing harmonic and rhythmic progression and its general sound seem to image the lovers' changing state of consciousness, a growing awareness of comedy on returning to normality, rather than the pregnant tensions represented in Britten's other tonality sets in the *Dream*.

The transition march in act 3 from the wood to the palace is discussed in chapter 9 as an extended passage of instrumental music with a striking layered structure. At one level, Britten incorporates an important, but not preeminent, complete, broadly spaced twelve-tone row that, for comparative purposes, is shown in example 7.3(g).

According to Britten's precedent of introducing a tonality set at dramatic high points, the tradesmen's joy and excitement when Bottom rematerializes and proclaims "our play is preferred" should be complemented by a distinctive tonal adventure (376–84). So it is, but one might venture to term the resulting tonality set "monstrous," a compliment to the composer's ingenuity. Britten brings back the downward octave cadential figure, the *Pyramus and Thisby* motive, and the formerly used harmonic seconds in snatches of scales. The orchestra begins a twelve-tone series, but gives up halfway—resorting to repetitions—after featuring roots squeezed into a tritone G to D♭ (see example 7.3[f] and example 7.5). The six tonalities are confirmed by the sounded fifths of the roots, but the triadic quality of each, major or minor, is left open. Even the roots and fifths together omit A♭ and E♭ from the twelve-tone set, and the supplying of these tones by the out-of-tune singers does not make the set sound complete. Possibly Britten deliberately uses an incomplete, less clear tonality set to characterize again the tradesmen's unprofessional activities and to indicate their confused excitement. The passage has other significant formal features not shown in example 7.5: variety in the vocal textures—homophonic and contrapuntal—and the use of repeated bass notes as common tones in greatly different chords.

Some of the tonality sets have additional functional characteristics that will be discussed when Britten's use of voices and instruments is examined in the next two chapters. The *Dream* contains some uses of all the twelve tones of the chromatic scale that do not amount to tonality sets in the sense just discussed. The opera concludes with a burst of dodecaphony: the final three measures feature predominantly diatonic scales in contrary motion in different, changing keys, scattering all twelve tones. As, by this time, the audience, at Puck's instigation, is supposed to be applauding, Britten presumably invites approval of the dodecaphonic sound.

Simple, small-scale examples of meaningful shapes that can be classified as of a humorous nature occur in Britten's *Dream* when he indulges in word painting or the related devices of action painting and sound effects. When Tytania, telling that "the ox hath stretched his yoke in vain," decorates the verb with a downward *portamento* prolonged over a full octave (26), and when Oberon, citing the fields as drowned, underlines the first syllable by a tortuously sinking eight-note melisma, the significant forms are melodic and direc-

Example 7.5. "Monstrous" Tonality Set, the Tradesmen Reunited; "Our play is preferred" in Britten's Opera *A Midsummer Night's Dream* (376[4]–381[3])

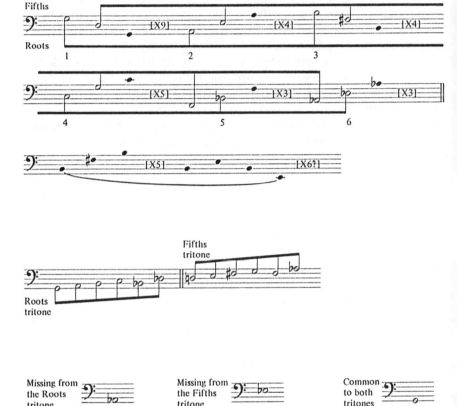

tional, cooperating with the dialogue in describing actions and attributes (27). Having contextually acquired a sinister significant form, this melisma, although inverted, can serve Tytania to show "murrion" flock as repulsive, even though much of the audience may not realize the word designates a disease (26–28). Tytania repeats the falling octave glide on "mortal," to stress the unhappy fate of her votress (38). In other uses of this classical device, Britten reverses the directional significance: Hermia, in two ascending phrases forming a rising sequence, slides up to the top final notes portraying the "height" she deems Helena to have unfairly urged (see example 7.6[a]).

Example 7.6. Humorous Significant Forms in Britten's Opera *A Midsummer Night's Dream*

(a) Word Painting: "height" (279)

She hath urg'd her height, She hath urg'd her height

(b) Ironic Word Painting: "bead" and "dwarf" (282)

You bead. Get you gone you dwarf

(c) Word Painting: "moon-light" (172)

by moon - light

(d) Ironic Word Painting: "Moon-shine" (173)

the per - son of Moon - shine

(e) *Sprechstimme* (425)

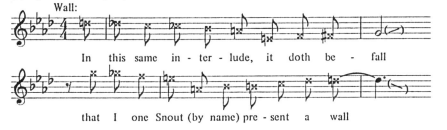

In this same in - ter - lude, it doth be - fall

that I one Snout (by name) pre - sent a wall

Word painting can be used ironically for humorous effect and un-flattering characterization, as when Bottom, describing his own por-trayal of "a part to tear a cat in," swoops down a full tenth to land on the word "lofty" (90); or when Helena, on the top notes of a long, angry, ascending scale dismissing Hermia, announces: "you dwarf" (see example 7.6[b]). Again, Quince, trying to stress the tradesmen's theatrical prospects, sings of a "sweet" comedy on a keenly disso-nant A♯ within a B major triad (383).

Word painting shades of into musical sound effects, accompanying or replacing a verbal mention of the noise. Bottom's anticipation of the Duke's "Let him roar again" evokes a leonine image from the trombone (99), and Flute's expressed fears of the ladies' shrieks are punctuated by dissonant piccolo and oboe figures (100–101) that prove Mitchell's comment on Britten's singular descriptive gift. When Bottom claims to roar like any nightingale, Britten cannot re-sist contrasting the muted trombone's roars with an onomatopoeic passage in the woodwinds: the mildly dissonant glissando major sec-onds in the clarinets are complemented by semitonal clashes when, fluttertonguing, the flutes join in to continue the upward chromatic scale fragments—even the bird's agony from the thorn is expressed (103). When Oberon, in a rage, drags Puck in after the second misdi-rected anointing, the timpani glissandi seem to represent cries of pain by Puck (288): at least the director of the 1967 Decca recording (with Britten conducting) thinks so, adding to the script by having Puck shout "Ow!" Britten generally does not trust sound effects alone, although the music may precede the verbal mention, as when the piccolo trill lark sings twice before Puck warns Oberon of the approaching dawn (336). In the awakening of the sleepers in the wood by Theseus's hunting horns, Britten uses sound effects as a major structural component, described later (341).

Action painting, in moderation, can be pleasantly amusing, as when Britten makes Quince, offering the playbill for the tradesmen's interlude, bow to Hippolyta accompanied by an extensive down-and-up-again arpeggio on the harpsichord (411). Peter Evans points out a satirical example when Wall demonstrates his narrow chink with his fingers, and Britten portrays it with a sudden, huge two-octave gap in the instrumental texture between a harp and the lower strings (*Music*, 253; S425). This musical joke also qualifies as another example of Britten's intensifying procedures, for the chink, on its earlier appearance during rehearsals, was shown musically only by separated taps on the small wood block and the bass drum as Bottom demonstrated "thus . . . thus" (175). Some obvious sonic imagery appears inevitable. Britten's orchestra rests a couple of bars while

Oberon bids "Silence, awhile" (330), and the orchestral clock strikes at midnight are de rigueur (466).

Another of Britten's humorous significant forms depends for its climax on a single, outstanding sonority, an augmented triad, harmonizing a single vocable, "moon." More than clever word painting is involved. Britten no doubt noticed how often Shakespeare used the word "moon" and its compounds, especially "moonlight" and "moonshine," particularly for the tradesmen when performing *Pyramus and Thisby* and its stage audience; he apparently decided to have some good-natured vocal fun at the expense of the performers, both when rehearsing in the wood and playing in Theseus's court. As librettist, despite the repetitions—or, better, because of them— he excised the word in these contexts sparingly. As composer, his usual device is to prescribe a substantial leap up to a long note high in the singer's range and make it more prominent by distinctive harmony. At rehearsal, citing one of the "hard things" to do, Quince, a bass, sets the pattern by dropping his voice to a whisper and dwelling on a high D♭ for the first syllable of "moonlight" while the bassoon sustains a D a semitone higher and the horns hold an A and a B♭ below and above it (171). Quince repeats the same high, strained syllable, with the flute starting a more consonant long B and C♯ trill. Quince approaches these long high D♭s from the F below and quits them by leaping down a third to A (see example 7.6[c]); perhaps Debussy should be thanked on Britten's behalf for two borrowed impressionistic sounds: augmented triads and the quivering reflections of his *Clair de lune.*

Starveling emphasizes the protruding pitch for "moon" by singing the word on a long dotted quarter note, which Bottom immediately stresses again in his repeated demand to "find out moonshine," extending the "moon-," on C♯, to a longer dotted half note, capped by a higher flute trill on E and F (172). Britten also added text here, having the five others sing "moonshine, moonshine" in chorus, the tenors, Flute and Snout, going higher still, to A and completing a distinctive, unearthly augmented triad with the others' C♯ and F, while the flute trills on (173). Bottom, in his solution to the awkward stage requirements, insisting on the introduction of the folkloric Man-in-the-Moon and his appurtenances, sings his C♯ in the lower octave while a clarinet provides the E and F trill a third above (173). He refuses to go up to the moon, but, dwelling on a full dotted half note, he still perpetrates an overlong, now-bovine "moo" (see example 7.6[d]). Did Britten seek to cow Bully Bottom? Only Shakespeare could get away with such a retranslation.

In the court performance, Moonshine himself, a baritone, outdoing his colleagues' demonstrations during the rehearsals, whispers "moon" on a long high F four times, thrice leaping up a full octave, once a diminished octave (442–44). Britten exploits the paradox of low but tense dynamics: the quieter note is particularly outstanding when Moonshine, annoyed at the audience's discourteous interruptions, shouts his line except for the crucial word. The vibraphone accentuates the high pitch and adds a sustained shimmer, striking a D♭ and an F precisely on each "moon." As is to be expected, Britten makes Pyramus, on finding Thisby's blood-stained mantle, leap up to his three "moon's" on the highest, longest notes in the phrases, top Es, not quite up to Moonshine's pitch or the dissonant Fs on the glockenspiel and the first violins' ghostly harmonic (449, 453). Britten wrings a final drop of humor from this device by making the mannerism catching: he has Demetrius, singing the infectious word, leap up to a middle C with a harpsichord flourish (443), and he has Hippolyta, congratulating the players with "well shone moon," cadence from a dissonant diminished seventh (A in the bass, she singing the C) onto a D♭ augmented triad, the vibraphone with a D♭ and an F and Lion with an A completing the impressionistic sonority again (448). It is even possible that here is an example of a composer, for comical effect, exploiting overambitious but untrained singers' problems in producing accurate vowels at high pitches: the distorted "oo's" surely sound outlandish in production—an esoteric joke indeed.

Wall, uttering the initial ten syllables of his first *Sprechstimme* aria, "In this same in-ter-lude it doth be-fall," attacks ten different tones arranged in mechanical, unexciting six- and four-note snatches of the chromatic scale, which amount to an uninspired, incomplete tone row. They are immediately followed by their retrograde (see example 7.6[e]). Britten completes the twelve-tone pitch repertory with an accompanying double pedal consisting of a low A♭ and a high E♭ iterated in the double basses and cellos (425). This use of the distinct timbred A♭ with E♭ interval more effectively completes the dodecaphonic sound than its use in the "monstrous" tonality set discussed earlier. Wall's second aria is his parting speech in the interlude, repeating the incomplete tone row and its retrograde in *Sprechstimme*, still in regular wooden rhythm, accompanied by the tonal double pedal and also the percussion—wood block and bass drum—taps that highlighted the chink (436). As a result of a textual excision from the play, this exit aria is immediately followed by Hippolyta's exclamation: "This is the silliest stuff that I ever heard" (437). Peter Evans sees Britten ribbing Schoenberg, "not with too malicious an intent," he hopes (254).

Perhaps, too, the percussion taps are a dig at the pointillistic developments featured by the more thorough-going serialists after Schoenberg. One can see, also, Britten demonstrating how twelve-tone and major-minor techniques can be combined to achieve a greater expressiveness. What he does here in miniature, he also does on the grand scale throughout the opera, producing a mosaic of simultaneous and successive sounds that is tonally richer than either technique used separately.

It was noted earlier that the wood music incorporates both the precise pitches of the tonality set and the vague, shifting pitches of the string *portamenti* that are outside the twelve-tone vocabulary: Wall's *Sprechstimme,* where the voice hits its note and immediately wanders off it, does something similar. Britten thus accentuates, both at the beginning and near the end of his *Dream,* similar tonally comprehensive musical structures, establishing a grand-scale musical balance. Musically, he sets the dramatically different arcadian woodland and urban "lime and hair" side by side, and, wryly, he invites an alternative, derogatory appraisal of his masterly opening tour de force by those who agree with Hippolyta's snap judgment of moonstruck Wall's delivery *au Pierrot Lunaire.*

Britten uses other small significant musical figures. The first to note is a pair of forms used throughout the opera that are remarkable, on the one hand, for their audibility, frequency, and consistency, and, on the other, for the subtlety of their connection with the drama. On twenty or more occasions, he uses a downward instrumental passage to announce or confirm the entrances of certain characters, or an upward one for their exits, thereby unobtrusively unifying the musico-dramatic developments and challenging the observant auditor-spectator to find a psychological association. Descending instrumental passages go with fairies' entrances. Perhaps Britten makes sure that Shakespeare's partly airy, partly earthy fairies really come down to earth. A descending scale is featured on several instruments when the first group appears (5), and the royal fairies' motive for Oberon and Tytania, consisting of half that scale, occurs and stands out as downward whenever they are introduced (20). The fairies go out to an ascending scale in thirds extending over nearly two octaves at the end of act 2 (319), and they presumably come to the fore again when Tytania awakes early in act 3, for the morning music is decorated with long descending scales on parallel high woodwinds with top-to-bottom glissandi on the harps (327). During the fairies' final exeunt, the last dozen or so Scotch snaps on the first harp inexorably climb by step and small leaps over a melodic tenth, out of the mortal world (490). The fairies all hide on Tytania's order ("skip hence," sung twice to increasing upward leaps), and the upper winds play quick upward scales (24–25); but when, earlier, according to stage directions, the fairies scattered to the side, flying neither in nor out, those instruments twice played rapid figures and scales that simultaneously rushed both up and down (15 and 16). Expecting an inversion of the royal fairies' motive with an exit, one finds it twice as Tytania calls "Fairies away, away": F♯, G♯, A in the double basses (40), the instruments that earlier featured the original downward G♯, F♯, E entry figure.

Puck is similarly greeted and dismissed, usually by the trumpet that designates him. It soars up as he flies off to girdle the earth (43), down as he flies in (74), up, with a rattling xylophone, as he flies off (251), and down as he files in again (253). His trumpet plays lower and lower snatches as he comes in swinging his broom to sweep the dust behind the door (481), and, as the final curtain falls, twelve upward instrumental voices, by their higher pitches and sheer numbers, easily dominate two downward bass lines (495). With his mode of locomotion generally described in Britten's stage directions as flying, in or off, the downs and ups in the orchestral figures approach action painting.

When the tradesmen first appear, the trombone tries an upward figure but concludes by inverting it into a downward motive (84). Later, the down-for-entrance connection is consistently used. Bottom has merely to suggest that "one must come in with a bush of thorns and a lantern" (173) for a flute, the oboe, and a clarinet— all marked *clearly* by the composer—to join in and jiggle down a full three octaves: it is a long way from the moon. Bottom's slow, confused reentry into the normal world is preceded by a syncopated downward converging figure in the two clarinets, supported by the basses (355), and the other tradesmen come in as the English horn jerkily moves down (368). A long descent on the strings anticipates Bottom's offstage "Where are these lads?" as he rejoins them (373). As they all leave, among other level melodic lines there are unmistakable upward movements: in Flute's, Snout's, and Bottom's voices, in the quadruple stops on the violins, and in the first poundings of the timpani, cellos, and basses (384).

A false exit deserves a contrary, downward movement. As Pyramus, having acted the ultimate exit by uttering "Now am I dead," denies his exit from the world with the five-fold "die," Britten has the accompanying clarinets appropriately proclaim the bogus demise by breaking into a derogatory downward figure (453). Then

Britten caps this subtlety. After raising himself, Bottom really expires and settles on the stage floor (and Moon goes out): the instrumental comment that catches and holds attention is an unexpected rapid upward cadenza on the glockenspiel, authenticating Bottom's "my soul is in heaven" (453). As Pyramus and Thisby get up and exit the theatrical world, the bassoon practices a chromatic scale in seven-, five-, and three-note snatches, climbing upwards fourteen steps, from bass clef low F♯ to G♯. In context, this is clearly not another dodecaphonic tonal device, but a form significant for an exit (458).

Britten's instrumental support for both the belated appearance and the conclusive exit of Theseus and Hippolyta conforms to the pattern. The harpsichord's ceremonial proclamation of their entry is firmly downward (394 and 398); whereas their midnight retirement with the lovers is made to progressively higher and louder notes plucked from the first harp with quiet, upward, higher tones in the treble woodwinds (471).

Although Britten uses this directional association often, he does so with restraint. With the lovers, there is no figure clearly confirming or contradicting the pattern—except when Demetrius abandons Helena to upward scales on the woodwinds covering three-and-a-half octaves (121). The model does not generally apply to falling asleep or awakening, which are mental rather than physical exits and entries, or to Oberon's vanishing and reappearing on the spot. In fact, there is a contradiction of the pattern when Oberon disappears after dispatching Puck for the herb, saying he will anoint Tytania's eyes: a solo violin finds a descending melody in the celesta accompaniment (44). When he makes his special reappearance (Britten's innovation) to become present but invisible and watch Demetrius and Helena, the same instrument discovers an upward passage in the same source (63). This pattern-reversal indicates that Oberon's magic disembodiment and reembodiment are indeed a different thing from physical coming and going—that he was present in spirit all the time. Cooke's speculation, which was earlier endorsed, that the two pairs of lovers' actions occur simultaneously, gains additional, supernaturally based support.

There are different reasons, unconnected with exits and entrances, for some upward or downward passages, such as the frantic scales and other figures in both directions during the lovers' irrational declarations and quarrels (128 and 259) and those when the tradesmen see Bottom with the ass-head, think themselves haunted, and disperse, as Puck narrated in the play (186–89). The harp glissandi framing Puck's "I will lead them up and down" ditty are clearly word painting (295). Fanfares, whether on Puck's trumpet or Theseus's horns, conventionally and consistently rise and fall.

It is plausible, but superficial, to explain the directions of the instrumental passages by suggesting that certain characters they accompany come in by descending from their normal abode above and go out by returning back up there: the fairies might come down to earth; Bottom, relieved of his ass-head certainly does. On further reflection, however, there is a rationale for the instrumental and vocal musics to soar on an exit—the higher, rising pitch produces an increase in tension, cooperating with the dramatic situation in a multiplot work; for the audience, compelled to switch attention to additional, different stressful events, is indeed left in suspense, wondering what is happening in the absent characters' plot. Britten's use of this simple, significant form contributes to the success of the *Dream* in several ways: it is subtle, thus challenging; it is consistent, making for organic unity; and it is varied in that he employs different instruments and musical figures, making for variety. It is the interesting legacy of a composer who can devise resources and control them completely.

The Scotch snap is another simple, rhythmically based significant form that Britten uses structurally to define sectional passages at the beginning and end of the opera. It is reasonable to assume from Britten's admitted precompositional ability to describe the music—and from the fact that he had taken part in the restructuring of the play to make the libretto—that, although he might make his composition sketches in their dramatic chronological order, he always had a good idea, when writing earlier scenes, how a musical idea would make a significant later return. Thus, almost at the beginning of the opera (10), the fairies in their first number, when describing the "cowslips tall," catch attention by changing rhythm to a Scotch snap in the second half of each bar (see example 7.7[a]) and then intensifying the jerkiness (see example 7.7[b]). Britten keeps alive the idea of the Scotch snap as audience attention-getter during Oberon's "I know a bank" aria (see example 7.7[c]) and when absurd Quince enters court with the tradesmen's playbill to a harpsichord passage that carries inverted dotting to the point of absurdity (see example 7.7[d]). Then, almost at the end of the opera (484), the fairy chorus, supported by the harps and joined by Oberon, in their benison "now until the break of day," slowly and solemnly reintroduce this Lombardic style (see example 7.7[e]), catching attention again and forging a link with their earlier pas-

Example 7.7. Scotch Snap and Saraband Rhythm in Britten's Opera *A Midsummer Night's Dream*

(a) Scotch Snap: Fairies (10)

Cow - slips   tall   her   pen - sion - ers   be.

(b) Scotch Snap: Fairies (13)

In   those   freck - les   live   their   sa - vours.

(c) Scotch Snap: Oberon (75)

wild   thyme   blows

(d) Scotch Snap: Harpsichord (411, left hand not shown)

(e) Scotch Snap: Fairies (485)

Now un - til the break of   day   Through the   house each   Fair - y   stray

(f) Saraband Rhythm: Lower Woodwinds and Harps (334)

(g) Saraband Rhythm: Strings (212)

sage, promising even wider environmental and human benefits. Willi Apel, in "Dotted Notes III" in the *Harvard Dictionary of Music,* points out that this rhythm figures prominently in the music of Henry Purcell, "where it is used effectively to bring out the short but accented first syllable that occurs in so many English dissyllables."

Britten confessed he learned much from Purcell in setting English words, but, in this second passage, the "silent innovator" even stands this scansion ideal on its head by wrenching the unstressed speech syllables onto the agogically accented music tones, adding to the unworldly aura and further foregrounding the fairies in their role of framing the operatic action. Britten, innovator as well as architect in sound, not only foresaw this development when highlighting the early cowslips with the snap; he shows how music can legitimize a prosodic trick that would be incongruously ridiculous in plain speech.

This fairies' Scotch snap rhythm is the reverse of that of Oberon's and Tytania's saraband (see example 7.7[f]), differentiating the junior from the senior characters and confirming the class gap that exists even in the fairy kingdom. The snap is also the reverse of the dotted Purcellian rhythm in the accompaniment to the fairies when they are under Tytania's orders to do Bottom courtesies (see example 7.7[g]). A footnote in the score, page 212, reads: "The semiquaver [sixteenth note] marked and delayed—Purcellian style" and advocates a quintuplet division of the quarternote. Only when unsupervised are the fairies innovative. White saw the returned Scotch snap as "a musical trick in reserve" (232): indeed it is more.

Britten uses several other small-scale significant forms that are less dependent for their impact on their likeness to the formal properties of "inner life" in Langer's hypothesis than on tension arising from the simultaneous similarity and difference between

Example 7.8. Significant Forms Simultaneously Similar and Different, in Britten's Opera *A Midsummer Night's Dream*

(a) Imitation (30)

(b) Inversion, in Canon (31)

(c) Inversion, Bitonal (334)

two or more closely related musical figures. Britten, for example, frequently associates a melodic strain with its inversion. In Shakespeare, only Tytania proclaims that "the mazed world . . . now knows not which is which" (36; 2.1.113); in the score Oberon joins in—indeed he begins. In the first phrase, waiting for his final note, Tytania echoes his musical figure in a tonal sequence a minor seventh higher (see example 7.8[a]), tensing as a straightforward repetition; in the second phrase (see example 7.8[b]), she does three things differently to increase the tension: she does not wait until he has finished before mixing her words with his; she features a diabolical tritone, D♯ first over and then under A; and, particularly relevant in this discussion, she exactly inverts his melodic line, adding a musical contrapuntal family quarrel to the personal royal dissension. When reconciled later, Oberon and Tytania "rock the ground" whereon the lovers and Bottom still sleep. The English horn and the clarinets accompany the dances with four measures of counterpoint comprising an expressive phrase and its upside-down mirror image, the instrumental parts well matched to the eye, but keenly dissonant to the ear (see example 7.8[c]). This Brittenesque introduction of a second original-with-mirror structure, representing Tytania over Oberon—with them still going in different directions although saying the same thing—has a heightened potency: amity enforced by trickery and torment perhaps retains hidden stresses, even between royal fairies.

Still other small-scale forms, dependent for tension or release on superposed like or different versions, are retrogrades, transpositions, augmentations and diminutions, ascents and descents of pitch, voice exchanges, and even *Sprechstimme;* they occur in Britten's *Dream* in larger-scale directional, rhythmic, harmonic, melodic, or tonal contexts, as will be seen later.

Significant forms can be misused. Too frequent imitative tricks in the music result in misguided "Mickeymousing," to use the filmmakers' term. Britten's use of this device is restrained, even when depicting the tradesmen as overanxious in explaining the meanings they fear the audience will miss. Related to this potential danger is the possibility of using significant forms, particularly small-scale ones, mechanistically, so that the association of the form with a particular musical or dramatic situation becomes banal rather than surprising. Britten avoids this weakness, even when dealing with the so-called "mechanicals" themselves, by making subtle variations in one or more musical elements of a form when it is repeated or brought back, altering its significance. The change may be as little as different instrumentation, as when Puck leads the duelists astray and apart. When each is exhausted and ready to sleep, Britten brings back the *cambiata* motive; but for Lysander it is in the two clarinets, inverted (303), while for Demetrius it is in the second clarinet and the bassoon, in original form (306).

The discussions and examples in this chapter have identified concepts of musical meaning expounded in the literature and applied by Britten in his *Dream*. Although devices are repeatedly cited as "significant form," the observations are not so much formal analyses as recognitions of links between shapes and psychological responses, particularly tensing and releasing. In the next chapters some particular operatic procedures for combining, or not combining, voices and instruments are examined. In addition, cultural aspects of the work are considered before the thesis of this study is reviewed.

8

Vocal Passages

Then cold, and hot, and moist, and dry,
In order to their stations leap,
and MUSIC's pow'r obey.

—John Dryden,
A Song for S^t. Cecilia's
Day, 1687

A matter that particularly concerned Britten, as it concerned all his modern opera-making predecessors—from the Florentine Camerata to the present,—is the stylistic handling of vocal passages that are sung rather than spoken. The requirements for textual intelligibility fluctuate according to the drama of the situation—a matter largely beyond the composer's control—but the need for frequent though intermittent musical interest is inherent in opera, and the composer must satisfy it without violating the supreme criterion for attractive drama. Four special things stand out in setting voices: the assignment of voice classes to roles, the use of recitative and aria, textual changes, and the combination of two or more voices.

The choice of vocal ranges for the characters—even of specific singers for the first performance—had been made at the libretto stage, with some unconventional decisions. The unusual countertenor voice for Oberon clearly marks him as supernatural—a characterization Britten would repeat thirteen years later in *Death in Venice* when the voice of Apollo was required—but it carries potentially distracting implications unless his masculinity is obvious in performance. Tytania's abilities as a coloratura soprano give her vocal power, which, according to Howard, is something for Oberon to master (169). Her voice provides the quality required to impress the stolid Bottom.

Britten's inspiration for Puck's role as a speaking acrobat came from watching some Swedish child acrobats with extraordinary

agility and powers of mimicry (Palmer, 179). The choice is mani-
foldly apt. That Robin Goodfellow was not an authentic fairy is
confirmed by his failure to sing in Shakespeare's play. Britten cast
him as a boy, admirably suited to be Oberon's obedient though
mischievous servant, his treble timbre distinguishing him from the
other high-pitched voices—especially if his voice is breaking. As
in Shakespeare's day, there would be little problem in finding a
competent boy actor, even a fine treble singer, but the acrobatics
would play havoc with a singer's breath control; thus, making Puck
a speaking role avoids this conflict and completes his individuality.
The speaking part can be articulated and accompanied by music
as desired; Britten designates Puck's speech rhythms accu-
rately on a staff without clef, allowing him to adopt normal
speech pitches.

Other voice range assignments are conventional, albeit establishing links and contrasts between and within social groups,
and humorously characterizing individuals. Theseus and Hippolyta, heavies, are bass and contralto, and the lovers can make a
balanced mixed quartet, within which Hermia is "lower" than Helena. The tradesmen, too, can make a balanced male sextet, including Flute as a tenor. Apart from noting that Thisby's role was made
for *the* tenor, colibrettist Pears, one wonders whether Britten,
steeped in English poetry and born on St. Cecilia's Day, smilingly
recollected another passage from the song that furnishes the epigraph to this chapter:

> The soft complaining FLUTE
> In dying Notes discovers
> The woes of hopeless lovers. (2. 539)

Britten, with youthful voices in mind, designates the named fairies
as trebles, whereas the fairy chorus may less restrictively consist
of trebles or sopranos.

When making the libretto Britten no doubt foresaw that certain
passages would need to be set in recitative and others in aria,
recognizing the availability of variants of these basic musical vocal
forms. Other passages might need different styles of utterance
altogether. Britten's use of recitative and aria is artistically conventional. Simply put, even in a play on stage, the spoken words may
either work with the characters' movements to bring about an
event that moves the plot forward, which one might loosely call
narration, or they may comment on that event or describe the

setting. In both functions, the words are intended to be immediately intelligible, even if the full meaning is made or left unclear in order to mystify. In opera, still primarily drama, the immediate intelligibility of text for narration is vital and must be preserved, but the straightforward apprehensibility of commentative words can be sacrificed on the altar of musical interest, especially when other media contribute to the meaning. The tendency of music— either singing or instrumental accompaniment—to obscure the words must be regulated: minimized in narration, but perhaps extensively tolerated in commentary. Hence, simplifying again, the fundamental distinction between the musical kinds normally used to present the different textual classes are: recitative for narration, aria for commentary.

Britten consistently adopts the first of two main operatic formulas for making the sung words as intelligible as possible; he keeps the rhythms and pitches of the sung vocal line near those of ordinary speech, recognizing that momentary departures, if kept intelligible, can be effective for emphasis. An example is when Bottom demands "a ca-len-dar, [pause] a ca-len-dar, [pause] look in the Alma-nac" (172), in which the emphasized dactyllic syllables fall on stressed beats in the matching $\frac{6}{8}$ musical meter, and the rising final intonation that would enliven his excited spoken word is reflected in the upward terminal leaps of a fourth in each musical phrase.

Another convention is to rely on a delivery mainly in monotone and in even rhythm, which suggests that a precedent might be found in Western European medieval antiphonal psalmody. Monotone gives an archaic, ceremonial flavor to the utterance; it also imitates the still-living spoken device of resorting to even pitched syllabification for forceful emphasis and clarity. Example 8.1 shows a comparison of an example of the ancient practice with Britten's treatment of part of the raven-for-a-dove exchange between bewitched Lysander and astonished Helena (130–31). Details of Britten's rhythms are not shown; a breve signifies multiple syllables sung on one note. Hoppin states that "psalms . . . are not normally sung alone but in combination with additional texts—either antiphons or responses—for which the melody is freely composed, . . . [a] union of recitative and free composition in a single musical item" (*Medieval Music*, 80). The similarities revealed in the example suggest that requirements for verbal intelligibility and musical variety were met more than a thousand years ago in a process that endures. The florid antiphon and Lysander's rhetorical question each provide an ornamental attention-getter to set off the recited central statement. Alternatively, a repetition of the antiphon

Example 8.1. Psalmody and Recitative in Britten's Opera *A Midsummer Night's Dream*

(a) Antiphon and Psalm Chant: Psalm Tone 3 (Related to the Hypomixolydian Church Mode)

(b) Lysander Woos Unresponsive Helena (130–31)

Source of Psalmody: **Richard H. Hoppin, ed.,** *Anthology of Medieval Music* **(New York: Norton, 1978), 2: "Vota mea Domino reddam,": Second Antiphon for Monday at Vespers, with Psalm 115 (116:10–19). Hoppin cites the** *Liber Usualis,* **pp. 281 and 163, as his source.**

against Helena's exit phrase could be shown, completing the decorative frames and reinforcing the parallel. The falling melodic fourths, ornamented in the antiphon, plain on Lysander's "dove," each imply that an important statement follows.

The inconclusive melodic minor third defining the psalmodic flex (a respite for breath in a long phrase) and concluding the mediant (a break between complementary statements) persists at corresponding points in Helena's complaint. The differences between the ancient and the modern passages confirm Britten's eclecticism as innovative. He uses additional tenor tones, for which the medieval *tonus peregrinus* is a precedent, making them rise by small leaps or steps for growing tension. For the same reason, he inverts the direction of the flex. The chant's termination culminates in a conclusive A descending to G: Britten's ending features an A♭ to G♭ progression, but he makes it upward, more tensing and conforming to his pattern of up-and-out discovered earlier. Britten's stylistically different settings here have overtones of the carefree serenader and of the devotional barren sister whom Egeus denounced and Theseus equivocally extolled in the excised opening court scene (23; 1.1.72 and 22; 1.1.30).

After Oberon's and Tytania's initial recriminations and their acknowledgment of joint responsibility for the environmental disasters—largely in colorfully jumbled canonically sung texts (see example 7.8[b])—Britten ends the musical turbulence with repetitions of the *Urmotiv* and the royal fairies' motive constructed from segments of outlandish whole-tone scale. A dramatic pause inconclusively cadences on F♯, suggesting that the audience listen carefully for something important to follow. On that note, Oberon loudly—"with force" but "always in tempo"—iterates his demand of his Queen, "Do **you** a-**mend** it **then**," in even eighth notes. Oberon goes on: "it **lies** in **you**," further emphasizing "you" by an upward leap to a longer note, pausing for the orchestra to repeat the royal fairies' motive in a harmonically remote, tenser B♭ seventh chord. He then dwells on longer notes to stress the key words "changeling boy" and "henchman" (35–36). As set, these crucial phrases rightly stand out, and future dramatic developments turn on them: had Tytania then yielded to Oberon's arrogant, male chauvinist proposal, there would have been no fairy plot.

Britten also consistently uses the second main guideline for verbal intelligibility: keep the orchestral sounds from interfering with the speech. The orchestra can be temporarily subdued or silenced, be given simple melody and rhythm, and be differentiated from the voices in pitch. Having voice and orchestral melody follow the same line helps the singer, but may obscure the words by modifying the timbre. Orchestra and voice can alternate in short passages, providing continuous music, a requisite of opera. Some of the foregoing examples illustrate these devices. A further clear instance occurs just after Oberon has announced his intention of dancing with Tytania in Duke Theseus's house (334). Although Puck speaks rather than singing, the vocal-instrumental alternations and other accommodations still apply to the following carefully planned sequence of sounds: (1) two piccolo lark-trills over a saraband played by other instruments; (2) two quiet tamburo ruffs with celesta *tremolo* chords, while Puck says, forte, *crescendo,* "Fairy King attend and mark"; (3) return of larks and saraband; (4) return of tamburo, celesta, and Puck: "I do hear the morning lark"; and (5) finally, many lark-trills and saraband, as Puck disappears (336–37). Here Britten's sequence respects the sense of what is heard and avoids conflicting superpositions.

Still within the realm of functional recitative, Britten's ingenuity with varieties of declamation produces other passages worth citing to illustrate a composer's resources. He adds the full orchestra when Theseus closes the court scene, pronouncing "the ir-on tongue of mid-night . . ." to a simple recitative melody containing mostly repeated tones of equal duration. His authoritative bass voice can prevail over the string basses, harps, and trombone that attack with him on the main beats but in lower octaves, while several other orchestral nonchord tones fall between the beats, missing his syllables. Both he and Hippolyta then, in turn, borrow the tradesmen's octave cadence and strengthen it by extending it to a major ninth and inverting it, naturally, to go upwards for an exit: "to bed" (468–71). Deeming a bass voice penetrating may appear to contradict Johan Sundberg's view that high voices conflict less with the pitch range wherein the orchestra's highest level of sound lies, "in the vicinity of 450 hertz; above . . . [which] the amplitude decreases sharply with frequency" (88). This pitch is central to the soprano's range, a fraction sharp of the violin's A string. Sundberg's point is particularly true in fully orchestrated arias. But, in production, another resource is available to the singer, profundo or coloratura alike: he or she can move downstage or to a spot producing maximum resonance in the auditorium, while the conductor holds the orchestra in check.

In isolation and at first sight, many of the foregoing and the following examples of Britten's meticulous attention to the details of marrying music and words might appear trivial, but it is not so. Every page of the score reveals instances of similar care, cumulatively overwhelming in importance, all a testament to the vital need for the music to serve the drama.

The greater part of the tradesmen's scene is in recitative: verbal humor must be intelligible. Since these men's voices have less trouble with vowel formants, however, Britten can make his dialogue less declamatory, less wooden, using more ornate final phrase inflections and more irregular rhythms, and he can add more frequent and adventurous orchestral accompaniments. Moreover, when an idea is repeated, as when Flute echoes the ladies' fear of the lion (170), or when a word recurs, such as "moonlight" (see examples 7.[c]), the later appearances can be decorated into obscurity, allowing the music a fairer share of the joint sonic transmission without impairing intelligibility overall.

It is interesting to ponder why certain passages, lengthy and important dramatically, are intelligible despite a full accompaniment that, by itself, might command undue attention. Britten makes Oberon sing two of his early passages, "having once the juice" and "take thou some of it," fully accompanied. These indispensable words compete with his celesta theme and countermelodies, the first time by the glockenspiel (43), the second time (marked "clearly") with full woodwinds and strings (80). Apart from the low dynamic levels of the orchestra, other cooperating features favor the voice. Because of an imperfect cadence to the preceding section, Oberon is obviously about to utter something that ought to be attended to, so the audience attends. Moreover, the orchestral passage, repetitive and without forceful harmonic rhythm, has been heard for some time, and, no longer novel, can be dismissed from full consciousness.

The ducal couple use recitative extensively, possibly because they have lost their philosophical sententiae,—written in the play in a manner perfect to become arias,—to the librettists' blue pencils. Their exit was noted above; their entrance shows more variety. When Theseus enters, proclaiming "Now fair Hippolyta," the notes in his opening eight bars range over a diminished eleventh and vary from half notes to sixteenths (398). But the passage clearly retains an image of him talking rather than singing, while the full orchestral sound remains more of a background than an accompaniment. Next, in imaging the moon's lingering of his desires by citing a dowager's withering of a young man's revenue (a tricky, archaic simile, surprisingly not cut), he changes to a more monotonic line, which Britten marks "clearly" (400). But the change of style is not obtrusive: he is always talking—pompously. Hippolyta's reply is similarly declaratory and patrician, although the orchestral figures increase in density and complexity. In the opening of the Theseus passage just cited, the composer gives more, but not prime, importance to the musical components of his utterance, so that the sung line becomes more florid melodically and more uneven rhythmically: a critic might apply the label "arioso,"—more properly "recitativo arioso,"—but the distinction does not denote a departure from the main function of intelligible narration.

In the examples cited so far, Britten has matched the verbal style of solo singing to the dominant dramatic need for intelligibility and the subordinate musical need for variety. When the dramatic need is less, he can indulge the operagoer's desire for musical artistry in arias. In the *Dream,* though not as blatantly as in opera seria, most of the leads get an aria or at least an arietta to display their skills. Britten had different opportunities to follow his natural impetus—to move upwards on Schmidgall's scale, from normal speech through declamation, recitative, and aria to coloratura, from the realistic through rising emotional intensity to the operatic occasion (11). Throughout the opera, he can let himself go musically, composing in a probably more congenial style, creating arias, each a detachable unit, involving music as the major partner. As a climax, Britten can pack even more into the tradesmen's interlude, burlesquing hyperartificial operatic formulae that continue to attract patrons who, some critics think, should know better.

Outside the ironic *Pyramus and Thisby* performance, Britten is to be judged as an opera composer writing for his contemporary audience, striving to tell them, in music, what he thinks and feels about a substantial part of Shakespeare's comedy. In the process, no doubt grateful for the opportunity, he wrote five mostly short, unmistakeable arias for select characters: Helena, inviting Demetrius's physical abuse (69), Oberon, visualizing Tytania's sleeping-place (75), Hermia, awakening from a nightmare (136), Bottom, building up courage (198), and Tytania, currying Bottom's favor (206). Shakespeare, making the male lovers indistinguishable and inconstant, seems to think less of them than he does of the faithful women; perhaps Britten, denying both men room for an arietta, shows the same scorn.

Helena's pose as Demetrius's spaniel is quite unnecessary for the plot, but it is sufficiently striking for Britten to keep the text, set it as an arietta, and hold up the action while she elicits pity and, probably, smiles. The passage is marked "more quietly," and stands between sections designated "impetuous" and "agitated." The accompaniment temporarily abandons the spluttering string

motive in favor of a smooth, trochaic $\frac{3}{4}$ woodwind strain with hints
of a barcarolle. Most importantly, Helena is given the opportunity
to display her downward arpeggii that gradually expand as the
words intensify: "beat me, . . . spurn me, . . . strike me, . . . neglect me, . . . lose me" (69–70). Both the stronger words and the
arpeggio musical figures expand on the downward motion by steps
used in the archetypical "Batti, batti" aria in *Don Giovanni*, although Helena is more serious and not as aware as Zerlina of the
humor in her pose. Demetrius's callous indifference is emphasized
by Helena's figurative digression, and it becomes evident again
when Helena finishes her aria.

Had the opera required it, Britten would have been bold enough
to cut a favorite passage like Oberon's "I know a bank", but he
left it in and highlighted it as one of the two most extended, tightly
structured vocal numbers in the work (75–80). Others have analysed it musically from several approaches, noting the melodic and
harmonic features (described elsewhere in this book) and the A B
C B¹ A¹ form. It paints a charming fairy vignette, but also makes
the important announcement that he will streak Tytania's eyes and
make her full of hateful fantasies. This is kept intelligible in the B¹
section by bringing back the simpler melody and accompaniment
made familiar in B; in the final A¹ section, the words "hateful" and
"fantasies" are sung twice. Despite Oberon's turn to important
narration, Britten continues to portray him as singing rather than
talking, even adding nine-note melismas on the two "fantasies,"
the second an inversion of the first. But then, switching to a pure
monotonic recitative, marked "clearly," he orders Puck to take
some of the herb and find the sweet Athenian in love with the
disdainful youth (80). Britten's skillful integration of functional recitative and aria adds to the credibility of singing in the operatic
genre.

On awakening, Hermia expresses sheer terror—both of the ser-
pent in her nightmare and from Lysander's absence (136). With a
frequently meandering melody and an insistent, agitated, detached,
rapid quintuplet accompaniment figure in the woodwinds (see example 7.2[g]), her utterance is more an arresting commentary on her feelings than a narration of an event. In a typical
aria situation, Britten even begins with a built-in recitative introduction to announce the addressee—Lysander—her dream, and
her quaking.

When Bottom, just translated and deserted by his colleagues,
decides he will sing "that they shall hear I am not afraid," he breaks
into the strophic ballad "The woosell cock . . ." (196). He is at

first unaware of awakening Tytania's approving recitatives between and after his verses. Thus Britten preserves the number's Shakespearean status, a solo song, more detachable than an aria, a pleasurable interlude characterizing Bottom specifically as an English rustic. The bogus "artistry," both of the fluid rhythm, written out in alternate quarter-note triplets and pairs and of the kaleidoscopic multitonality, stands out from its context and from Tytania's fairy harp accompaniment. Britten also teases him by incongruously enriching the ballad with a through-composed second stanza permitting an onomatopaeic "plainsong cuckoo" phrase (C♯, A; C♯, A), the interval a shade too wide for realism—unless, in June, the bird has characteristically changed his tune.

Tytania's aria instructing her fairies to be kind and courteous to Bottom (206–12) has many features that, by similarity and contrast, complement Oberon's "I know a bank" (75). These two arias provide opportunities for the singers to characterize themselves, often ironically, as in a literary dramatic monologue. The Fairy King and Queen do not disappoint. Apart from the unlike contents,—since Oberon is bent on torment and Tytania on courtesies—their musics are different: his melody is tortuous and his rhythm irregular, hers quietly patterned; his harmony is chromatic and modal, hers mainly diatonic; his form is five-fold, hers simply tertian, A B A; his aria proper leads down to a dark, low note on [hateful] "fantasies," hers up to a bright high note on "arise." One must wait until act 2 for this musical comparison and revelation, but another side of the relationship between the froward married pair is then clear: the male beneficent would-be righter of human love tangles harbors a complex, sinister streak, whereas his female victim radiates a simple generosity. In Britten's usage, aria is not simply a musical decoration.

Britten's departures from normal speech in either direction, toward level incantation or undulating melisma, as illustrated, are masterfully applied operatic conventions, providing not only required intelligibility in recitative and acceptable colourful confusion in aria, but a handsome contribution to the *Dream*'s variety in unity.

The discussion of Britten's treatment of recitative and aria, one voice singing at a time, has indicated certain changes the composer makes to the libretto text, particularly the repetition of a word or phrase. Since modifications of this nature occur also, even more so, when two or more characters sing together, it is appropriate to examine the composer's textual alterations now, before studying his procedures in a duet, a trio, or a more populous number, including a chorus or an extended ensemble. The numerous kinds of change made to the libretto text by the composer are generally of local, short-term impact, but they may be for the benefit of either intelligible words or well-turned music. An opera composer's skills may be evaluated according to his ability to minimize the adverse effects of the inevitable mutilation of the text and to maximize the dramatic impact of the combined operation. Britten, by common consent, does well indeed.

In the *Dream,* as elsewhere, the most prevalent musical effect is not to change the text on the score's page (except by hyphenation to clarify the assignment of syllables to notes), but to discipline it. Music's imposed rhythms and pitches are often at variance with natural speech tones, although dynamics generally match the normal spoken volumes. Drastic exaggerations of speech inflections occur in arias, even noncoloratura ones, as when Tytania instructs her named attendants to "be kind and courteous to this gentleman," typically arresting the expected verbal flow and elaborating her sentiments—bewitched, loving, incongruous, ridiculous—for the audience's greater enjoyment (206).

Britten uses not only exaggerations but also drastic diminutions of spoken pitch inflections in opera's recitatives. When Lysander describes his widowed aunt's house as a refuge from the sharp Athenian law, he does so largely in single-tone, even-rhythmed dialogue, which remains plainly intelligible, as the action demands (53).

Britten's (or Pears's) own line, "Compelling thee to marry with Demetrius," is in unvaried eighth notes on a single, midtessitura pitch, G (53). This kind of level diction ultimately becomes an incantation, a speech-act, functionally and intelligibly promoting the plot, as when Oberon disenchants Tytania: "Be as thou was wont to be . . ." (324).

Word repetitions are legion. Two-and-a-half lines of the fairies' opening, "Over hill, over dale," are immediately repeated, avoiding an inappropriate frantic start and affording the music time to drive home the *Urmotiv* (7). The two words "Skip hence" in Tytania's orders to her attendants are repeated, the second time with an increased leap upward, emphasizing the statement (24); Oberon soon balances the device with a less spontaneous duplication of "the winds" (25). When Oberon and Tytania round out their now-shared catalog of terrestrial disasters in the admission "We are their parents and original," Britten brings back the "We are," the final word of which he suggestively drowns with a loud, *tutti* chord, its B♭ root a dramatic tritone removed from that of the previous sonority (34).

This special emphasis neatly culminates the confused, contrapuntal quarrel, clearing the way for Oberon to recite his selfish proposed solution and for her to reject it, both of which are required to be heard distinctly.

Severe excisions were required to produce a proper length text for Britten's *Dream;* thus it might appear counterproductive for the composer to repeat words that functioned adequately singly in the play. The paradox disappears when it is acknowledged that music requires time to make its point, to establish a mood or to display a significant form. Cooperation between musical elements and textual repetitions is well illustrated in Oberon's aria and song, "I know a bank . . .": in the score he will make Tytania "full of hateful, *hateful*" fantasies, *of fantasies*." The words italicized are emphasized in performance not only by being repeated but by musical changes. The composer decreases the tempo on the first "hateful," introduces the celesta figure and a cross-rhythm, imposes a rapid melisma on the first "fan-" syllable that outlines the false relations in the celesta sonority, and inverts the melisma when that syllable is repeated (80).

Following conventional operatic procedures, Britten achieves various effects by reassigning text to different characters in distinct ways. In the play, the environmental disasters from the royal fairies' estrangement are all cited by Titania: in the libretto, abbreviated and reassigned, they become ominous intersexual *stychomythia*, a prelude to an intensifying musical number about which more later. There are canonic entries where the confusion of words is only partially mitigated by staggering the pair's verbal attacks.

The stuttering effect heard in "change, change, Their, Their, wonted, wonted" is particularly jumbled and effective because of the high tessitura of Oberon's countertenor voice (25–33). Characterizations also are subtly changed. In the play, only Titania explicitly admitted to parentage of the progeny of evils (36; 2.1.17), whereas, in the opera, Oberon expresses his share of the blame: through this admission and Tytania's equal if not superior vocal powers, Britten's musical changes erode the aloof dominance Shakespeare's text suggested for the male fairy patriarch.

Fixing the libretto determines the successive presences on stage of single characters or groups, and the composer is faced with making music for different numbers of performers. The particular number has become a label for the operatic number: a duet, a trio, a quartet, and so on, or, more vaguely as to numbers, an ensemble or a chorus. Most of these labels, also designate operatic scenes with different

dramatic functions demanding certain distinctive musical characteristics.

Britten, in the *Dream,* frequently has to compose extended passages for dialogue between two active, independent characters—Oberon and Tytania, Lysander and Hermia, Demetrius and Helena,
Tytania and Bottom, Theseus and Hippolyta—and for larger groups,
with each character still functioning independently rather than as a
member of a chorus. There are some constraints. The dramatic situation may require a readily understandable plot advancement, and,
thus, a form of recitative is mandatory; or it may call for a contempla-
tion of the characters' emotions or their attitudes towards each other,
friendly or hostile, in which case a form of aria is appropriate. Britten's respect for the Shakespearean text imposed another restric-
tion, but he did not hesitate to repeat words or phrases or to reassign
them to other characters for musical reasons when the plot permitted. There is a danger of unattractive sameness if duets prevail, but
the composer has significant musical options. First, a melody to be
sung can be given its own innate character. Lysander's agreeing to
patience followed by his description of his widowed aunt has a melody ranging over a ninth, containing nine of the twelve musical tones,
proceeding by a mixture of repeated tones and eight different intervals in varied rhythms, suggesting A major and G minor tonalities—
an interesting line, attracting and holding Hermia's and the audience's attention while important information is offered, and providing variety in the *secco* and the more florid passages in the scene
(52). Second, as the dramatic situation permits, and with only minor
textual modifications, the composer can have the phrases, whether
consisting of the same or different words, sung by the characters in
a number of distinct patterns: solo and alternately, or together and
synchronized, or together but "distanced," one starting later but
overlapping the first. Britten freely exercises these textual options,
simultaneously making the characters' melodic lines either the same,
related, or quite different. Third, the accompaniment can be a mere
background or it can take a prominent, perhaps independent, part in
the total presentation.

The tense Oberon-Tytania meeting scene was mentioned earlier in
limited connections, such as the reassignments among characters:
as a duet it reveals further aspects of Britten's convincing musical
dramaturgy. After entering slowly from opposite wings, both sing
"I'll met by moonlight," a leaping melody with alternate syllables in
unisons and octaves: they express the same sentiment of animosity,
but she, a coloratura soprano, can dominate his countertenor vocally
at will by singing higher, at a pitch that comes through the orchestra

better. They sing the rest of their greeting, her "jealous Oberon" and his "proud Tytania," in unison, to the royal fairies' motive that preceded their exchange; the superposed, mutually obliterating different words and the common melody reinforce the hostile but shared attitude and add a connotation of marital disruption to the motive (23).

Britten enriches Oberon's and Tytania's elaboration of the disasters resulting from their debate and dissension with a variety of expressive textual and melodic structures. At first they sing alternately; then they combine, a development reflecting the rising dramatic tension. The key summarizing phrase, "the seasons alter," is sung clearly in unison and repeated after an expressive pause, a Phrygian cadence ending the first statement and providing an abnormal temporary point of release. From this they depart by the same contrary steps they used in cadencing, Tytania's high F♯ (clashing with F's in the orchestra) over Oberon's D♯ a minor tenth below again displaying her dominance and inviting his revenge (28).

They each sing the words "and this same progeny of evils" to melodies of very similar shape, his, in E Phrygian mode, a transposed imitation of hers in C major, but distant by half a bar (32). In this two-part fugal stretto, Britten, by many dull secundal, quartal, and quintal harmonic intervals on accented beats, acentuates the unhappy antisocial outcome of their debate.

At the climax of the scene, Britten constructs a peak of dissension by combining several of these textual and melodic devices. In the libretto, Titania says, "and for her sake I will not part with him," Oberon following with "Give me that boy and I will go with thee." This sequence is tenser than the play's, for Titania's intervening conciliatory invitation to Oberon to "patiently dance in our round" (36; 2.1.140) is omitted from the opera. Adding to the tension, Britten has them sing the phrases twice, the entries of the different words unsynchronized and on pitches a dissonant major seventh apart, the tonality fluctuating between E and F, and the beat irregularly subdivided, producing polyrhythmic patterns. Subtly but most tellingly of all, Oberon's line is a recognizably close relative of Tytania's, a strict inversion, portraying their dispute as an interfamily quarrel, fresher and no less bitter than a feud among long-standing enemies (39).

This melee of textual and musical conflicts to support a dramatic quarrel is but a rehearsal for the coup Britten brings off by stacking the same devices when the four lovers, awake and properly paired, have just left the stage on their way to the palace. Offstage, each says, "let us recount our dreams," just half a line in the libretto. Helena starts with the six notes F, E, C♯, D, F, E—the first four plainly the cambiata, the last four, beginning on C♯, its inversion (354). The others enter at half-measure distances with transpositions or inversions of this row, creating a mounting confusion of clashing words and a succession of ever-changing dissonances, prominent in contrast to the occasional consonances—disciplined "reckless counterpoint." Their vocal sound fades away to a more restful chord, which nevertheless contains a major seventh, a tritone, and two tones that are dissonant with the *sostenuto* morning-music chord that accompanies them (354). In particular, Lysander's middle C and the women's A and E above it are perfectly consonant, but Demetrius's B♭, a whole tone below Lysander (the whole audible as a highly unstable third inversion of a dominant thirteenth in F), quietly and gently reminds the audience, as Shakespeare does not, that he retains potentially disruptive traits (354). The dramatic instability is plain; the lovers had just announced, in chorus, their questionable unities, "mine own and not mine own" (351); Britten's masterstroke is his matching this with a musical paradox—using well matched components in a centuries-old orderly procedure designed for harmonic results, he produces a dissonant cadential release (354).

Unlike many earlier opera composers who perhaps stressed the musical component, only rarely in the *Dream* does Britten portray the singers' agreement or difference by an extended passage with two or more strongly contrasted melodies. During the four lovers' quarrel, Helena does have a slow melodic passage for "but fare ye well . . ." while Lysander, after singing "stay" on a long note, goes on "gentle Helena" in a rapid recitative (268). Helena does address Demetrius, "sweet do not scorn," on a slow downward G minor scale while he rattles off a quick "if she cannot entreat . . ." (269). But a combination of simultaneous melodies contrasted in form portrays antagonism no more effectively than a union of structurally similar lines. As was mentioned above in dealing with small-scale significant forms, in which the each-against-each quarrel reaches a midscene climax, Britten relocates four textual couplets and tellingly reverts to a recognizable fugal stretto, the voices even beginning on the same E♭ tone (275). Uncomfortably yoked likes create more tension than well harnessed unlikes: aural lilies that fester. . . .

Arguably, the most important intermediate-range operatic form is the ensemble, in which several characters, probably from two or more distinct actions, in changing styles of delivery, interact, advancing the plots by complication or denouement, all nonstop over a considerable time by the stage clock. The musical form, forged by both instruments and voices, must support the dramatic action, by alternate cooperation and counteraction. The *Dream* afforded Britten only attenuated situations of this kind. The contacts between the court and the lovers in the play, the scenes that would have engendered the best ensembles, are reduced in the libretto to a brief, one-sided ruling by Theseus. Oberon and Puck operate on, but are unseen by, the lovers and the tradesmen. In *Pyramus and Thisby,* the two-way relations between the tradesmen players and the court-and-lovers audience are richer than in real theatre, but they do not at the time affect each others' plots.

There are shorter situations when there is musical support for dramatic ensemble action within a single group of characters, supporting the excitement. In the tradesmen's casting and rehearsal sessions, Bottom musically enriches his Ercles demonstration and his lion and nightingale acts, while Flute practises his Thisby role in the background. In the four-way lovers' quarrel, their kaleidoscopic confrontations, abbreviated from the play, are refocused by the integrated instrumental motives and the four-part vocal fugal stretto of scrambled, disputatious couplets. Britten inserted a partially relaxing musical silence, a *reculer pour mieux sauter,* before the women's statures become an issue on Helena's "you puppet" accusation (276).

The most interesting ensemble episode occurs when the six tradesmen have completed their mispunctuated, *pomposo* announcement, "If we offend . . .," in harmonized recitative and canon, addressed to the seated court and lovers (414–19). Responding, each of the six stage audience members is given a separate staff and different text, some relocated. They begin singing separately, at short time intervals, each repeating his or her line as required, to the following direction in the score: "This Recitative Ensemble is not to be sung in strict time. Each character sings his line at the natural speed of diction, repeating it until silenced by Theseus' 'Who's next'" (419). Britten not only has the stage audience itself demonstrate how "these fellows do not stand upon points," he moves towards a "controlled aleatoric" form, similar to the oriental heterophonic techniques he employed in earlier and later works, *Paul Bunyan* (1941) and *Curlew River* (1964), described by Mitchell in his 1988 Italian article as constructive innovations (32).

Shakespeare's *Dream* does not call for a functional chorus in the sense of numerous characters behaving as a crowd acting and reacting as the general populace or a faction of it, or in the sense of the classical Greek dramatic chorus. By contrast, in the opera, Britten calls for a chorus of fairies, trebles or sopranos, and uses them, in place of single fairy, to announce the measures for beautifying the countryside preparatory to Tytania's coming (5). He brings them back to lullaby her (145) and to join Oberon in planning the final blessings (485). Britten uses these chorus deployments conventionally for musical and dramatic interest; he has the group singing along with solo fairies or alternating with them (144), and he subdivides the group into antiphonal subgroups (5). Occasionally the tradesmen and the lovers provide textural variety by singing snatches, en masse, as a chorus rather than, say, a quartet with independent parts.

9

Instrumental Passages, Music by Characters, and Metaopera

> See the conq'ring hero comes,
> Sound the trumpets, beat the drums.
> —Thomas Morell, librettist of
> Handel's *Joshua*

Five extended, wordless instrumental passages play a major structural role in the opera, not only in determining its changing moods and settings, but also in musically articulating the dramatic action and helping to suggest an organic, concentrated interpretation of the complex work. They establish their own forms to do this, free from textual influences.

The first of the passages that portray an atmosphere and a place rather than a movement is the opening wood music. In it, Britten achieves his aim of setting a mysterious, awesome, haunted wood mood mainly by three devices. First, the ubiquitous, long, up-and-down portamenti introduce pitch-classes foreign to the familiar twelve in an equal temperament domain. Progressively more and more of the muted strings exude these strange, mobile sounds, higher and higher, denser and denser, louder and louder, finally retreating to accomodate Tytania's fairies entering in groups. The tremolo, the quick reiteration of the tones (Monteverdi's artifice), expresses excitement and danger. Second, between the swooping portamenti noises, the single tones, intervals, and triads—in varied textures—dwell momentarily on different degrees of the chromatic scale, producing a cycle of the twelve possible tonic centres, depicted above as a tonality set in example 7.3(a). Within the variegated context of mid-twentieth-century new music, this complete succession, an unpredictable mixture of closely and distantly related root movements, projects a *déjà-entendu* strangeness. The prominent initial alternating G and F♯ tonal centers introduce a construct of tonalities separated by a half-step that results in vertical and horizontal bitonalities, inviting double readings. The G/F♯ juxtaposition is repeated in the second full cycle and is continued alone thereafter; it and similarly related tonal pairs are used in several other tense situations. One critic, obviously with the portamenti in mind, colorfully proclaimed "that Britten expects the ear like the eye to travel up and down the tall tapering trunks" (White, 224), while others imply that the wood is a living character, breathing (Peter Evans, 239), sighing (Kennedy, 220), groaning (Bach, 40), even eructating (Conrad, *A Song,* 216). Its widely recognized distinctiveness makes the passage effective as it returns, to articulate the scenes within the opera's first act, to recharge the wood with a persisting aura of mystery, and to round out the act. Britten suppresses his melodic gifts in this wood music, allowing unhindered scope to the forceful devices based on the musical elements of tonality and texture.

The sleep music in act 2 appears less frequently than does the wood music in act 1. Only an orchestral prelude, an interlude, and a short postlude are needed to introduce, replenish, and leave suspended the atmosphere of deceptive moonlit calmness that lures Tytania and Bottom into an enchanted love affair, provokes the lovers into acrimonious quarrels, and finally releases them into a healing sleep. Differences in timbre are the immediate expressive device. The twelve pitch-classes are arranged in four chords and appear in progressively higher segments of the instrumental range (see example 7.3[d]): first, D♭, F, and A♭, close and low in the muted strings; second, D, F♯, A, and B in the brass; third, Gs, E♭s, and B♭ opened out in the woodwinds; and, fourth, E over C high on the harpsichord, harps, and vibraphone, garnished with a tap on the suspended cymbal. The allocation of instruments to chords hints at the characterizing connections already made between different instruments and dramatis personae. Dodecaphonic tonality and shifting grouped instrumental colors image the all-inclusiveness of personality-changing slumber. The clear, compact root progression, D♭, D, E♭, C, establishes a ground for a passacaglia with varied repetitions that define recognizable small-scale forms and a bipartite structure for the whole act. Melodic and rhythmic figures—but not such as to destroy the deceptive tranquility—appear in the four preludial restatements of the ground (157), in its four returns in the interlude (236), and eventually in the nine accompanying postludial appearances, the first in retrograde (312). Britten may have thought of the opening four "moonlight" chords in Mendelssohn's first Overture to the play (E: I, V, iv, I), but Britten's chord sequence is structurally more potent, not only within act 2, but in connecting with the wood music of act 1 and the morning music of act 3: all are different and contrasted, yet all are related as extended solo orchestral passages. Finally, the sleep music returns in act 3 to depict the land of lost content when Bottom awakes (366).

When act 3 opens after the second interval in the opera, Britten uses other resources in the morning music to advance the drama to another stage. He divides the first and second violins equally into three parts in order to make three sonic strands with indistinguishable timbres. They enter in sequence, followed by the violas, but, despite the structure, the sound is quite unlike that of a fugal exposition. Example 9.1(a) shows the levels, instruments, bars of entry, and pitch-class sets of each part.

Each part mostly moves by wide melodic leaps that make it appear to wander aimlessly on two levels—for instance, the second violins meander both between C and D on the staff and between A, B♭, and C above it. But the parts interlock, and the general result is a seemingly random selection of diatonic notes, progressively denser and higher in pitch. The slow, even movement, "gently flowing crotchets," confirms an image of lack of concentration and direction on awakening. The strictly diatonic pitch resources are shown in Example 9.1(b), and the severe limit holds for sixtynine measures, imposing a remarkable tonal stasis, particularly in the context of what Britten wrote before.

Charles Osborne recorded a statement of Britten's in 1963: "certainly I use key-centres, melodic and rhythmic patterns still" (92–93); a special application of this conservatism can be seen here. Within the pandiatonicism of this morning music, Britten establishes or hints at tonalities and modalities by iteration and durations. From the tabulation of durations of tones shown in example 9.1[c] and analysed in table E.6 of appendix E, and from an inspection of the held tones in the score, which act as finals, the foci in the first three sections of the first thirty measures are on G, B♭, and E, suggesting modalities of G♯ Dorian, B♭ Lydian, and E♯ Locrian. In the fourth section, the C root tone temporarily suggests a dominant seventh or ninth of F major, but a resolution never materializes. By the fifth section and later, at curtain-up, the focus is changing, particularly when the cellos and double basses enter with low seconds on F with G and G with A, each climbing eventually to A with B♭ and B♭ with C.

Working against this short-term, sleep-laden blandness, how-

Example 9.1. Pitch Organization in the Pandiatonic "Morning Music" before Curtain-up in Act 3 of Britten's Opera *A Midsummer Night's Dream* (321–22)

(a) Entries of Pitch-classes: first entry ○; later ●

(b) Pitch content in scalar form (first 69 measures)

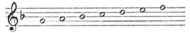

(c) Pitch-classes Ranked According to Durations Sounded (first 30 measures; for analysis, see table E.6)

ever, is an intensification: more textural levels, faster movement in eighth rather than quarter notes, extended range, added instruments, and louder dynamics. Then the violas invert their motives to move downwards, and Oberon and Puck appear. Despite its distinctive style, Britten ensures that this distinctive music fits into the grand plan. Coming after the second interval between acts, it does not jar with the previous music; although "the wood early next mornng" is a silent stage direction, the audience can see "Tytania with Bottom and the four lovers lying asleep" in changed lighting.

The avoidance of clear tonality pays a rich dividend when two new pitches are suprisingly introduced at the dramatic moment when Oberon would undo the imperfection of Tytania's eyes: his word "hateful" wanders to E♭ while one of the *divisi* cellos discovers A♭ (324). This particular interval, formed of tones somewhat distinct from the surrounding tones, was met earlier when it completed, not always with complete success, the twelve-tone set. These flatted new pitches with subdominant or even Phrygian flavor momentarily ruffle the pandiatonic calm and cause one to experience anew the placid morning music, soon to be restored and epitomized. A *rallentando* introduces a prolonged *pianissimo* diatonic trill on F by the third violins.

The next extended instrumental passage portrays movement, a change of scene, rather than the atmosphere of one place. After waking, all the characters had announced a move from the wood to the palace. Dramatically, the time of transition is one of expectation, the audience hoping to see the court in all its glory. Arguably, the impact of the spectacle, a staple ingredient of opera, when it appears, is increased by its postponement and consequent newness, not familiarized by an earlier court scene as in the play. There are obvious reasons why Britten inserted an orchestral interlude between the awakenings in the enchanted wood and the celebrations in court. A formal interact break would upset the balanced act divisions, and it would not indicate the link between the locales. There is time to be bridged: a whole morning and afternoon. The change of scene should not be perceived as taking place either abruptly, after the reunited tradesmen leave, or suddenly, before the ducal couple enter; therefore Britten breaks the interval into two parts: a lengthy transition (385–94) and a brief introduction shortly before "the lights are up on Theseus' Palace" and the ducal couple enter with their court to a new soaring, leaping melody on the strings with the *Urmotiv* on the harpsichord (394). Table 9.1 identifies sections of the interlude, naming characters and things possibly represented.

According to a line cut from the play (26; 1.1.165), there is a league to be traversed on foot; what more appropriate transition passage than a quick march to suggest a happy, expectant journey? The success of the "Sea Interludes" in *Peter Grimes* probably convinced Britten that extended, organized, functional orchestral passages are welcome to operatic audiences. The transition passage is basically a dialogue—a pattern fitting easily into an opera— between a pair of horns and different groups of other instruments that respond to and comment on the horns' propositional fanfares: the Duke can speak at will, but one does not address him unless spoken to. At the opening of the opera Britten had already made

Table 9.1 Sections of the Orchestral Interlude, from Wood to Palace, in Britten's Opera, *A Midsummer Night's Dream* (Analysed in example 9.2).

Section of Ex. 9.2	Page and measure number [in brackets] in the score	Instrumentation	Stage directions; characters and things possibly represented
Transition from wood to palace			
(a)	384[7]	Trombone, Timpani, Cellos, Double Basses	SD: The lights go down on the wood
(b)	385[3]	Tbne., Harps, Vcs. Dbs.	Quick March
(c)	385[4]	Horns (muted)	Theseus
(d)	385[5]	Flutes 1 & 2	[Fairies]
(e)	386[8]	Horns	Theseus
(f)	386[3]	Clarinets 1 & 2	[Lovers]
(g)	386[7]	Horns (open)	Theseus
(h)	387[2]	English Horn, Bassoon	[Tradesmen]
(i)	388[2]	Horns	Theseus
(j)	389[1]	Fls., Cls.	[Fairies and Lovers]
(k)	390[3]	Horns	Theseus
(l)	391[1]	E.H., Cls., Bsn.	[Tradesmen and Lovers]
(m)	391[2]	Horns	Theseus
(n)	391[3]	Fls., Cls., E.H., Bsn.	[All the Marchers]
(o)	392[1]	Horns, within *tutti*	[Palace comes into sight]
Introduction of the court			
(p)	394[3]	Fls., E.H., Cls., Harpsichord, Strings	[Theseus's presence is sensed]
(q)	395[8]	Horns enter followed by *tutti*	[Theseus's entry fanfare is heard] SD: By now the lights are up on Theseus's palace

Puck arrogate the usual conquering hero's fanfare, instrumented according to Morell: now, when the Theseus-horn imagery sinks in, one can further approve of Britten's second switch, assigning the wider-ranged, rounder-timbred instrument to the head of state. The dialogue unfolds over a background: the harpsichord and the gong accentuate a dynamic tonality set enclosed in a static pedal point articulated by the harps, lower strings, and timpani; change occurs within stability. Example 9.2 emphasizes the layered structure, the authoritative horns on larger staff, their commentative respondents on smaller staff, and the background instruments below. As the passage portrays a movement towards a goal (each character group had announced the palace as its destination), a Schenkerian type of analysis is particularly appropriate: hence the figure portrays the tonal foreground and middlegrounds of the landscape, part (A), leading to several background features, part (B).

Britten gives the horn passages in this interchange their own plan of development, based on prominent high points and low points, some with an anacrusis. The first and second fanfares climb up to peaks on E and F♯, respectively; the third and fourth mount higher to G♯ and A. The upper instrument climbs the scale by steps and the lower instrument mounts by leaps of a third as the interval between the horns decreases from a minor seventh to a unison. The next—fifth and sixth—fanfares are half-length, properly regarded as parts of a single utterance; they fall short of the peak in their respective climaxes of F♯ and G♯ (390–91). The final, seventh, flourish, the longest, getting louder, climbs to a *fortissimo* A, *a 2*, together with the other instruments. Bass Fs are prominent in the introductory and accompanying harps' and basses' lines, and the horns' three Lydian sharpings from those Fs, the B, F♯, and G♯, proclaim that here is a sound struggling to burst out from the confines of the natural harmonics, even from the seven-tone domain. But the two tones still missed from the twelve-tone set, C♯ and D♯, announce that the horns have not yet achieved complete dodecaphony. This reads like the description of an intensification, as, texturally and melodically it certainly is. But the development is also a progressive closure to the transition, releasing harmonic and tonal stresses into a *tutti* A major sonority. Then, from that climax, the orchestra, in a conjoined introduction passage, can descend by the whole tone steps of the *Urmotiv* to the F tonality, which, as a frame, both began the transition and will reveal the ducal couple. The horns set out from the wood, via the summits of their fanfares, to explore the upward, E, F♯, G♯, A, route toward the court; they partially retreat to consider its implications; and

Example 9.2. Analysis of Orchestra Transition Passage from Wood to Palace in Britten's Opera *A Midsummer Night's Dream* (385–94) (Accidentals are written as in the score and apply only to the following note.)

(A) Layered Structure of Foreground and Middleground

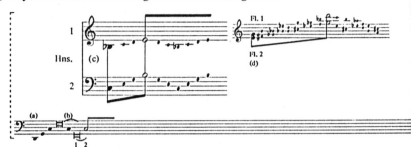

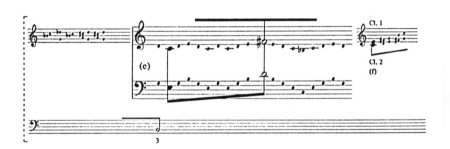

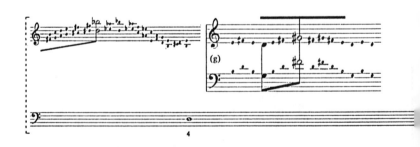

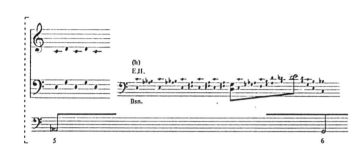

(h)
E.II.

Bsn.

5   6

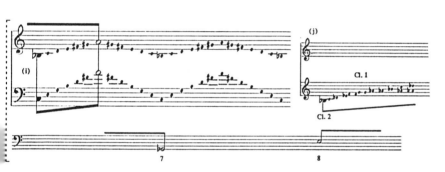

(i)

(j)

Cl. 1

Cl. 2

7   8

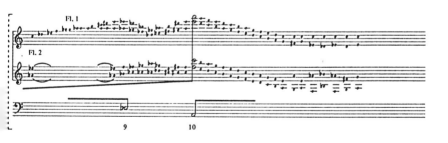

Fl. 1

Fl. 2

9   10

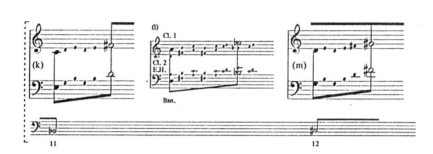

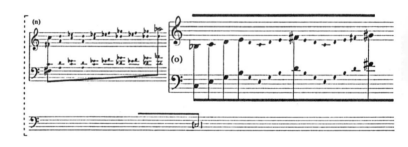

(B) Backgrounds

(1) Horn Fanfares

(2) Linear Progressions: High Points of Horn Fanfares Climb through a Fourth, Minor and Major Thirds, and a Major Seventh

(3) Progressions of Thirds: Low Points of Horn Fanfares Climb through a Seventh, Fifths, and a Thirteenth

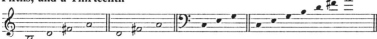

(4) Dynamic Tonality Set within a Static Pedal Point

they finally agree that it was the right way to bring the whole orchestra to a point affording a clear view of the palace. Then the courtly introduction can be sounded.

The instrument groups that answer the horns in the transition, too, have their own different pattern of development, featuring increasing density. The composer introduces, in turn: flutes, clarinets, English horn with bassoon, flutes with clarinets, English horn with clarinets and bassoon, then flutes with clarinets, English horns, and bassoon; and finally these four with trumpets, strings (except basses), and the horns themselves. Whereas the pair of horns begin their fanfares a seventh apart and converge to smaller intervals as they ascend, their imitators tend to diverge to larger intervals as their pitches rise. This structural element projects a continuous increase in tension and closes, with the horns, in a rhythmic stacking of A's. Yet the dialoguing instruments together still constitute only part, an upper layer, of the piece.

Additional, growing suspense is built into an underlying layer of the structure by three tensing processes. First is the repeated pounding of a pedal point by the basses, timpani, and harps with occasional help from other instruments, insisting on stable, unaltering F tonality. The second tensing process is the sounding by the pedaling instruments, between their Fs an octave apart, of the other eleven different notes that complete the twelve-tone alphabet. There are thus, alternately, pedal notes and row notes, contending for stable and vagrant tonality. The progression differs from the earlier ones in containing no less than five semitonal steps, four downward, and the tonal shifts are more widely spaced. Third, the meter of these lower-story notes is 𝄴 ‖: ♩ 𝄽 ♩ ♩ :‖, projecting, in each four-bar section, a high or a low F every five or six beats and a tone from the row every two or three beats, each varied between strong and weak accents. Guillaume de Machaut and his fourteenth-century colleagues might feel flattered by Britten's use of isorhythm, but the Suffolk composer's dodecaphonic enrichment to make his own brand of tense and intensifying *ars nova* would have tested the old Rheims canon's faith in the value of innovation, perhaps goading him to anticipate what Britten himself said in 1962: "the craze for originality, . . . has driven many artists into using a language to which few hold the key, and that is a pity." ("Speech," Hull, 90).

The transition passage is another of Britten's surveys of tonal resources. He uses four rival formal elements, the horns, their mimickers, the pedal, and the row, operating on upper and lower pitch levels. He varies the texture, tonality, and other elements, to produce music of fluctuating but overall increasing intensity in an organic form. From its context, following the lovers' and the tradesmen's announced departures from the wood for the palace, the music's destination becomes certain—the court, where the purpose of the musical intensification becomes clear: the Duke and his bride-to-be are persons of awe. The second, courtly introduction section of the interlude, including the court harpsichord motive (See example 7.1[g]), were examined earlier.

It is easy to share Peter Evans's apparently mixed feelings about the effectiveness of the interlude. The composer's objective is to set the stage for Theseus, and thus the horn passages that earlier represented him a-hunting in the wood offstage when the lovers awoke are a natural choice of material for the transition. Evans sees the progressive foregrounding of the horn theme, in the wood and in the quick march, as Britten's creating "in advance the musical necessity for some corresponding stage representation," making Theseus's and his court's appearance an expectation fulfilled rather than a belated adventitious deus ex machina device. Seemingly, Evan's insight into Britten's ingenious preparation is not fully matched by his satisfaction with the result, for, he says, "even so, a considerable effort is called for at this point," and Theseus's releasing of Hermia from her father's choice of husband and ordering the triple wedding "is bound to appear a somewhat cursory way of sorting out the lovers' tangle" (253). The double use of the horn passages helps unify the work, but Britten is, perhaps, relying too heavily on music to compensate for the lost clarity of Shakespeare's plan following the librettists' paratactic restructuring and counting too much on retrospective intelligibility.

In review, the diverse collection of extended orchestral passages that frame and articulate the opera show Britten fully exercising his distinctive, highly developed procedures for achieving variety and unity. An occasional difficult challenge can be welcomed. The wood music combines horizontal dodecaphony projected by a cycle of major triads in tertian harmony, with an "omniphony," the continuum of additional pitches in the ubiquitous extended portamenti. The sleep music features vertical and horizontal, two-dimensional dodecaphony, also projected by a set of sonorities from the "common practice" period—clearly tertian, enriched by an added sixth and a first inversion. The set is short in range and more often repeated. The pandiatonic morning music represents a pause in the debate between twelve-tone structures and major-mirror organisms. The wood-to-palace transition combines on different levels a tonally static pedal point, a twelve-tone row, and a modulating diatonic progression.

Moreover, in this transition passage the horns, alternating with their mimickers, establish a tensing and relaxing formal music process, matching the common, effective pattern that Wallace Berry cited. The passage has an introduction that also dismisses the tradesmen in its opening bars. Britten produced Berry's "expectant intensity," frequent in introductions, by beginning and quickly abandoning a stable pounding of Es and Bs, then, after seeming to embark on a twelve-tone cycle, prematurely slipping into a D, G, C sequence—moving counterclockwise on the cycle of fifths—to herald the quick march in F (384–85). The next two stages of the passage, the first and second fanfares and their answers, make up Berry's "statement and restatement." They are indeed relatively stable, for, although the tone cycle note punctuating the double pedal slips from C to B, there is yet no sense of having gone anywhere, and, although the restatement does involve variation in that the second horn passage is longer and the anwering woodwinds passage is handed down from flutes to clarinets, the development is slight (385–86). The next group of fanfares and answers, the third to the sixth, form Berry's "transition and development," expected to be "normally relatively fluctuant." The achievement of the fanfares' peak, to G♯ then A, the lesser achievement of the curtailed figures' reaching only to F♯ and G♯, and the varied groupings of the different answering instruments are truly fluctuant. Finally, the seventh fanfare, in reaching and foregrounding the A tonality with the other instruments, is a form of the cadence Berry sees to complete the process.

By the time of the transition passage, the Brittenesque tonality set has lost its strangeness and become a norm that, through its consistent association with dramatic highlights, has acquired an aura of expectancy: it can now stand alone, without words, as a tensing implication of significant change. Possibly its nurtured familiarity has made it less unworldly—and thus fitter to participate in heralding the worldly court's belated appearance.

There is no extended nonvocal passage to conclude and prolong the opera, though perhaps the epilogue, mentioned earlier for its dodecaphony, qualifies for direct comparison with the purely instrumental passages, since Puck refrains from pitched, rhythmic song. Indeed his closing speeches have an additional direction: "(no beat)." Fanfares reproduce and vary slightly the rhythm that first announced him (see example 7.2[a]), between which he speaks. Punctuating the final speech, his trumpet reproduces its initial figures with further slight variations, using all twelve tones while capering into and out of its home base, D major. Other accompanying instruments are similarly inclusive. Puck claps his hands, a hint to the audience, and, while *tremolo tutti* scales briefly continue rushing up and down to attain a unison cadential D, a quick curtain drops on the magician's multicolored flash and smoke cloud. The music does not linger to become tedious.

The first two acts of the opera began in clear G major and D♭ major tonalities respectively, which were echoed in the G Dorian mode and the F tonality openings of the two scenes in act 3. The opera ends squarely in D major, an unmistakable overall sharping that—some would say—matches the dramatic comedic progress toward brightness, with better things expected to follow.

In conceptualizing and setting his *Dream,* Britten would have been concerned with the extensive presence in Shakespeare's play of music by or for the characters. Most of the opera's music is designed to be heard by the operagoers seated in the opera house, but to be inaudible to the characters; it is commentative on the drama, the dialogue, and the movement—which is not to say that that music is not an integral part of the opera. On the other hand, some music heard in an opera is—to borrow a filmmaker's term—"reality" music performed by or for a character, such as a song (as distinct from an aria), a performer's or performers' instrumental number, music to accompany a dance, or a fanfare (intended to be heard as such) before an entry. Other aural phenomena, too, are "reality" in this sense: noises heard by the characters as part of the action, such as a midnight clock strike. These musical numbers and sounds create a double impression on members of the audience, who are listening to dramatis personae listening to sounds and also hearing them themselves unfiltered by the personalities on stage. The *Dream's* librettists tended not to excise music that was part of the play; the composer tends to feature it. The wide choice of style available for inherent sound is a powerful tool for characterizing the performer on stage—as when Bottom sings, roughly, "The woosell cock"—or for defining the setting—as when Theseus's horns are used to portray the wood as a hunting ground after the enchanted ones have fallen asleep. The ability to mock the situation by a deliberately incongruous sound allows the composer, like the playwright, to utter a critical "voice" without obtruding. "Real" episodes provide a convenient means of articulating the drama and the musical whole.

Specifically, as play and opera, the *Dream* is built around the relation between reality and unreality, portrayed, for example, through the paradoxical distinctions and similarities between day and night, being awake and dreaming, rationality and enchantment, even, perhaps, between reason and emotion. To develop this theme, the dramatist, frequently without comment, makes a character "act," stepping outside his or her expected role to bring something potentially contradictory into it, such as a surprising philosophical argument, a song, or even a complete drama. Not all characters are complex. Theseus and Hipployta never leave their roles of exhibiting superior socal status and celebrating a dynastic marriage. Similarly, the lovers do nothing uncharacteristic, merely seeking desired partners in marriage and, too, keeping their station by ridiculing the tradesmen's theatricals. Oberon and Titania sing and dance, and the tradesmen dance; but these actions may be quite in character for fairies and humans. On the other hand, the tradesmen in *Pyramus and Thisby* (except, at times, Snug the Lion) deliberately try to quit their everyday functions to become "other" in their endeavours to be tragedians. Clearly, Puck, in his epilogue, changes from the mischievous character he has so successfully been into a praise-seeking thespian.

When, in an opera made from a well-known play, a character's departure from plain speech and pedestrian movement involves his or her presentation of music, the composer must decide whether the operatic music is to be authentic to the period of the play or is to conform to the norms of the new opera. He must, too, select his attitude towards it: neutral, praising, or deprecatory. In the *Dream*, Britten displays his usual inventiveness in composing songs and dances for the fairies and the tradesmen incorporating stylistic features of the Renaissance prototypes that are yet modern—probably necessarily so since the songs and dances of Shakespeare's stage were changeable and are not now known beyond dispute. Nothing need be added to what has been said about the songs and dances and about Puck's realistic epilogue. But the setting of *Pyramus and Thisby* was a wide-open option that Britten boldly exercised in a striking, even controversial manner, making a burlesque metaopera, a feature equal in importance to the restructuring in differentiating the opera from the play.

On close examination, *Pyramus and Thisby* may be regarded as essentially metaopera. In the opera-within-the-opera, Britten kept all essentials of Shakespeare's slight modification of the story from Ovid's *Metamorphoses,* adding an instrumental prelude and postlude. The following list indicates one way of dividing Britten's small-scale work, showing a new scene when the characters change, but omitting references to the stage audience's comments that terminate scenes 2 to 11 and occur during some of them:

1. Instrumental prelude (413–14)
2. Tradesmen (414–20)
3. Prologue; Quince and Wall (420–26)
4. Pyramus (427–31)
5. Thisby and Pyramus; Wall (432–38)
6. Lion (438–42)
7. Moon (442–45)
8. Thisby and Lion (445–48)
9. Pyramus (449–54)
10. Thisby; Bottom (454–58)

11. Bottom (458–59)
12. Instrumental postlude (459)

Britten had several contemporary popular operatic subgenres to parody. Although the story would be apt, he seemingly rejected the Wagnerian *Gesamtkunstwerk* model as too far from his own style to permit subtle comparisons—and possibly because of limited orchestral resources. As between certain styles commonly used for simple tragic plots, he chose to parody the earlier Italian bel canto models of Rossini, Donnizetti, Bellini, and the young Verdi, rather than the later verismo models of the older Verdi, Puccini, and others. Probably he could have more fun associating the homespun tradesmen with the greater artificiality of the bel canto high plateau of singer's opera.

At the outset of the entertainment, in sections 1 and 2, Britten's main targets are the simple functional harmony and catchy tunes of much bel canto opera. He composes a sequence of musical phrases (shown in reduced score in example 9.3):

1. An introductory fanfare for trumpet and timpani, modulating temporarily twice from D major to A major: expendable, an obsolete concession to patrons who would not take their places until the music had begun (example 9.3[a]).
2. A full-bodied exchange between orchestra and tradesmen's chorus, as they mispunctuate their dedication, far too humble in 1960. It features two departures from the tonic D major, all in full, simple triads in root position. The I-V-I excursion is clearly a dig at conventionality; the I-♭VII-I trip may be a bow to the prefunctional modality current when English composers were formerly in the van (example 9.3[b]).
3. A vocal montage, when each tradesman, in canon, sings "All for your delight, We are not here"; although the entries are distanced by five quarter notes in $\frac{4}{4}$ meter, the regularity mocks scholastic species counterpoint. But the main thrust is at the cycle of fifths, shown in harmonic reduction in example 9.3(c). Britten ingeniously relents in his satire by making Starveling end his phrase flat, breaking the pattern, so that Snout and Flute—on a top note requiring falsetto—can short-circuit the cycle, cutting it in half, and returning to D, now minor in quality.
4. A mechanical I-V-IV-V-I harmonic progression as the tradesmen conclude their choral dedication. After the too quick

Example 9.3. Metaopera: Functional Harmony Satirized in *Pryamus and Thisby* in Britten's Opera *A Midsummer Night's Dream* (413–24)

(a) Tonic, D Major, Established by Temporary Modulation (413)

(b) Tonic Confirmed by Excursions to Dominant and Subtonic (414)

(c) Defective Cycle of Fifths in Scholastic Counterpoint (417)

(d) Tonic Reconfirmed by Dominant and Subdominant (418)

(e) Vagrant Tonality in Aleatoric, Unscholastic Counterpoint (419)

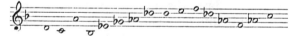

(f) New Tonal Region, E♭ Major, Established by Tonic and Dominant (420)

(g) New Tonality Overclarified by Mechanistic Melody and Subtonic Modality Proposed (421)

Three times, and variations

modulation in passage 3, Britten again shows the banality of mechanically used primary triads (example 9.3[d]).

5. A number by the other sextet, the court and the lovers in which Britten goes to the opposite extreme: their jumbled text, although musically notated, is aleatoric, and the new D minor key signature is a poor guide to the many sonorities resulting from the accidental E♭s (perhaps Neapolitan), G♭ (perhaps F♯), D♭ (perhaps C♯, and A♭ (Lydian G♯, or F minor thirds) (example 9.3[e]).

6. Quince's warning "Gentles, . . . Gentles," is incorporated into an instrumental I-I-V-I sequence in E♭ major (reduced in example 9.3[f]), another semitone root movement between sections; thus Britten completes his organization of classical functional tonality.

7. Quince's aria, in which a slavishly repeated melodic phrase is an even more obvious butt for Britten's parody (example 9.3[g]).

Even before the tragic characters appear, Britten has invited his audience to compare obtrusive traditional functional tonality unfavorably with his assimilation of it with twelve-tone and pandiatonic developments. If the passages are viewed together, Britten has used a typical classical last movement form, the rondo, to make his point: in example 9.3, items (b), (d), and (f) are the returning theme of unfashionable, plain tonality; items (c) and (e) are episodes of unstable modulation and confusing lack of control.

Britten exaggerated the distinct structure of number opera by keeping the sections abruptly short and by inserting some fifteen groups of comments from the court and the lovers, perhaps endorsing by reductio ad absurdum his own middle-of-the-road course, modeled on the mature Mozart, between distracting fragmentation and wearing continuity.

Britten manipulated the recitative-aria dichotomy by improving on Shakespeare's witty reversal, which had made the tradesmen speak verse and the court and the lovers speak prose during the performance. Although the stage audience's remarks are commentary, Britten sets them in recitative, a secondary reversal, necessary for the verbal humor to be understandable. The actors conventionally sing both recitative and aria (better, arietta, since the numbers are so brief), but Britten slips in several amusing refinements. Wall's arias are in the *Sprechstimme* Hippolyta found so silly. Lion's second aria is a lengthy vocalise, a roar, written "Oh!" in comically repeated rhythmic snatches and banal harmonic changes, ending as a background for the stage audience's enthusiastic congratulations and furnishing a vital tone for the glowing augmented triad on Hippolyta's "Moon."

In the tradition of singer's opera, the temperamental stars must have enough arias to gratify their overweening pride of showmanship, but not so many as to arouse costars' jealousies. Britten shows the tradesmen breaking this convention. He furnishes Pyramus and Thisby overhandsomely, and Prologue gets a special, fully fashionable three-stanza aria; Lion has his "quasi-polka" quatrain and his roar; Wall "sings" twice; but poor Moon gets no further than some four audience-interrupted recitatives.

Britten does not forget functional operatic choruses. The tradesmen unsuccessfully try to imitate his techniques by singing "all for your delight" (417–18) in imperfect dodecaphony (no $A\flat$) with two overorganized cycles of fourths (D^7 to F^7, and A^7 to D minor). The lovers and Theseus in chorus check Hippolyta, reciting "but silence, here comes Thisby" (445) in simple unison $B\flat$ and $A\flat$, harmonically V^7 for her impending signature tune, in $E\flat$.

Britten uses still other musical features to give *Pyramus and Thisby* its Italianate feel. The melodies of several of the ariettas—Prologue's (422), Bottom's (428 and 450), Thisby's (432, 433, and 455), and even Lion's (439)—by their largely diatonic regularity powerfully suggest quotations from bel canto, particularly in the arching lines of the first example from Bottom and the last from Thisby. Bottom, one might quip, "mis-Handels" his last arietta. The ariettas are incongruous coming from the tradesmen's mouths, but the chromatic and modal distortions from the bel canto style not only characterize the untrained singers, but suggest that the posturing style is outworn. "For my part, I want singers who can act," Britten said (Palmer, 180). The harmony of the players' set pieces is noticeably more in the major-minor tradition than is that of the main opera. There are conservative, sometimes functional, diminshed and augmental triads. Secundal root movements, D major to C major (414–17) and E♭ major to D♭ major (421–24), stand out more than similar progressions occasionally used before. Rhythms tend to be more regular, even four-square; this anachronistic regularity, with "ham" singing piled on "ham" acting, becomes the mechanically encrusted elements that Bergson identified with humor.

Fundamentally, Britten's jokes at the expense of Beethoven's choral "Joy" movement mentioned earlier and at bel canto opera are directed at romanticism's abandonment to self-indulgent emotional expression, or, in Schmidgall's words, its "escape from the bonds of Neo-Classicism on the one hand or realism on the other, as well as escape from the customary restraints of society" (*Literature*, 111). In this sense, Britten's generally faithful preservation of the spirit of Shakespeare's *Dream* not only defines that work as, in Ben Jonson's phrase, "for all time," but makes Britten an eclecticist who is constructively discerning. In the *Dream* Britten acknowledges aspects of both the Wagnerian and the Verdian traditions. He reflects the former in that he emphasizes the powers of the supernatural and makes prominent use of motives. But he tends more strongly towards the latter in that his central actions are by the mortal lovers and the earthy tradesmen, in a number opera that both emulates and parodies the style of that subgenre.

Ovid's tale was a simple, straight tragedy. It presented, in turn: Babylonian normality, onerous to the young lovers; their escape to the watered, "Green World," blind to the tomb's imagery; a potentially tragic misunderstanding by Thisbe, running away, thinking the lioness ravenous; a fatal misunderstanding by Pyramus, finding the blood-stained veil and killing himself; and a perfect love-in-death gesture by Thisbe. Shakespeare simplified the tale, dropping Ovid's metamorphosis of the mulberry that imaged the "Green World" turned bloodred, the lovers' common burial urn, and the parental reconciliation. The remaining parallels to the Athenian lovers' adventures were sufficiently self-evident and telling. Britten expands the tale in two distinct directions. First, he enhances Shakespeare's parody by musical rhetoric: the actors' deliveries are heightened in ariettas and by word painting, while the patrician stage audience's comments are confirmed as lapses into the plebian by their prosaic recitative. Second, he superposes on the lamentable tragedy a parody of the artificiality of bel canto opera, making a prodoxical, ambivalent comment on his own style and achievement: the *Dream* rejects bel canto traditions, to which his own recognized lyrical compositional gifts must be related.

Not all critics approve wholeheartedly of the spoof. Winton Dean, apparently noting some lack of musical cohesion, considers *Pyramus and Thisby* the weakest part of the opera, the "loosest in design": no *Urmotiv*, perhaps? He compares it unfavorably with the rest of the opera, where, with equal justification, he finds that "a high degree of motivic organization . . . united so many diverse dramatic elements in a satisfactory whole of moderate length" (Hartnoll, 119). A simple trick characterizes Thisby as a would-be but incompetent diva: on her entry she misses her opening pitch three times, singing in C major, A♭ major, and B major during an outrageously traditional passage in E♭ major. This produces humorous bitonalities, but Peter Evans sees it as too unsubtle to wear well (254). Mitchell, in 1960, after three hearings, saw "a pretty major flaw . . . [in] Britten's conception of the rustic play" and explains, pointedly: whereas Shakespeare

> managed to keep the language of his parody within the bounds of rustic possibility . . . Britten seems to throw characterization and dramatic truth to the winds. . . . [The rustics] reveal themselves, dismayingly, to be the smartest and most knowing of cabaret teams. . . . The hangover from this extravaganza makes it difficult to reclaim the mood and style to which, fortunately, the opera returns ("In and Out," 798–99).

This is undeniably a valid critical stance; but, especially in this era of multilayered perception, others would allow Britten such latitude, just as they applaud the quasi-polka quality of Lion's entry song, anachronism and all. Schmidgall, developing his analogy between "Shakespearean" and "operatic," very recently praised *Pyramus and Thisby* highly, pointing out that "Britten uses every part of Shakespeare's parody of his own style and dramaturgy to parody the methods of composers from the heydey of grand opera" (*Shakespeare,* 290–91).

It was noted earlier that Britten rarely combined themes to make

Example 9.4. Themes Combined to Reclaim the Enchanted Mood in Britten's Opera *A Midsummer Night's Dream:* **Combination of** *Urmotiv, cambiata,* **and clock strikes (473–80)**

Played three times

a predominantly musical occasion. He does, however, do this at the end of the opera, when the court and the lovers retire, reclaiming the supernatural mood Mitchell welcomed (472–80). In the manner already mentioned, the twelve-fold midnight clock strokes are extended by different instruments at varied pitches and tempos. Simultaneously, pairs of the named fairies sing their frightening nocturne, "Now the hungry lion roars," along with a flute, a clarinet, and the muted first violins. Of the five stanzas, the first three are to the melody shown in example 9.4. Britten features the *Urmotiv* in agogic accents and works the cambiata motive in twice, first decorated by an A♭, second inverted and compressed. The disturbing images of the cambiata unite with the tonal vagaries of the melody and the rogue chimes to recreate an atmosphere for the fairies' awesome catalog of terrors of the night. But there is no way to tell whether they are gloating or themselves terrorized.

The major musical influences have been examined; the next chapter concludes with a summary of the positive and negative effects of the librettists' and the composer's adaptation of Shakespeare's play and an evaluation of the consequences for the opera as a whole.

10

Conclusion

Titania: Come my Lord, and in our flight,
Tell me how it came this night,
That I sleeping here was found,
With these mortals on the ground.

(72; 4.1.99–102)

In the play, the reconciled Oberon and Titania leave to compass the globe. With memories of being enamored of an ass and victim of dramatic irony, she demands, "tell me how. . . ." Shakespeare does not need to make Oberon tell, his audience has already seen all; Britten, the silent innovator, would similarly have refused to say how his music worked to enhance the impact of Oberon's and Tytania's roles. The attempt in this book to do this and to understand generally the popularity and artistic merit of the work now concludes with a summary and evaluation of the whole opera-making process. The examination of the libretto-making process included a study and illustration of credible reasons for the textual changes made in that step. The criteria used then can now be applied to the completed opera score, comprising words, music, and directions for production. Ultimately, evaluation must be based on a comparison between the source play and the opera. Certain statements by Britten and others suggested specific questions about the opera. These are now addressed, and a few other observations are made.

Appropriate length for the libretto text, both bare and when set into music, was demonstrated earlier. The score shows an optional cut of some twenty bars made, for unexplained reasons, at the first performance, shortening the lovers' awakening scene (343–45). Peter Evans disapproves because the spacious timing of the captivating return to normality was lost (252).

Intelligibility of the opera to an aesthetically sympathetic but critical operagoer remains a central requirement. The setting into music complicates any adjudication. Undoubtedly the act of singing and the presence of instrumental accompaniment obscure, even obliterate, many words, despite their repetition, the use of recitative, and subordination of the orchestra. It is equally certain that music, independently of any textual associations, adds denotations to the combined aural media that can aid apprehension: melodies, harmonies, rhythms, and other elements present significant forms that mean things, both rationally and emotionally. Porter, in his article on Benjamin Britten's librettos, looks forward to the complete opera and concludes: *"A Midsummer Night's Dream* is a brilliant biopsy of the play, where Britten's music miraculously replaces Shakespeare's poetry without damaging the original drama" (10). But the respective losses and gains of intelligibility should be segregated only for analytical purposes; the crucial question is the apprehensibility of the cofunctioning words and music— indeed of them supported by the other media heard and seen on stage.

Editing Shakespeare's text for intelligibility consisted largely of removing matter that had become obscure in the 1960 context; the composer had a somewhat different aim, to offer musical language easy to grasp. With the expansion, not to say disintegration, of musical language in the mid-twentieth century, the opportunity for lack of communication through musical obscurities was unprecedentedly great. Britten's avoidance of this pitfall was largely due to his successful integration of diverse compositional procedures, particularly those involving functional tonality, an achievement mentioned, for instance, in connection with the transition march in act 3. He avoids, even in purely instrumental passages, the opposite extremes of full and no precompositional control of variables, and he even excuses the moderately esoteric device of Wall's *Sprechstimme* by criticizing it vicariously—although whether sincerely or tongue-in-cheek is difficult to determine. In his tonality sets, Britten adds a new dimension to dodecaphony as a partner for drama.

There is no received notation of Renaissance music in the play for Britten to adjudge intelligible or otherwise and thus adopt or reject; therefore, if the opera is to keep the play's staged and implied loci, any "reality" music in it must be his invention or a "foreign" quotation, both potentially incongruous. Within Britten's normal language, the bel canto style ariettas in *Pyramus and Thisby* are archaisms, foreign but still intelligible in the broader operatic repertory. But they are plausible *because* they are used to portray incongruous traits in the players. Britten deemed the conservative taste of many operagoers for obtrusive vocal virtuosity at the expense of well-acted drama to be, like Pyramus, too long in dying; so he makes the stage and theater audiences treat misapplied artistry as a joke. The nursery rhyme element, "Boys and girls come out to play," in Bottom's tongs-and-bones number, while not Shakespearean or Brittenesque, has other relevancies: it makes Bottom lovably childlike, confirms that "the moon doth shine as bright as day," and invites the theater audience to join in the playfulness, to be in the enchanted, moonlit wood. It justifies Puck's speculation in his epilogue that they "have but slumber'd" (492).

Britten frequently leaves intelligibility to the text, refraining from an allusive but inept musical intervention. Matching the unseasonable weather with a topical musical lament would have trivialized the disasters. At "Jack shall have Jill" (317), he eschewed the obviouis nursery rhyme tune gloss that might have been one too many, perversely suggesting their misfortune.

Textual intelligibility, which is essential, was distinguished from clarity, which may be withheld for suspense, and from simplicity, which, if excessive, is condescending. Musical intelligibility, clarity, and simplicity must similarly be distinguished. One can assume, with Peter Evans, that the early morning fanfares in the wood were meant to be intelligible, denoting Theseus a-hunting rather than the horns of Elfland faintly blowing; it is acceptable that their meaning is not immediately clear, that only hindsight will elicit the connotation that Theseus was an authoritative figure present all along though unintroduced. One can similarly accept as intelligible the celesta passages indicating the spiritual presence of the absent Oberon, which Britten adds to the trumpet fanfares, intelligibly characterizing Puck and reminding the audience that he might be committing mischief when he anoints Lysander's eyes—though unintentionally, for a change. The resulting increased musical complexity is another matter, modest and acceptable.

Situations such as the following are encountered: the textual reference to the recondite "triple Hecate's team" (89; 5.1.384) had to stay in the libretto because it was inextricably embedded in necessary, alternately rhymed lines. Britten added no musical symbol in an attempt to make it intelligible—how could he?—but, he has it sung by all four of Tytania's named attendants, "we Fairies that do run," so that it becomes more plausible than when spoken in the play only by the Puck, not a true fairy at all.

All in all, there are opposing influences on intelligibility: Renaissance obscurities are gone, but some words are lost in the music; significant musical forms support the action and the dramatic pace is slower, but there are fewer explicit causal linkages within and between the plots. Arguably, the opera is, on balance, at least as intelligible as the comedy, a compliment to any librettist or operatic composer.

Simplicity is another criterion dependent on there being adequate material to apprehend, rather than too little or too much. The librettists simplified Puck's soliloquy and his two uncomfortable exchanges with Oberon in the play concerning the ill-fated anointings of Lysander and Demetrius. Britten does not attempt an impracticable musical restoration of the excised Shakespearean references to the sleeping maiden—part of the scenario that understandably misled Puck—but the music is charged with significant features that compensate for simplification. Through repetition, Puck emphasizes the pregnant "night and silence" and his delighted "who is here?" on spotting Lysander's weeds of Athens. A single, loud celesta figure, rushing down from and back up to E in a pair of E major septuplet runs harboring a cankerous Phrygian F♮, hints at Oberon's influence, although he is physically absent (117). When Puck has erroneously concluded that he has found his patient, Oberon's image returns for nine more conjoined down-up excursions, quietly overseeing Puck's ceremonious incantation, specially marked "slowly (without tempo)," until a final *crescendo* outburst snaps, leaving a prolonged dramatic silence. The suspended cymbal and F♯ tamburo have *ppp tremolandos,* while Puck's trumpet quietly flutters a meandering, constricted, cross-rhythmic melody that even traces a cambiata before bursting into a climactic five-note whole-tone scale, A♭ up to E, where it joins the celesta (118). Britten repeats this trick when Puck, the self-confessed "knavish lad, thus to make poor females mad," sees Hermia, exhausted, crawl to join the other sleeping lovers (310). The absent Oberon is even more influential: the celesta figure is an octave higher, sounded twice, louder, and features C and C♯ in false relation. The drastically reduced libretto text is handsomely rescued from oversimplification by the complex music.

When, finally out of patience, Oberon upbraids Puck for the repeated mishaps (289), Britten introduces a musical sequel to the climax just mentioned, in the form of a reconstructed whole-tone scale. Oberon recites his accusation, "this is thy negligence . . . ," on A♭, B♭, and C, the *Urmotiv* upside-down. There are wide gaps between the accompanying *fortissimo* A♭, B♭, and C major triads, their tonics in the outer voices, in harps and harpsichord; into these the timpani pound, four times, a quick *glissando* G♯, F♯, and E figure completing a transposition of the five-note whole-tone scale on Puck's trumpet mentioned in the preceding paragraph. The full meaning of these last triple *Urmotiv* tones on timpani is revealed when Oberon uses them for the crucial, accusatory word "wilfully" (290). Thus Britten adds interesting complexity on two levels: locally in the final Oberon-Puck showdown through the extended, tenser return of the whole-tone scale, and globally by tonally linking that with their previous discovery of wrong anointing where the impressionistic scale was introduced.

Britten follows operatic conventions in retaining musically inspired digressions from the drama and plot in the form of songs, dances, and purely instrumental numbers. These are not merely different from the speeches, movements, sets, and other media essential in a play; they react with them, adding a modicum of complexity to a basic libretto.

Making a libretto by halving a play, as in the *Dream,* necessarily simplifies the source; setting the text into music necessarily complicates the libretto. If the many varied subtleties of Britten's music and its functionality are understood, the opera is obviously not simpler, criteria other than the right degree of simplicity bear on the work's aesthetic worth and attractiveness.

Like exciting action and simplicity, clarity can be insultingly excessive or lacking, whereas it should be pleasingly veiled, suspenseful, and challenging. As a result of the librettists' restructuring and their excising of speeches commenting on connections between events, it was earlier adjudged that the libretto is more paratactic and that the immediate slight loss of clarity generates positive interpretative speculations, but a final assessment was withheld pending the consideration of the music's role. Granted the intelligibility of Britten's music and its thematic nature, it cannot fail to complement the librettists' achievement. Thematic repetitions and returns of musical passages establish or clarify links between the dramatic events and situations they accompany, integrating a plot or coupling plots, while the variations in the recurrences demonstrate that circumstances never repeat themselves exactly. Musical impulses and developments supplement dramatic progress, confirm likenesses, and discover differences; in short, they clarify.

Britten's added music deserves no charge of offensiveness. It is serious, in a language used and accepted before without offense. It is courteous to the words and action, deferential or taking the lead as occasion demands. The occasional apparent poke at the music of others—Beethoven, Schoenberg, the bel canto opera composers—is restrained and kindly; Britten's wit is often self-questioning, even self-mocking. Many in his audience, male and female World War II veterans, now respectable operagoers, would recollect the ribald and bawdy songs they enjoyed singing in the armed services a couple of decades earlier. Britten and Pears, although "Puritans both" according to Mitchell (*Britten and Auden*, 157), tolerated some of Shakespeare's sexual jokes, but Britten refrained from even hinting at available modern ribald musical glosses, wisely, because the carefully cultivated atmosphere of enchantment would have been dissipated. This kind of topicality is the worst for rapidly dating a composition, threatening early oblivion or unsatisfactory updating.

In discussing the need for drama in the libretto—for it to be excitingly eventful and psychologically plausible—the value of a happy mean, to be neither placidly boring nor sensationally overwhelming was emphasized. Without the music, which needs its own time to be functional at all, a libretto cannot establish an optimum pace for the dramatic elements, but Britten's and Pears's text did appear to be a sound basis for a satisfactorily paced score. The slower pace of events and situations caused by singing must be accepted, but their impact can be intensified by the music, and thus, in a way, the overall effect of the drama can be readjusted to a more attractive level by the musical devices that can go with singing. It was stated earlier, in effect, citing Doran, that acclaimed Renaissance drama by achieving multiple unity had outgrown the Aristotelian ideal of one action. Britten noted the distinct character groups in distinct actions, nevertheless interacting, and he welcomed the chance to use a different kind of texture and orchestral color for each section (Palmer, 177). Although this music does differentiate the actions, its ultimate effect is not to break them apart but to integrate them through the successive and the occasionally simultaneous deployment of themes and motives including the *Ur-motiv*'s derivatives, the recurrence of distinctive new devices such as the tonality sets and the consistency of style. The operatic *Dream*'s drama, put into Britten's music, acquires a pleasing pace and impressive variety in unity.

In the interests of dramatic pace, Britten excised or greatly shortened the great majority of the eighteen expanded images that David P. Young has designated as "full landscapes with a remarkable sense of spaciousness and distance . . . 'panoramas.'" Young sees them as functional in the play, providing "sketches of human activity" and "a contrast to the confinement of the woods." They contribute significantly "to the play's atmosphere of magic, spaciousness and limitless possibility, all attributes of the power of imagination" (75–81). Young refers to such things as Puck's pranks (33; 2.1.45), Titania's votaress's miming of pregnant sails (36; 2.1.132), and Hippolyta's hounds' musical discord (72; 4.1.118), all excised, no doubt for brevity's sake.

Britten occasionally relies on music alone to portray things cut from the play. Theseus's excursion from his hidebound court into the "Green World" to hunt and his return to civic responsibilities prepared to bend the patriarchal law on compassionate grounds is a sweeping dramatic movement in the play, interwoven with the lovers' own sylvan excursion, each with parallel, self-revealing results. Theseus's initial adamant posture and his retreat into nature (in which Hippolyta takes part) are cut from the libretto, but Britten subtly slips them back in. First, the significance of Peter Evans's interpretation of the two sets of horn passages, in the awakening and transitional scenes, can readily be extended further back to image the hunting prince as also lawgiver and administrator of justice. Second, as noted, the music played between the wood and the palace consists not only of the march but also of a noble *tutti* passage heralding a truly ducal couple into court. These additions create *dramma per musica,* "drama by means of music," one of the definitions of the very earliest operas, still fundamentally applicable.

Oberon's repentance for tormenting Tytania is a small-scale instance of a dramatic event portrayed briefly by music instead of tediously by text. In dialogue, the identities of the speaker and the person spoken to are certain; but when music functions as the commentator, it is not always clear which character, if any, is hearing it. Britten utilizes this unrestricted impact. As Oberon and Puck apear early in act 3, the normalizing morning music is playing, with the subtle modification that the viola figures are inverted to run downwards, the direction for an arrival. Tytania, perhaps, cannot hear the music because she is still asleep, but it does affect Oberon who, having received the changeling boy, begins to pity her dotage and will undo the hateful imperfection of her eyes (323). In the play (70; 4.1.47), he gives Puck a wordy account of how she came to give him the boy; Britten cut this retrospective explanation, making the disenchanting music help to dispel Oberon's vindictiveness and turn the plot.

Related to the topic of cuts to make the libretto is the attribute of opera described in chapter 1: "Music of an orchestra may reinstate rhetoric cut from the source." Much of Shakespeare's rhetoric was excised; did Britten's music put a form of rhetoric back into the opera? Britten certainly uses musical rhetoric in the sense of artistic significant forms designed to heighten the meaning and force of the musical elements of the opera, but they bear little direct reference to specific lost Renaissance figures, such as classical allusions, repetitions, or epic similes. Certainly Britten's appropriate association of textual and musical images falls short of archaic *Affektenlehre*. This, of course, is not to deny that, in the broader sense, operatic music is a rhetoric, making the plain words impress and persuade us mightily.

Although Britten rarely attempts a musical restoration of literal content, he often adds a characterizing gesture, which may confirm or vary Shakespeare's picture. The prankish rhythm and melody of Puck's trumpet's figures provide an open-ended substitute for his boastful account of his peccadillos, and Tytania's exercise of her dominant coloratura voice says more for her firmness than the excised logic of her devotion to the changeling's mother. Hippolyta loses other things than her patrician agreement with Theseus over the hounds; one misses more her disagreement with him over the poet's imagination. But promoting her by Britten to dramatic and musical critic of *Pyramus and Thisby* partially restores her lost status; she becomes a leading stage audience participant rather than an exotic ornament. These musically inspired changes in characterization react positively on the drama, and they, with the many others mentioned earlier, illustrate the frequently exercized operatic prerogative of altering the absolute and relative importance of elements of the source play.

Britten subtly introduces changes of these kinds into his *Dream* with noticeable scope for varied audience interpretation that probably reflects his deliberate ambiguity of artistic vision, which Mitchell describes (*L'innovatore* 45). But, wait; it was stated earlier, among the operatic attributes under "didacticism," that Britten had strong points of view to which he found opera could give expression. In this lighthearted comedy, Britten is reticent with his views, gently respectful of his audience's opinions; in other works, such as the antimilitaristic *Owen Wingrave,* his message is blatant. Following upon this point, one may wonder how the deliberate ambiguity of artistic vision, which Mitchell ascribes to Britten, squares with the apparently opposite vision, which Howard detected (described in chapter 2). In her opinion, the opera "presents a singie interpretation of the comprehensive material of the play, . . . its narrow reading reveals some aspects in compensatingly greater depth"?

Howard is right. The play has two mortal wedding plots: the

ducal nuptials celebrating a victory by the sword superseded by rational love, and the lovers' nuptials entailing self-directed amours leading to verbal combat. The ducal wedding, where the wishes of authority and power prevail, is declared to be the ideal state by its preceding and following festivities, and it is strategically announced and presented as a model for the emotionally immature lovers. The opera fails to set the ducal marriage up as an ideal, and, without the model, the lovers (unaware of the faery interventions) themselves achieve their desired pairings unaided. No Egeus on stage, a harsh law barely touched on, no nunnery looming in the background—there is a single interpretation of the main dramatic theme, "love aspiring to and consummated in marriage" (Brooks, cxxx). The interplay with musical themes, culminating in the tonality set as the lovers awake (see example, 7.3[e]), adds depth to the central action.

Mitchell can simultaneously maintain Britten's deliberate ambiguity of artistic vision. Britten leaves it open to the audience to approve or disapprove of the decline, even disappearance, of parental authority. Indeed, by reducing the tragic rebellious elopement of Pyramus and Thisbe to a farce, he seems to say that the members of the theater audience, patriarchs or otherwise, must, like himself but unlike the predominantly frivolous stage audience, see the possible different messages emanating from the action, evaluate them, and take sides.

Generally speaking, Britten matches the textual dramatic events with musical meanings, rather than counteracting them. Naming a few previously discovered examples will suffice to demonstrate this: varied, unstable tonality sets raise the tension in dramatic crises; word, action, and sound paintings add a further touch of humor to amusing moments; slithering portamenti project the wood's elusive influences; imperfect cadences precede changes of direction that should not be missed; full closes do more than finalize a movement, they leave an impression to be pondered, or they suggest a sequel; and organized musical confusion aggravates textual complication, rendering it partially or wholly unintelligible. There appear to be no small-scale musical counteractions to the libretto's dramatic situations, but an extended ironic intermedia relationship is brilliantly portrayed in the *Pyramus and Thisby* metaopera. From the broader perspective, significant musical forms unify the drama by their thematic appearances, producing a unity that, by virtue of the generative function of the *Urmotiv* and the developmental variations in the motives on their repetitions and returns, is organic.

Following the conclusion that Britten generally matches the textual dramatic events with the musical meaning, one can critically examine some of the statements in his *Observer* article (Palmer, 198), referred to earlier, and their implications. In chapter 1, Britten was quoted as saying that the "strong verbal music" in Shakespeare's *Dream* and the music he had written for it "are at two quite different levels"; it was noted that it remains to be seen whether he did manage to preserve both musics. Britten's music, like all music, is organized sound, just as Shakespeare's poetry, particularly his verse, is organized sound, but the one disciplines the sounds of many different instruments, while the other disciplines only the sounds of the human voice while speaking. Because the human voice is a medium common to spoken drama and opera and because the musical organization, by significant sung and orchestral forms, can powerfully supplement the tones of voice available to a speaker, there exists a potential for rational and emotional meanings between the different "levels." With Shakespeare's own "musical" words preserved in the libretto and the composer's music generally supporting them, Britten's "different levels" concept can be seen as a pregnant truism that he makes productive.

Immediately after his "different levels" opinion, Britten continues: "I haven't tried to put across any particular idea of the play that I could not equally well express in words, but although one doesn't intend to make any special interpretation, one cannot avoid it" (Palmer, 178). This somewhat unclear statement is taken to signify that he intended to let the text of the libretto express the meaning, essentially the same meaning, as the words of the source play, but that his music unavoidably changed emphases. That this happened is revealed by the conclusion that Britten usually makes his music match textual meanings rather than counteract them, and by the contrary opinion, which others support, that, for instance, supernatural forces are emphasized in the opera at the expense of traditional hereditary or military authority.

Like any well-structured music, Britten's builds a hierarchy of large- and small-scale forms that regulate the dramatic actions through the tensing and releasing characteristics Wallace Berry noted in successive stages of a typical passage. Obvious longer-term articulatory passages that clarify the *Dream*'s progress from one atmosphere to another and from one setting to another are the wood music, sleep music, morning music, and transition march, as they reveal stereotyical or distinctive structures such as ritornelli or binary forms in solo instrumental and accompanimental functions. Britten's featuring of the celesta to indicate Oberon's spiritual presence when Puck anoints Lysander was cited as a complication: it is also a small-scale musical clarification, obviating a time-consuming soliloquy. The later repetition of the figure, when Puck observes Hermia's exhaustion, performs a third function, a unification, connecting separated scenes of impending confusion and hopeful denouement. But the highest dividend from the formal hierarchy is the unity of the opera as a whole derived from such progressions as the overall tonal sharping and the pianissimo to forte dynamics, cemented by the rondo of such forms as the Scotch snap and the tonality set.

The almost complete loss of philosophical statements and other merely conceptual, commentative material from the text must, in a sense, make the opera immediately less philosophical; it requires an accommodation to accept without complaint the excision of such famous passages as Theseus's on imagination. But can one not philosophically recognize, without being explicitly told, that both works, comedy and opera, as wholes are demonstrations of the immense power of imagination?

A statement of Linderberger's that probes behind the simple loss of philosophical statements needs examination. He stated that two things in opera cause it to "impress its audience as ultimately more philosophical than spoken drama." First, "the composer subjects human actions to the tight logic of musical form." Britten surely does this in the examples given of humorous and other short significant constructs, and in the ritornello and the passacaglia that unify and articulate the scenes in acts 1 and 2, respectively. Second, "the composer seems to raise these [human] actions to a more mythical, more universal level." As to this philosophical operatic feature, Britten's changes are less emphatic. In a literal sense, much of the play's mythology is excised as obscure, and Theseus's control is drastically reduced. On the other hand, the influence of the fairies, particularly Oberon's, is increased, and the substitution of a framing supernatural aura for that of a particular legend can be treated as setting the drama on a more universal level. Arguably, Lindenberger's general view obtains in Britten's *Dream,* but it remains subtle and elusive.

Lindenberger's further view of "opera's ability to impose inevitability on action" (54), can be argued. One expects from the comedic opening of Shakespeare's *Dream* that young love will triumph—

unless the *Romeo and Juliet* story, also featuring disobedience to parental plans, intrudes as a likely pattern. Through the loss of Theseus's specific threatened punishments for Hermia, the opera already seems more likely to end by endorsing inherent youthful freedom of choice. But perhaps the most powerful operatic feature making for an expected resolution is the simple need for the music to end promptly with the dialogue. When, as is usually the case, that ending supports the ending of the story, comedic or tragic, the outcome seems more than ever to have been unavoidable. In the operatic *Dream,* musical moods supporting the verbally narrated behests at the end of both Oberon's and Puck's comedic dismissals are present. Finally, one remembers that Britten, the artist who declared himself deeply, inextricably within society, had called opera the most powerful medium of communication he knew.

Britten and conventions?—he carefully said only that he noted them; it was pondered at the outset how far he and Pears respected or defied them. A review of the attributes applicable to an opera of this type listed in chapter 1 (some seventy, although a few are similar) shows that, except to conserve the source—surprisingly maintaining those challenging Shakespearean words, such great poetry—they adhered to all but the trivial norms. Peter Evans's observation that Britten was "fairly near a norm of indebtedness to past practice" was interpreted as circuitously labeling him as mainstream. This study of Britten making his *Dream* confirms this, but, emphatically, not with any pejorative overtones. Citing many instances of musical originality, following Mitchell, Britten has been dubbed "the silent innovator," a status perfectly consistent with a mainstream artist, although it is not the business of this study to incorporate here details of the evidence Mitchell adduces for Britten's musical creativity and eclecticism in other works.

In the opinion of Frank Kermode, *A Midsummer Night's Dream* was "Shakespeare's best comedy" by virtue of an intense sophistication, marked intellectual content, elaborate and ingenious thematic development, and comic equilibrium (214, 216). A reordered synthesis of the foregoing specialized evaluations of the opera that Britten and Pears made from it clearly designates it as a modern work, different in impact, but at least as attractive as the Renaissance masterpiece. With its fewer words put into music, the opera is full-length, an economical production unit and neither too long nor too short for an audience seeking a complete afternoon's or evening's entertainment. With Shakespearean words retained and bowdlerization discredited, there is no real risk of offense in the mid-twentieth century with its greater freedom of expression.

Still summarizing, it is considered that the intelligibility of Britten's opera, to a sympathetic but critical operagoer is at least equal to the play's intelligibility to a playgoer with similar attitudes. As a result of the added music's supportive functioning with the attenuated words, the drama is, on balance, improved; the slightly fewer events are more exciting and richer in psychological implications. As between play and opera, the adaptation confers some acceptable complexity by musically inventing additional relations between actions. This additional content, like lovers' and madmen's shaping fantasies to Shakespeare's Theseus's mind, poses further questions to be apprehended. But the whole, when comprehended, is both clear yet ambivalent. As Hippolyta might conclude, it is "strange, and admirable" (78; 1.27).

An opera audience requires many sensory and intellectual skills to become satisfied with all aspects of works of "the extravagant art" (as Lindenberger approvingly labels opera), and the exercise of those skills is pleasurable irrespective of the works' aesthetic qualities. Since it is a highly refined chamber opera, Britten's *Dream* is perhaps less extravagant than most other works in the current repertoire, but the challenge of adequately responding to the rich depth of his musical setting succeeds in making the work genuinely attractive, attesting that Britten has, as aimed, written "dramatically effective music for the theatre."

Appendix A
Performances of Britten's Opera
A Midsummer Night's Dream

Table A.1 Performances of Britten's Opera A Midsummer Night's Dream, 1960–1988.

Country	Number of score leasings, and "seasons" (S)[1]	Number of performances
United Kingdom[2]	67	101
		+ 348 (estimated)[3]
United States	54	175
Italy	3 (S)	13
Austria	6 (S)	40
		+ 40 (estimated)[4]
Canada	5	16
Australia and New Zealand	6 (S)	42
Argentina	1 (S)	7
Total	142	782

Source: Boosey & Hawkes Music Publishers Limited, England, and their overseas branches and agents. Agents in Germany and Sweden did not reply to inquiries.

1. In order to maximize the number of replies received, raw data or summaries was requested in the format most readily available. The data gathered, therefore, often indicated different units of performance. A "leasing" of the opera score and parts to a renter is the best available index of performance; in fact, it usually indicates a group of performances. It appears to be roughly equivalent, for our purpose, to a "season" in which an opera company performs the work several times, possibly using company-owned scores and parts; hence the selection of these units and their combination in the tabulation. Doubtful data, such as performances indicated as possibly less than fully staged, are excluded.

2. Of these leasings, ten were to countries in continental Europe other than Italy and Austria. Four were to companies in Japan.

3. Estimated on the basis of fifty-two leasings with an average of 6.7 performances per leasing—the average for the fifteen leasings in the United Kingdom for which the number of performances was stated.

4. Estimated on the basis of three seasons with an average of 13.3 performances

209

per season, the average for the three seasons in Austria for which the number of performances was stated.

The steady success of this opera is proven by the 142 leasings and "seasons" and their distribution among the quinquennia elapsed since its composition, namely: in the period beginning 1960, 25; 1965, 18; 1970, 24; 1975, 32; 1980, 25; and 1985, 18. The peak in the 1975 period is possibly explained by renewed interest following Britten's death in 1976; the 1985 figures are for fewer than five years. The locations of the estimated 782 performances were widely distributed: in the United Kingdom, in many different centers in England, Scotland, and Wales; in the United States, in twenty-two continental states and the District of Columbia. Forty of the leasings in these two countries were to universities and other teaching institutions where, most probably, public performances were given. Of the Metropolitan Opera House (New York), the Royal Opera House, Covent Garden, La Scala, Milan, and the Vienna State Opera (the "big four," [Harries and Harries, 3], only the "Met" did not appear in the gathered data. The New York City Opera, however, was cited with leasings in two separate years.

A supplement to the foregoing statistics, confined to the two leading countries in the table, shows the following additional performances between 1988 and mid-1992:

	Number of score leasings	Number of performances
United Kingdom (from mid-1987)	6	30
United States (from mid-1988)	16	44

The average number of performances per year for the two countries are:

	Earlier period	Later period
United Kingdom	17	6
United States	6	11

Reasons for the changes in popularity have not been sought.

Appendix B
Biographical Notes

Benjamin Britten

Edward Benjamin Britten was born in the year 1913, on 22 November, St. Cecilia's day, in the town of Lowestoft in the county of Suffolk, England, and died at The Red House, Aldeburgh, in the same county, aged 63, on 4 December 1976. His first forename was unused in practice; it does not even appear on his black marble tombstone in the churchyard of the parish church of SS Peter and Paul, appropriately named after the biblical fishermen, in the North Sea fishing town of Aldeburgh.

He was famous as performer (piano), conductor, and, especially, composer. Peter Evans's *The Music of Benjamin Britten* lists works published from 1932 (op. 1) to 1975 (op. 95) and other musical works (551–59), while Kennedy's *Britten,* in the Master Musician Series, in its classified list of works, lists twelve operas from *Paul Bunyan* (1941) and *Peter Grimes* (1945) to *Owen Wingrave* (1970) and *Death in Venice* (1973), including the tenth, *A Midsummer Night's Dream* (op. 64, 1960) (297–98).

Britten was much honored in his own country: he was created a Companion of Honour in 1953, received the Order of Merit in 1965, and was created a life peer, Baron Britten of Aldeburgh in the county of Suffolk, in 1976. In 1964, at Aspen, Colorado, he received the first Aspen Award to honor "the individual anywhere in the world judged to have made the greatest contribution to the advancement of the humanities." The citation read: "To Benjamin Britten, who, as a brilliant composer, performer, and interpreter through music of human feelings, moods, and thoughts, has truly inspired man to understand, clarify and appreciate more fully his own nature, purpose and destiny" (Britten, *Aspen,* 8).

This award has a twofold relevance in this book: it is one instance among many showing that Britten's success in composing *A Midsummer Night's Dream* was something to be expected from a supremely competent composer, rendering the opera's popularity and artistic value unsurprising. Second, the award elicited valuable statements from Britten in his acceptance speech, which, according to E. M. Forster, was a rare "confession of faith from a great musician" and which, according to Mitchell, "remains the only statement of its kind that Britten made" (Britten, *Aspen,* front cover, 7).

Jeremy Cullum

Jeremy Cullum, interviewed at the Britten-Pears Library on 12 August 1988, was Britten's secretary from ca. 1952 to 1970. He was a cathedral chorister in St. Paul's, London, and, as a World War II child evacuee, in Truro, Cornwall. He was organist of the Aldeburch parish church. Britten created a special part for him in the first performance of the *Dream*, recorded in the program as an Attendant upon Theseus. Notes of the interview appear in Appendix C.

Imogen Holst

Palmer, editor of *The Britten Companion*, describing his contributors states (457–58): "[She] was . . . Britten's amanuensis and music assistant from 1952 to 1964. . . . Her book on Britten in Faber's Great Composers series was revised for a third edition in 1980." In her 1977 article for *Musical Times*, (reproduced in Palmer as "Working for Benjamin Britten (I)" [46–50]), she convinces one that she is his faithful biographer and that she was personally, conscientiously, even meticulously, involved in ensuring that his scores were exact expressions of his clearly stated intentions. One of her unexpected jobs was "rehearsing the 'tongs and bones' number in *A Midsummer Night's Dream*," the instrumental performance by Tytania's fairies in response to Bottom's request for music. Her grave is near those of Britten and Pears in Aldeburgh, reflecting the dates 1907–84.

Donald Mitchell

Kennedy, in his appendix C: "Personalia" (322), introduces Donald Mitchell:

(b. 1925), English publisher, critic and writer. Joint editor, with Hans Keller, of symposium on Britten's music, 1952. Music critic for *Musical Times* 1953–57 *Daily Telegraph* 1959–64. Editor of *Tempo* 1958–62.

Palmer ("Contributors," 458–59) adds: "Mitchell is engaged in writing the authorized biography and critical study of Britten's works."

Mitchell was the composer's close friend and publisher from the 1960s but has been a student and advocate of his music for far longer. He was professor of music at the University of Sussex. His many publications include works on Mozart, Mahler, and Britten.

Peter Pears

Peter (Neville Luard) Pears was born on 10 June 1910, at Farnham Surrey, England, and died on 3 April 1986 at Orford, near Aldeburgh. His fame as a tenor, both in lieder and opera, is international, particularly as an interpreter of the works of Britten, who wrote many of his compositions with a view to their performance by Pears. He was knighted in 1977. His friendship with Britten began in 1937; they lived together in Aldeburgh (Crag House from 1947, The Red House from 1957) and lie in adjacent graves with matching memorial headstones.

Pears played a significant part in writing the working libretto for Britten's *A Midsummer Night's Dream*. Of his literary activities, apart from the *Dream* libretto, the *New Grove Dictionary of Music* mentions that he translated works by Schutz and Bach, and Paul Wilson's bibliography in *A Britten Source Book* lists well over a hundred articles, principally in the Aldeburgh Festival programme books from 1949 to 1985. Persons who knew them both said that he and Britten never traveled without volumes of English poetry in their pockets.

Rosamund Strode

Palmer's notes on his contributors reveal (459–50) that

Rosamund Strode studied at the Royal College of Music, and at Dartington Hall under Imogen Holst. After some years as a freelance musician, she came to work for Britten in 1963, succeeding Imogen Holst as his music assistant the following year. Since the composer's death she has continued to work for the Britten Estate and, as the Britten-Pears Library's Keeper of Manuscripts and Archivist, for the Britten-Pears Foundation.

She worked for Britten during the composition of the *Dream*. Her article in Palmer's book, "Working for Benjamin Britten (II)" (51–1), confirms her hero's control over the grand and minute aspects of all the many musical tasks he undertook. Her description of the intricacies of composing and publishing an opera score reveal the problems that would arise in a textual analysis of materials pertinent and peripheral to this study. Notes of interviews with her appear in appendix C.

Paul Wilson

Paul S. Wilson, MA, ALA, Librarian, The Britten-Pears Library (as styled in letters and in person during the author's visits to Aldeburgh in 1987 and 1988), displayed for inspection and supplied details of archival and other material in the library. He gave invaluable leads to additional personal and material sources, and, in other professional and personal ways, greatly assisted the researches. He is joint compiler, with John Evans and Philip Reed, of *A Britten Source Book*.

Appendix C
Interviews with Resource Persons

Jeremy Cullum

The author talked with Jeremy Cullum at the Britten-Pears Library on 12 August 1989 with the working libretto and Benjamin Britten's and Peter Pears's Penguin Shakespeare *A Midsummer Night's Dream* texts before us. The author pointed out that one of his aims was to identify respective changes to the text made before and during composition. Following is a report of the substance of the topics discussed in the order in which they arose. Parenthetical numerical references are to the working libretto in the Britten-Pears Library.

Cullum colorfully defined his period of secretaryship to Britten as from *Gloriana* [1953] to *Owen Wingrave* [1971].

Concerning the *Dream,* he had worked partly at Britten's residence, the Red House, with the librettists, and partly at his own home. No one else had helped with the typing. The number of typings varied, sometime once was enough, sometimes retyping was required. He indicated that there were probably two copies of each typing, a top copy and a carbon copy. (But see below.)

Asked what was his "copy" for the working libretto of the *Dream* and what was its quality, Cullum stated that it was Pears's Penguin copy of the play and that it was much annotated.

He stated that he dealt mainly with Pears, but also with Britten—with no one else. Concerning procedures, Cullum recollected that he received the copy from Pears and that, when typed and proofread by himself, he gave it to Britten. He indicated that mistakes were corrected from Britten's notes or instructions.

The author asked if Cullum could identify his own hand among the many diverse manuscript corrections. He pointed out some of his amendments, including one to "the honey-bags steal . . . humble bees" (47).

Cullum was asked to comment on the "Attendant" role given to him by Britten in the first performance. He said that he carried the umbrella for Hippolyta, as depicted in the photographic illustration on the cover of the vocal score.

Concerning the obviously fewer manuscript amendments to the typing in act 1 as compared to acts 2 and 3, Cullum thought that act 1 was probably retyped to go into the printed libretto. He could not recollect why acts 2 and 3 were not retyped.

Cullum stated that Britten was composing the opera while typing was going on and that the act 1 retyping was probably done during composition.

The author pointed to some ensemble brackets in the left margins (e.g., 26), some ruled, some freehand, asking who inserted them, librettists or composer. Cullum stated that if the brackets were ruled they were by him, if freehand, by Britten.

Concerning carbon copies, Cullum thought a page (25a) in the working libretto was a carbon. This suggests, in view of the use by Imogen Holst of a carbon copy to prepare the vocal score, that *two* carbon copies were made, rather than one, contrary to the report above. The page looked to the author like a top copy made with a different typewriter ribbon.

Not surprisingly, even if he had participated, Cullum could not now explain how there came to be manuscript, two-stage corrections to the typescript, for example, ink corrections over pencil ones (44, 69, and 75 verso), or how speeches separate in Harrison came to be conflated in the libretto (18).

The author did not get the opportunity to ask Cullum how the Holst carbon copy, used to prepare the vocal score, was kept in step with the master copy which was constantly being changed by librettists and composer. Cullum did some proofreading of the vocal score for Holst and found a wrong note.

Rosamund Strode

The author had a number of interviews with Rosamund Strode during a visit to the Britten-Pears Library, 8–18 August 1988. She volunteered many vivid recollections (not all reported here, and none verbatim) of events during the incident packed periods she worked for Britten.

RS: The vocal score was printed by Boosey & Hawkes before the first performance, a procedure generally disapproved of by Britten, who liked to get things quite right before publishing.

RS: Moth was given a small part by Britten so that he would not feel left out when the other fairies sang. [The score calls for an "M . . ." (220) and an "H . . ." (226), both oversung by Tytania; Harrison's Shakespeare has nothing for Moth in the corresponding places (52; 3.1.196 and 69; 4.1.26)].

RS: Britten was strong on planning well integrated programs.

RS: Britten was reluctant to write about his own music, holding that the music should function without verbal explanation.

RS: Britten paid no attention to critics: he never read them.

Strode was unable to keep a further appointment at which some clarifications and further information were due, including her opinion as a singer whether certain of Britten's changes, for example between "you" and "thee," had been made to permit more accurate vowel enunciation at certain pitches. It was arranged that the author would write to her later, if found necessary.

Appendix D
The Britten-Pears Library

An explanatory leaflet (July 1992) describes the Britten-Pears Library. The library was assembled over the years by Benjamin Britten and Peter Pears and is now the property of the Britten-Pears Foundation. It is housed in specially designed premises, adjacent to the Red House in Aldeburgh.

The main areas of holdings are:

1. **music manuscripts:** "a unique collection of the manuscripts of Benjamin Britten's compositions, comprising the vast majority of the works written from early boyhood until his death," [including] "a number of important manuscripts belonging to the national collection at the British Library, which are deposited in the Britten-Pears Library on permanent loan.";

2. **other papers:** a large collection of Britten's correspondence and several draft librettos;

3. **the general library** of English song, literature, annotated scores, "poetry, drama and other subjects, among which there is important source material for students of Britten's life and works"; and

4. **the general archive:** printed ephemera, etc., photographs, sound and film, and the archive of the English Opera Group/English Music Theatre Company from 1947 to 1981)

The Library is open to scholars and research students by appointment. Enquiries are to be addressed to the Librarian, The Britten-Pears Library, The Red House, Aldeburgh, Suffolk, IP15 5PZ, England. Tel: (0728) 452615; Fax: (0728) 453076.

Appendix E
Statistical Analyses of Tonality Sets and Pandiatonic Passage

Tonality Sets

Table E.1. Root Movements within Tonality Sets in Britten's Opera *A Midsummer Night's Dream*. (In number of semitones, up [+] or down [−] (e.g., 7 shown as 5, 8 as 4, 9 as 3, 10 as 2, 11 as 1.)

Item number in set	1	2	3	4	5	6	7	8	9	10	11	12[1]
Tonality set												
(a)	−1	−4	+2	+5	+4	−5	−5	−3	−2	−5	6	
(b)	−5	+3	+4	+3	−1	+4	+3	+4	+3	+3	+4	
(c)	6	+1	+2	−4	−4	−5	+3	+4	−5	+4	+2	
(d)[2]	+4	+3	6	+4	+3	+2	−4	−4	−5	+2	+4	
(e)	−2	+1	−2	+4	+2	+2	−3	+4	+1	−3	+4	
(g)	−5	−1	+3	6	−1	−1	−2	−1	6	+1	+3	

Source: Example 7.3
1. Sonorities not numbered in the examples are ignored.
2. These figures, not true root movements, record the movements between tones, highest to lowest, within each of the four chords and from chord to chord.

Table E-1 shows the variety within and between the tonality sets.

Table E.2. Frequencies of Root Movements within Tonality Sets in Britten's Opera *A Midsummer Night's Dream*, by Size of Movement. (The headings show tonal equivalents of semitonal movements: up [+] or down [−]; TT = tritone, M = major, m = minor.)

Root movement	6 +TT −TT	+5 +P4 −P5	+4 +M3 −m6	+3 +m3 −M6	+2 +M2 −m7	+1 +m2 −M7	−1 −m2 +M7	−2 −M2 +m7	−3 −m3 +M6	−4 −M3 +m6	−5 −P4 +P5
Tonality set											
(a)	1	1	1	·	1	·	1	1	1	1	3
(b)	·	·	4	5	·	·	1	·	·	·	1
(c)	1	·	2	1	2	1	·	·	·	2	2
(e)	·	·	3	·	2	2	·	2	2	·	·
(g)	2	·	·	2	·	1	4	1	·	·	1
Total[1] [55]	4	1	10	8	5	4	6	4	3	3	7

Source: Table E.1
1. The harmonic tonality set (d) is excluded.

Table E.3. Repeated Root Movements within Tonality Sets in Britten's Opera *A Midsummer Night's Dream*. (In number of semitones and tonal equivalents, up [+] or down [−].)

Repeated root movement, by size and nature	Set	Location Between items
−3, +3; +m3 (or −M6), +m3 (or −M6) [outlines a diminished triad]	(b)	9–11
+2, +2; +M2 (or −m7), +M2 (or −m7)	(e)	5–7
−1, −1 −m2 (or −M7), −m2 (or +M7)	(g)	5–7
−4, −4 −M3 (or +m6), −M3 (or +m6) [outlines an augmented triad]	(c)[1]	4–6
−5, −5 −P4 (or +P5), −P4 (or +P5)	(a)	6–8[2]

Source: Table E.1

1. A pseudorepetition between items 7 and 9 of harmonic tonality set (d) is excluded from this figure.

2. This table shows a total of five repeated root movements out of a total of fifty (ten possible in each of five sets).

Table E.4. Repeated Sequences of Root Movements within Tonality Sets in Britten's Opera *A Midsummer Night's Dream*. (In number of semitones and tonal equivalents, up [+] or down [−].)

Sequence of root movements repeated, by size	Set	Locations Between numbers
+3, +4, +3; +m3 (or −M6), +M3 (or −m6),	(b)	2–5
+m3 (or −M6)	(b)	7–10
−5, +3, +4; −P4 (or +P5), +m3 (or −M6),	(b)	1–4[1]
+M3 (or −m6)	(c)	6–9

Source: Table E.1

1. This table shows a total of two repeated sequences of root movements out of a total of forty-five (nine possible in each of five sets).

Table E.5. Number of Major and Minor Triads Outlined by Root Movements within Tonality Sets in Britten's Opera *A Midsummer Night's Dream.*

	Location	Number
Major triad, up:		
+4, +3;	Set (b)	3
+M3 (or −m6), +m3 (or −M6)		
Minor triad, up:	Set (b)	3[1]
+3, +4;		
+m3 (or −M6), +M3 (or −m6)	Set (c)	1

Source: Table E.1
1. This table shows a total of seven major or minor triads outlined within root movements out of a total of fifty (ten possible in each of five sets).

Pandiatonic Passage

Table E.6. Durations of Tones in the First Thirty Measures of Pandiatonic "Morning Music" Opening Act 3 of Britten's Opera *A Midsummer Night's Dream.* (By sections[1] and levels. Unit: levels 2–4 = quarter note sounding; level 1 = eighth note sounding. Predominant tones in **bold** figures; totals in brackets.)

Level(s)	Tone	Section(s) 1	2	3	4	5	1–5
4	E	—	—	**11**	**14**	3	28
Violins	D	—	—	1	1	1	3
I	C	—	—	—	—	—	—
	B♭	—	—	—	—	—	—
	A	—	—	—	—	2	2
	G	—	—	6	2	3	11
	F	—	—	6	1	3	10
				[24]	[18]	[12]	[54]
3	E	—	—	—	—	2	2
Violins	D	—	4	**8**	—	4	16
II	C	—	5	9	2	4	20
	B♭	—	**11**	6	**13**	1	31
	A	—	1	1	3	—	5
	G	—	—	—	—	—	—
	F	—	—	—	—	1	1
		[21]	[24]	[18]	[12]		[75]

		1	2	3	4	5	
2 Violins III	E	—	—	—	—	—	—
	D	—	—	—	—	1	1
	C	—	—	—	—	3	3
	B♭	2	5	6	1	3	17
	A	3	6	8	1	3	21
	G	9	10	9	15	2	45
	F	1	—	1	1	—	3
		[15]	[21]	[24]	[18]	[12]	[90]
1 Violas	E	—	—	—	—	3	3
	D	—	—	—	3	4	7
	C	—	—	—	3	5	8
	B♭	—	—	—	3	3	6
	A	—	—	—	—	—	—
	G	—	—	—	—	—	—
	F	—	—	—	—	1	1
					[9]	[16]	[25]
All levels combined	E	—	—	11	14	8	33
	D	—	4	9	4	10	27
	C	—	5	9	5	12	31
	B♭	2	16	12	17	7	54
	A	3	7	9	4	5	28
	G	9	10	15	17	5	56
	F	1	—	7	2	5	15
		[15]	[42]	[72]	[63]	[52]	[244]

1. Sections: 1 = 321[1–5]; 2 = 321[6–12]; 3 = 321[13–20]; 4 = 321[21]–322[3]; and 5 = 322[4–7].

Table E-6 shows the relative prominence of tones by agogic accent.

Works Cited

Editions: Britten

Britten, Benjamin. *A Midsummer Night's Dream: Opera in Three Acts, op. 64*. Libretto adapted from William Shakespeare by Benjamin Britten and Peter Pears. Score. London: Boosey & Hawkes, 1960.

———. *A Midsummer Night's Dream: An Opera in Three Acts Adapted from William Shakespeare by Benjamin Britten and Peter Pears*. Music by Benjamin Britten. Libretto. London: Boosey & Hawkes, 1960.

———. *A Midsummer Night's Dream: Opera in Three Acts, op. 64*. Cond. Benjamin Britten. London Symphony Orch. and vocalists. Decca, 3-LP records, SET/MET 338–40, 1967.

Britten, Benjamin, and Peter Pears. *A Midsummer Night's Dream*. Complete Libretto. Benjamin Britten's working copy. Typescript. Britten-Pears Library, Aldeburgh.

Editions: Shakespeare

Allen, Michael J. B., and Kenneth Muir, eds. *Shakespeare's Plays in Quarto: A Facsimile Edition of Copies Primarily from the Henry E. Huntington Library*. Berkeley and Los Angeles: University of California Press, 1981.

Blackwell, Basil. *The Works of William Shakespeare Gathered into One Volume*. Oxford: Shakespeare Head Press, 1934.

Evans, G. Blakemore, et al. *The Riverside Shakespeare*. Boston: Houghton, 1974.

Brooks, Harold F., ed. *A Midsummer Night's Dream*. The Arden Edition of the Works of William Shakespeare. London: Methuen, 1979.

Griggs, William. *Shakespeare's Midsummer Night's Dream, The First Quarto, 1600: A Facsimile in Photo-Lithography*. London: W. Griggs, 1880.

Harrison, G. B., ed. *A Midsummer Night's Dream*. Penguin Shakespeare. Revised edition 1937. Harmondsworth: Penguin, 1953.

Hinman, Charlton, preparer. *The First Folio of Shakespeare*. The Norton Facsimile. New York: Norton, 1968.

Quiller-Couch, Sir Authur, and John Dover Wilson, eds. *A Midsummer Night's Dream*. Cambridge: Cambridge University Press, 1924.

Shakespeare: A Reprint of his Collected Works as Put Forth in 1623: Part I Containing the Comedies. London: Lionel Booth, 1862.

Secondary Sources

Apel, Willi. "Dotted notes. III: Inverted dotting." *Harvard Dictionary of Music*. Cambridge: Harvard University Press, 1969.

Bach, Jan Morris. "An Analysis of Britten's *A Midsummer Night's Dream*" (with original composition by author: *Spectra*). D.M.A. diss., University of Illinois, 1971.

Barber, C. L. *Shakespeare's Festive Comedy: A Study of Dramatic Form and Its Relation to Social Custom.* Cleveland, Ohio: Meridian-World Publishing, 1963.

Berry, Ralph. *Shakespeare and Social Class.* Atlantic Highlands, N.J.: Humanities Press International, 1988.

Berry, Wallace. *Structural Functions in Music.* Englewood Cliffs, N.J.: Prentice-Hall, 1976.

Boosey & Hawkes. Letters to W. Godsalve, 23 Mar. 1988 to 17 Aug. 1992.

Brett, Philip. "'Fiery Visions' (and revisions): 'Peter Grimes' in progress." In *Benjamin Britten: Peter Grimes,* compiled by Philip Brett, 47–87. Cambridge Opera Handbooks. Cambridge: Cambridge University Press, 1983.

Britten, Benjamin. "Communicator: An Interview with England's Best-Known Composer" (In interview with Elizabeth Forbes). *Opera News* 31 (11 Feb. 1967):16.

———. "An Interview" (an interview with Charles Osborne). *London Magazine,* n.s. 3, no. 7 (1963):91–96.

———. "Introduction." In *Grand Opera: The Story of the World's Leading Opera Houses and Personalities,* edited by Anthony Gishford, 11–12. New York: Studio-Viking, 1972.

———. "Mapreading" (A conversation with Donald Mitchell). In *The Britten Companion,* edited by Christopher Palmer, 87–96. Cambridge: Cambridge University Press, 1984.

———. "A New Britten Opera." *Observer Weekend Review,* 5 June 1960. Reprinted as "The Composer's *Dream.*" In *The Britten Companion,* edited by Christopher Palmer, 177–80. Cambridge: Cambridge University Press, 1984.

———. *On Receiving the First Aspen Award* (Speech, 1964). London: Faber, 1978.

———. "On Writing English Opera." *Opera* 12 (1961):7–8.

———. "Speech, On Receiving an Honorary Degree from Hull University, 1962." *London Magazine,* n.s. 3, no. 7 (1963):89–91.

Browning, Alexandra. Interview, 1 Oct. 1989.

Burridge, Christina J. "'Music, Such as Charmeth Sleep': Benjamin Britten's *A Midsummer Night's Dream.*" *University of Toronto Quarterly* 51 (1981–82):149–60.

Conrad, Peter. *A Song of Love and Death: The Meaning of Opera.* New York: Poseidon Press, 1987.

———. *Romantic Opera and Literary Form.* Berkeley and Los Angeles: University of California Press, 1977.

Cooke, Mervyn. "Dramatic and musical cohesion in Britten's *A Midsummer Night's Dream.*" DPh. diss., Cambridge Music Tripos Part II, King's College, 1984.

Copland, Aaron. *What to Listen for in Music.* Revised edition 1939; reprinted New York: New American Library, n. d.

Cullum, Jeremy. Interview. 12 Aug. 1988. (In appendix C.)

Dean, Winton. "Shakespeare and Opera." In *Shakespeare in Music,* edited by Phyllis Hartnoll, 89–175. London: Macmillan, 1964.

Donington, Robert. *The Rise of Opera*. London: Faber, 1981.

Doran, Madeleine. *Endeavors of Art: A Study of Form* in *Elizabethan Drama*. Madison: University of Wisconsin Press, 1954.

Dryden, John. "A Song for Sᵗ CECILIA's Day, 1687." In his *The Poems of John Dryden*, edited by James Kinsley. 4 vols. Oxford: Clarendon, 1958.

Evans, John, Philip Reed, and Paul Wilson, comps. *A Britten Source Book*. Aldeburgh, Suffolk: Britten-Pears Library, 1987.

Evans, Peter. *The Music of Benjamin Britten*. London: Dent, 1979.

Frye, Northrop. *Anatomy of Criticism: Four Essays*. 1957; reprinted Princeton: Princeton University Press, 1971.

Grout, Donald Jay. *A Short History of Opera*. 2d edition. New York: Columbia University Press, 1965.

Hamm, Charles. *Opera*. 1966; reprinted New York: Da Capo Press, 1980.

Harries, Meirion, and Susie Harries. *Opera Today*. London: Michael Joseph, 1986.

Herbert, David, ed. *The Operas of Benjamin Britten*. New York: Columbia University Press, 1979.

Hoppin, Richard H. *Medieval Music*. New York: Norton, 1978.

———, ed. *Anthology of Medieval Music*. New York: Norton, 1978.

Howard, Patricia. *The Operas of Benjamin Britten: An Introduction*. New York: Praeger, 1969.

Keller, Hans. "Introduction: Operatic Music and Britten." In *The Operas of Benjamin Britten,* edited by David Herbert, xiii–xxxi. New York: Columbia University Press, 1979.

Kennedy, Michael. *Britten*. The Master Musician Series. London: Dent, 1981.

Kerman, Joseph. *Opera as Drama*. New York: Knopf, 1956.

———. *Opera as Drama*. New and revised edition. Berkeley and Los Angeles: University of California Press, 1988.

Kermode, Frank. "The Mature Comedies." In *Early Shakespeare,* edited by John Russell Brown and Bernard Harris, 214–27. Stratford-upon-Avon Studies, 3. London: Edward Arnold, 1961.

Kott, Jan. *Shakespeare Our Contemporary*. Translated by Boneslaw Taborski. Preface by Peter Brook. London: Methuen, 1965.

Langer, Susanne K. *Feeling and Form: A Theory of Art Developed from Philosophy in a New Key*. New York: Scribner, 1953.

———. *Philosophy in a New Key: A Study in the Symbolism of Reason, Rite, and Art*. 3d edition. Cambridge: Harvard University Press, 1969.

LaRue, Jan. *Guidelines for Style Analysis*. New York: Norton, 1970.

Levin, Richard. "Shakespeare or the Ideas of His Time." In *Shakespeare Today,* edited by Ralph Berry, 129–37. Winnipeg: University of Manitoba Press, 1977.

Lindenberger, Herbert. *Opera: The Extravagant Art*. Ithaca: Cornell University Press, 1984.

Marwick, Arthur. *British Society since 1945*. Penguin Social History of Britain. Harmondsworth: Penguin, 1982.

Meyer, Leonard B. *Emotion and Meaning in Music*. Chicago: University of Chicago Press, 1956.

Miller, Jonathan. Whelan Visiting Lectures. University of Saskatchewan, Saskatoon, Oct. 1989.

Mitchell, Donald. "Benjamin Britten: *l'innovatore silenzioso*." Program book of the Fifty-first Maggio Musicale Florentia 1988:31–63.

———. *Britten and Auden in the Thirties: The Year 1936*. Seattle: University of Washington Press, 1981.

———. "In and Out of Britten's 'Dream.'" *Opera* 11 (1960):797–801.

———. Interview, 16 Aug. 1988 and 12 Sept. 1988.

Mitchell, Donald, and Philip Reed. *Letters from a Life: The Selected Letters and Diaries of Benjamin Britten 1913–1976*. 2 vols. Berkeley and Los Angeles: University of California Press, 1991.

Morell, Thomas, librettist. *Joshua, an Oratorio,* by Georg Frideric Handel. Kalmus Classic Edition. Miami, Fl.: CPP Belwin, n.d.

Palmer, Christopher, ed. *The Britten Companion*. Cambridge: Cambridge University Press, 1984.

Partridge, Eric. *Shakespeare's Bawdy*. Revised edition. London: Routledge, 1968.

Porter, Peter. "Benjamin Britten's Librettos." In *Peter Grimes, Gloriana: Benjamin Britten,* edited by Nicholas John, 7–18. Opera Guide Series, No. 24. London: John Calder, 1983.

Salzer, Felix. "Introduction." In *Five Graphic Music Analyses,* by Heinrich Schenker. New York: Dover, 1969.

Schafer, Murray. *British Composers in Interview*. London: Faber, 1963.

Schenker, Heinrich. *Five Graphic Music Analyses*. New York: Dover, 1969.

Schmidgall, Gary. *Literature as Opera*. New York: Oxford University Press, 1977.

———. *Shakespeare and Opera*. New York: Oxford University Press, 1990.

Senior, Evan. "Is Britten's New Opera Really an Opera?" *Music and Musicians,* 8, no. 11 (July 1960):10.

Smith, Patrick J. *The Tenth Muse: A Historical Study of the Opera Libretto*. 1970; reprinted New York: Schirmer-Macmillan, 1975.

Spevack, Marvin. *A Complete and Systematic Concordance to the Works of Shakespeare*. 8 vols. Hildesheim: Georg Olms Verlagsbuchhandlung, 1968.

Strode, Rosamund. Interview, Aug. 1988. (In appendix C.)

———. "Working for Benjamin Britten (II)." In *The Britten Companion,* edited by Christopher Palmer, 51–61. Cambridge: Cambridge University Press, 1984.

Sundberg, Johan. "The Acoustics of the Singing Voice." *Scientific American* 263, no. 3 (1977):82–91.

Weiner, Andrew D. "'Multiformitie Uniforme': *A Midsummer Night's Dream*." *ELH* 38, no. 3 (Sept. 1971):329–49.

White, Eric Walter. *Benjamin Britten: His Life and Operas*. 2d edition. Edited by John Evans. Berkeley and Los Angeles: University of California Press, 1983.

Young, David P. *Something of Great Constancy: The Art of "A Midsummer Night's Dream."* New Haven: Yale University Press, 1966.

Zitner, S. P. "Hamlet, Duellist." *University of Toronto Quarterly* 39 (1969–70):1–18.

Zuckerkandl, Victor. "Schenker System." In *Harvarrd Dictionary of Music,* edited by Willi Arel. Cambridge: Harvard University Press, 1969.

Index

Recordings, 29, 144
Reed, Philip, 29
References, in play, 80, 90–92
Re-forming (reshaping, restructuring): Britten's objectives in, 40–42, 73–75; definition of, 39; elements as candidates for, 41; as preparatory, 39–40, 61, 110
Release, dissonant cadential, 170. *See also* Tension and release (Meyer)
Relocation of actions, 52, 55, 77, 108
Repetition, of text or of music, 79, 120, 166–68
Representation, 32; of reality, 44; of Theseus, 46, 50, 71, 77
Reshaping. *See* Re-forming
Responses to music, as obvious or unclear, 112–13
Restatement (a formal process in music) (Wallace Berry), 122, 185–86
Restoration of cuts by music, lack of, 199
Restructuring. *See* Re-forming
Retiming of actions, 56, 77, 98, 101–2
Return of text or of music, 79, 120, 166–67
Reversing order of statements, 63, 67–68, 77–78
Reworking of sources of operas by other librettists, 77
Rhetoric, music as, 194, 202–3
Rhyme, 83
Rhythm, a component of music, 125
Ring, The (Wagner), 88
Ritornello, 66, 120, 125, 139
Riverside Shakespeare, The, 15, 51
Robin Goodfellow, 52–53, 157
Romantic movement, overall: in operas, 105; in *Dream*, 71
Romanticism, 193
Romeo and Juliet (Shakespeare), 206–7
Rondo form, of *Pyramus and Thisby*, 191–92
Rosen, Charles, 123–24
Rossini, Gioacchimo, 189
Rounding off of a scene by music. *See* Build-up and rounding off of a scene by music
Royal Fairies: their entrance prelude, as tonality set, 134, 135, **136**, 137–38, **138**; their motive, **127**, 128
"Rustics" label, 50

St. Cecilia's Day, 156–57, 211
Salzer, Felix, 128
Saraband, **151–52**, 152–53
Satirization, of a displeasing thing, 48, 93
Scene break in denouement of *Dream*, 71
Scenery, 55, 85
Schafer, Murray, 86
Schenker, Heinrich, 126, 130, 179
Schmidgall, Gary: on character groups, 45; his criticism of *Dream*, 20, 194; on graduated scale of utterance styles, 163; on operatic conventions, 34–35, 37; on romantic decadence, 193; on Shakespeare and Verdi, 109–10
Schoenberg, Arnold, 79, 134–35; 146, 200–201; *Pierrot Lunaire* (1912), 147
Schubert, Franz, 119
Score: a key text, 25, 28; the printed, 28, 38n; rentals of the, 20
Scores, ancillary: the manuscript full, 25; the printer's proofs, 25; the vocal, 25, 28
Scotch snap, 147–48, **151**, 150–52
Scribe, Eugène, 77
Secco (recitative), 168
Senior, Evan, 31
Serenade (Britten), 23, 30
Setting: putting into music, 43, 156, 165–67; of place or time, 31, 45, 54–56, 85. (*See also* Music)
Sextet, 157, 191
Sexual matters, 99; concerning bawdy, 44, 92, 201; concerning male-female relations, 50, 58–59, 105, 167
Shakespeare, William, 23, 82, 84–85, 92; Britten on his words, 41, 45, 75–76, 84, 205. Works: Sonnet No. 43 (c. 1595), 48; *Romeo and Juliet* (1596), 206–7; *A Midsummer Night's Dream* (1596) (see *Midsummer Night's Dream, A* [Shakespeare]); *Much Ado about Nothing* (1599), 81; *Hamlet* (1601), 85; *Macbeth* (1606), 110
Shape. *See* Form
Sharping, overall tonal, in *Dream*, 186, 206
"Significant form" (Langer). *See* Form

Silence, dramatic, in music, 117, 144–45, 171, 199
"Silent innovator", Britten as the, 39; as taciturn about his music, 39, 44, 109, 112, 196; as composer of quiet, strange music, 63. See also Innovator, Britten as an
Simplicity: diminutions of 76, 199–200; doubtful results in, 50–52, 55, 89, 105; in Dream, 198–200; enhancements of, 48, 51–54, 65–66, 74, 90–92, 95–96, 99, 111, 208; in the libretto, 41–42, 74, 87, 89, 95–96, 99
Simplification, 45, 48, 51, 105, 199–200; and oversimplification, 76
Simultaneity: of similarity and difference, 152, **153**, 154; in utterances, 78–79
Singers, opera. See Britten, Benjamin: on opera singers
Singer's opera, 189, 192
Sleep. See Night, sleep, and dreams
Sleep music, 69, 174–75; as tonality set, 134, **136**, 140
Smith, Patrick J., 34–36, 40, 77
Society, the artist in, 24, 36, 207
Sonate caractéristique, op. 81a (Beethoven), 128
Song: general features of, 53, 83–84, 87, 187, 200; in Dream, 83–84, 105, 165; other uses of, 80, 94–95
Sonnet No. 43 (Shakespeare), 48
Sound, a component of music, 125
Sound effects, 112–13, 144, 187, 204
Source material as expendable, 43
Source text, 24–27, 47, 76
Speaking role, 156–57
Spectacle, 32, 48, 177
Speech, quiet or loud, 100
Speech–act, 166
Spelling, 76, 89
Spells, beastly, 67–68, 72, 79, 91
Spevack, Marvin, 97n
Sponsorship, 86
Sprechstimme, 79, **143**, 146–47, 192, 197
Stasis (Wallace Berry), 122, 176
Statement (a formal process in music) (Wallace Berry), 122, 185–86
"Strange and admirable," 208
Strauss, Richard, 34
Stretto, fugal, 125, 169–70

Striking passages, 80, 84–85
Strode, Rosamund, 29, 30, 73, 80, 213, 215–16
Structure. See Form
Stychomythia, 167
Sundberg, Johan, 161
Sung line and ordinary speech, 158
Supernatural: countertenor as, 156; fairies as, 63; forces, 205; mood, 194–95; music, 119
Superposition of different words, 168–69
Symmetries, formal, 53, 55, 64–65, 68, 139, 164
Symphony No. 9 ("Choral") (Beethoven), 129–30
Symphony No. 41 ("Jupiter") (Mozart), 121

Tensing and releasing, simultaneous, 121
Tension and release (Meyer), 119–22
Terminology, 21, 112
Terms, recondite, embedded in rhymes, 198
Terzzug, 126
Text: adjustments to, other than cutting, by librettists, 77–79, 87; changes in, in setting, 156, 165–67; discrepancies in, found by Holst, 25; influence (a component of music), 125
Texts, key, identification of: source text, 24–27; working libretto, 24, 27–28; score, 25, 28
Textures, Britten on, 45, 59, 201
Theme(s), 32, 126
Theseus: characterization of, 86, 157; remains a true aristocrat, 99–100; made less desirable, 48, 68, 90, 92–93; stripped of philosophy, 54, 206; role diminished, 46, 63–64, 71
Thesis (conclusion) of book, 21, 207–8
Thisbe, characterization of. See Pyramus and Thisbe, characterization of
Through-composed stanza, 165
Tippett, Michael, 36
Tonal movement, overall, 186
Tonal richness, from precise with shifting pitches, 147
Tonality: with atonality, 119; Brittenesque, 186